Table of contents

Introduction 11
Breakfast Recipes 12
    Cinnamon Berries Oatmeal 12
    Sausage and Potato Mix 12
    Coconut Quinoa 12
    Veggie Hash Brown Mix 13
    Hash Brown and Bacon Casserole 13
    Cinnamon French Toast 13
    Carrots Oatmeal 13
    Thyme Hash Browns 14
    Maple Banana Oatmeal 14
    Chia Oatmeal 14
    Buttery Oatmeal 14
    Ginger Raisins Oatmeal 15
    Apple and Chia Mix 15
    Pumpkin and Quinoa Mix 15
    Cocoa and Berries Quinoa 15
    Quinoa and Veggies Casserole 16
    Cauliflower and Eggs Bowls 16
    Sausage and Eggs Mix 16
    Parmesan Quinoa 17
    Broccoli Casserole 17
    Creamy Shrimp Bowls 17
    Peach, Vanilla and Oats Mix 18
    Hot Eggs Mix 18
    Potato and Ham Mix 18
    Spinach Frittata 18
    Chili Eggs Mix 19
    Cheesy Eggs 19
    Tomato and Zucchini Eggs Mix 19
    Chocolate Breakfast Bread 20
    Almond and Quinoa Bowls 20
    Carrots Casserole 20
    Cranberry Maple Oatmeal 20
    Mushroom Casserole 21
    Ginger Apple Bowls 21
    Granola Bowls 21
    Squash Bowls 21
    Lamb and Eggs Mix 22
    Cauliflower Casserole 22
    Beef Meatloaf 22
    Leek Casserole 22
    Eggs and Sweet Potato Mix 23
    Pork and Eggplant Casserole 23
    Apple Spread 23
    Cherries and Cocoa Oats 23
    Beans Salad 24
    Peppers Rice Mix 24
    Cashew Butter 24
    Pumpkin and Berries Bowls 24
    Quinoa and Chia Pudding 25
    Beans Breakfast Bowls 25
    Basil Sausage and Broccoli Mix 25
    Zucchini and Cauliflower Eggs Mix 26

- Mushroom Quiche ... 26
- Scallions Quinoa and Carrots Bowls ... 26
- Ham Omelet ... 27
- Peppers and Eggs Mix ... 27
- Baby Spinach Rice Mix ... 27
- Herbed Egg Scramble ... 28
- Peas and Rice Bowls ... 28
- Asparagus Casserole ... 28

Lunch Recipes ... 29
- Seafood Soup ... 29
- Sesame Salmon Bowls ... 29
- Shrimp Stew ... 29
- Garlic Shrimp and Spinach ... 30
- Ginger Salmon ... 30
- Creamy Cod Stew ... 30
- Sweet Potato and Clam Chowder ... 31
- Maple Chicken Mix ... 31
- Salsa Chicken ... 31
- Turkey and Mushrooms ... 32
- Indian Chicken and Tomato Mix ... 32
- Turkey and Figs ... 32
- Turkey and Walnuts ... 33
- Slow Cooked Thyme Chicken ... 33
- Roasted Beef and Cauliflower ... 33
- Soy Pork Chops ... 33
- Pork and Cranberries ... 34
- Lamb and Onion Stew ... 34
- Pork Roast and Olives ... 34
- Beef Stew ... 34
- Beef and Celery Stew ... 35
- Tomato Pasta Mix ... 35
- Honey Lamb Roast ... 35
- Worcestershire Beef Mix ... 35
- Chickpeas Stew ... 36
- Lentils Soup ... 36
- Chicken Soup ... 36
- Lime and Thyme Chicken ... 37
- Shrimp Gumbo ... 37
- Squash and Chicken Soup ... 37
- Pork Soup ... 38
- Mushroom Stew ... 38
- Beans Chili ... 38
- Parsley Chicken Stew ... 39
- Mustard Short Ribs ... 39
- Creamy Brisket ... 39
- Mushroom Soup ... 39
- Creamy Potato Soup ... 40
- Chicken with Corn and Wild Rice ... 40
- Mixed Pork and Beans ... 40
- Pork Chops and Butter Sauce ... 40
- Chicken and Peach Mix ... 41
- Chicken Drumsticks and Buffalo Sauce ... 41
- Mustard Pork Chops and Carrots ... 41
- Fennel Soup ... 41
- Artichoke Soup ... 42

- Beans and Mushroom Stew ... 42
- Chicken and Eggplant Stew ... 42
- Turmeric Lentils Stew ... 43
- Pork Chili ... 43
- Cinnamon Pork Ribs ... 43
- Pork and Mushroom Stew ... 44
- Pork and Tomatoes Mix ... 44
- Pesto Pork Shanks ... 44
- Potato Stew ... 44
- Chicken and Rice ... 45
- Salmon Stew ... 45
- Paprika Pork and Chickpeas ... 45
- Beef and Cabbage ... 46
- Balsamic Beef Stew ... 46
- Beef Curry ... 46
- Chicken and Brussels Sprouts Mix ... 46
- Chickpeas Stew ... 47
- Eggplant Curry ... 47
- Beef and Artichokes Stew ... 47
- Beef Soup ... 48
- Veggie Soup ... 48
- Oregano Turkey Stew ... 48
- Masala Beef Mix ... 49

Side Dish Recipes ... 50
- Cheddar Potatoes Mix ... 50
- Balsamic Cauliflower ... 50
- Italian Black Beans Mix ... 50
- Butter Green Beans ... 51
- Corn Sauté ... 51
- Sage Peas ... 51
- Tomato and Corn Mix ... 51
- Dill Mushroom Sauté ... 52
- Hot Zucchini Mix ... 52
- Butternut Squash and Eggplant Mix ... 52
- Carrots and Spinach Mix ... 53
- Creamy Coconut Potatoes ... 53
- Sage Sweet Potatoes ... 53
- Cauliflower and Almonds Mix ... 53
- Garlic Risotto ... 54
- Red Curry Veggie Mix ... 54
- Rosemary Leeks ... 54
- Mustard Brussels Sprouts ... 54
- Potatoes and Leeks Mix ... 55
- Black Beans Mix ... 55
- Orange Carrots Mix ... 55
- Hot Lentils ... 55
- Marjoram Rice Mix ... 56
- Mashed Potatoes ... 56
- Barley Mix ... 56
- Lime Beans Mix ... 56
- Creamy Beans ... 57
- Spinach Mix ... 57
- Bbq Beans ... 57
- White Beans Mix ... 57
- Sweet Potato and Cauliflower Mix ... 58

- Cabbage Mix 58
- Parsley Mushroom Mix 58
- Cinnamon Squash 58
- Zucchini Mix 59
- Kale Mix 59
- Buttery Spinach 59
- Bacon Potatoes Mix 59
- Cauliflower Mash 60
- Veggie Mix 60
- Farro Mix 60
- Cumin Quinoa Pilaf 60
- Saffron Risotto 61
- Mint Farro Pilaf 61
- Parmesan Rice 61
- Spinach Rice 61
- Mango Rice 62
- Lemon Artichokes 62
- Coconut Bok Choy 62
- Italian Eggplant 62
- Cabbage and Onion Mix 63
- Balsamic Okra Mix 63
- Garlic Carrots Mix 63
- Curry Broccoli Mix 63
- Rice and Corn 64
- Cauliflower and Potatoes Mix 64
- Asparagus Mix 64
- Garlic Squash Mix 64
- Baby Carrots and Parsnips Mix 65
- Lemon Kale Mix 65
- Brussels Sprouts and Cauliflower 65
- Cabbage and Kale Mix 66
- Thyme Mushrooms and Corn 66
- Veggie Medley 66
- Paprika Green Beans and Zucchinis 67
- Tarragon Sweet Potatoes 67
- Mustard Brussels Sprouts 67
- Parmesan Spinach Mix 68
- Minty Peas and Tomatoes 68
- Savoy Cabbage Mix 68

Snack Recipes 69
- Spinach Spread 69
- Artichoke Dip 69
- Crab Dip 69
- Lemon Shrimp Dip 69
- Squash Salsa 70
- Beans Spread 70
- Rice Snack Bowls 70
- Cauliflower Spread 70
- Mushroom Dip 71
- Chickpeas Spread 71
- Spinach Dip 71
- Dill Potato Salad 71
- Stuffed Peppers Platter 72
- Corn Dip 72
- Tomato and Mushroom Salsa 72

Recipe	Page
Salsa Beans Dip	72
Pineapple and Tofu Salsa	73
Chickpeas Salsa	73
Creamy Mushroom Spread	73
Bulgur and Beans Salsa	73
Beets Salad	74
Lentils Salsa	74
Tacos	74
Almond Bowls	74
Eggplant Salsa	75
Almond Spread	75
Onion Dip	75
Nuts Bowls	75
Eggplant Salad	76
Lentils Dip	76
Turkey Meatballs	76
Stuffed Mushrooms	76
Paprika Cod Sticks	77
Macadamia Nuts Snack	77
Salmon Bites	77
Spinach and Walnuts Dip	77
Curry Pork Meatballs	78
Calamari Rings Bowls	78
Shrimp Salad	78
Chicken Salad	79
Apple and Carrot Dip	79
Sweet Potato Dip	79
Spinach, Walnuts and Calamari Salad	80
Chicken Meatballs	80
Cinnamon Pecans Snack	80
Seasoned Peanuts	80
Broccoli Dip	81
Walnuts Bowls	81
Cauliflower Bites	81
Beef Dip	81
Zucchini Spread	82
Beef Dip	82
Eggplant Salsa	82
Carrots Spread	83
Cauliflower Dip	83
Lentils Hummus	83
Spinach Dip	83
Peppers Salsa	84
Artichoke Dip	84
Mushroom Salsa	84
Poultry Recipes	**85**
Garlic Chicken and Green Beans	85
Oregano Turkey and Tomatoes	85
Mustard Chicken Mix	85
Lemon Turkey and Spinach	86
Paprika Chicken and Artichokes	86
Chives Chicken Wings	86
Lime Chicken Mix	87
Chicken and Olives	87
Turkey, Tomato and Fennel Mix	87

Chicken with Tomatoes and Eggplant Mix 88
Chicken and Onions Mix 88
Pesto Chicken Mix 88
Ginger Turkey Mix 89
Turkey and Plums Mix 89
Creamy Turkey Mix 89
Chicken and Apples Mix 90
Chicken and Endives 90
Basil Chicken Wings 90
Chicken and Broccoli 91
Rosemary Chicken 91
Chicken Curry 91
Balsamic Turkey 91
Turkey and Scallions Mix 92
Parsley Chicken Mix 92
Turkey Chili 92
Masala Turkey 93
Chicken and Beans 93
Turkey and Corn 93
Coriander Turkey Mix 94
Turkey with Olives and Corn 94
Dill Turkey and Peas 94
Turkey with Rice 94
Italian Turkey 95
Duck and Mushrooms 95
Turkey and Tomato Sauce 95
Tomato Chicken and Chickpeas 95
Turkey with Leeks and Radishes 96
Coconut Turkey 96
Hot Chicken and Zucchinis 96
Turkey with Radishes 97
Chives Duck 97
Cilantro Chicken and Eggplant Mix 97
Chicken with Brussels Sprouts 98
Chicken and Mango Mix 98
Turkey and Avocado 98
Chicken and Peppers 99
Chicken and Cabbage Mix 99
Lime Turkey and Chard 99
BBQ Turkey mix 100
Chicken and Asparagus 100
Lemon Turkey and Potatoes 100
Turkey and Okra 101
Mustard Duck Mix 101
Orange Chicken Mix 101
Turkey and Carrots 102
Rosemary Chicken Thighs 102
Turkey and Kidney Beans 102
Coriander and Turmeric Chicken 103
Garlic Turkey 103
Cumin Chicken Mix 103
Meat Recipes 104
Pork Chops and Mango Mix 104
Beef and Zucchinis Mix 104
Pork and Olives Mix 104

Pork and Soy Sauce Mix	104
Beef and Sauce	105
Pork and Beans Mix	105
Beef with Spinach	105
Pork and Chilies Mix	105
Mustard Ribs	106
Beef and Corn Mix	106
Cider Beef Mix	106
Tarragon Pork Chops	106
Honey Pork Chops	107
Turmeric Lamb	107
Chili Lamb	107
Beef and Red Onions Mix	107
Pork and Okra	108
Chives Lamb	108
Oregano Beef	108
Pork and Green Beans	108
Mint Lamb Chops	109
Beef and Artichokes	109
Lamb and Potatoes	109
Lamb and Tomatoes Mix	110
Pork and Eggplant Mix	110
Lemon Lamb	110
Rosemary Lamb with Olives	110
Nutmeg Lamb and Squash	111
Lamb and Fennel Mix	111
Creamy Lamb	111
Beef and Capers Sauce	111
Masala Beef and Sauce	112
Lamb and Cabbage	112
Pork and Lentils	112
Balsamic Lamb Mix	112
Beef and Endives	113
Lamb and Lime Zucchinis	113
Beef and Peas	113
Maple Beef	113
Rosemary Beef	114
Parsley and Chili Lamb	114
Cumin Pork Chops	114
Paprika Lamb	114
Beef with Peas and Corn	115
Lime Pork Chops	115
Lamb with Capers	115
Lamb and Zucchini Mix	115
Beef and Peppers	116
Cayenne Lamb Mix	116
Cinnamon Lamb	116
Lamb and Kale	116
Beef and Sprouts	117
Pork Chops and Spinach	117
Green Curry Lamb	117
Oregano Lamb	117
Pesto Lamb Chops	118
Beef with Green Beans and Cilantro	118
Balsamic Lamb Chops	118

Creamy Beef 119
Walnut and Coconut Beef 119
Fish and Seafood Recipes 120
Lime Shrimp 120
Chili Salmon 120
Rosemary Shrimp 120
Paprika Cod 120
Spicy Tuna 121
Ginger Tuna 121
Chives Shrimp 121
Coriander Salmon Mix 121
Tuna and Green Beans 122
Cod and Corn 122
Turmeric Salmon 122
Sea Bass and Chickpeas 122
Creamy Shrimp 123
Parsley Cod 123
Pesto Cod and Tomatoes 123
Orange Cod 123
Garlic Sea Bass 124
Tuna and Brussels Sprouts 124
Shrimp with Spinach 124
Shrimp and Avocado 124
Chives Mackerel 125
Dill Cod 125
Shrimp and Mango Mix 125
Balsamic Tuna 126
Lime Trout Mix 126
Creamy Tuna and Scallions 126
Cod and Mustard Sauce 126
Shrimp and Pineapple Bowls 127
Lime Crab 127
Hot Salmon and Carrots 127
Shrimp and Eggplant 127
Sea Bass and Squash 128
Coconut Mackerel 128
Salmon and Peas 128
Chili Shrimp and Zucchinis 128
Italian Shrimp 129
Basil Cod and Olives 129
Tuna and Fennel 129
Shrimp and Mushrooms 129
Salmon and Berries 130
Cod and Artichokes 130
Salmon, Tomatoes and Green Beans 130
Shrimp and Rice Mix 131
Shrimp and Red Chard 131
Chives Mussels 131
Calamari and Sauce 132
Salmon Salad 132
Walnut Tuna Mix 132
Almond Shrimp and Cabbage 133
Indian Shrimp 133
Shrimp, Tomatoes and Kale 133
Trout Bowls 134

Calamari Curry	134
Balsamic Trout	134
Oregano Shrimp Bowls	134
Salmon and Strawberries Mix	135
Shrimp, Salmon and Tomatoes Mix	135
Shrimp and Cauliflower Bowls	135
Cod and Broccoli	136
Cinnamon Trout	136
Dessert Recipes	137
Cinnamon Apples	137
Vanilla Pears	137
Avocado Cake	137
Coconut Cream	137
Almond Rice Pudding	138
Cherry Bowls	138
Berry Cream	138
Maple Pudding	138
Chia and Orange Pudding	139
Creamy Berries Mix	139
Apple Compote	139
Plums Stew	139
Cinnamon Peach Mix	140
Strawberry Cake	140
Ginger Pears Mix	140
Raisin Cookies	140
Blueberries Jam	141
Orange Bowls	141
Quinoa Pudding	141
Chia and Avocado Pudding	141
Almond and Cherries Pudding	142
Vanilla Peach Cream	142
Cinnamon Plums	142
Cardamom Apples	142
Cherry and Rhubarb Mix	143
Peaches and Wine Sauce	143
Apricot and Peaches Cream	143
Vanilla Grapes Mix	143
Pomegranate and Mango Bowls	144
Mandarin Cream	144
Cranberries Cream	144
Buttery Pineapple	144
Strawberry and Orange Mix	145
Maple Plums and Mango	145
Cantaloupe Cream	145
Yogurt Cheesecake	145
Chocolate Mango Mix	146
Lemon Jam	146
Lemon Peach Mix	146
Rhubarb Stew	146
Strawberry and Blackberry Jam	147
Pear Cream	147
Rhubarb Jam	147
Apricot Marmalade	147
Apple, Avocado and Mango Bowls	148
Tomato Jam	148

Cinnamon and Chocolate Peaches 148
Coconut Jam 148
Bread and Berries Pudding 149
Tapioca and Chia Pudding 149
Dates and Rice Pudding 149
Almonds, Walnuts and Mango Bowls 149
Berries Salad 150
Pears and Apples Bowls 150
Creamy Rhubarb and Plums Bowls 150
Greek Cream Cheese Pudding 150
Greek Cream 151
Ginger Cream 151
Bread and Quinoa Pudding 151
Melon Pudding 151
Conclusion 152
Recipe Index 153

Introduction

Cooking in your slow cooker can be so much fun! You get some of the best flavors and textures and you don't need any special skills. You only need a good slow cooker and it will do all the work itself.

This brings us to the second part of our discussion: cooking for your loved one. We are sure that you would like a cooking guide that will bring to you some amazing recipes you could prepare for yourself and your loved one. Well, this is such a guide.
You now have the chance to discover a wonderful and easy to follow cooking journal. You now have the slow cooker recipes collection for 2!

Slow cookers have gained a lot of popularity over the last years because they are easy to use and they allow you to make some rich and hearty meals with minimum knowledge and effort.

Knowing these facts, all you have to do now is to get your hands on a copy of this slow cooker collection for 2 and start cooking.
Make some rich and flavored dishes for your loved one using simple ingredients and one useful tool: the slow cooker.

Don't hesitate anymore! Get a copy of this great slow cooker collection and have fun cooking for your loved one!
Enjoy this special guide and start this culinary journey right away! It will be the best one you've taken so far!

Slow Cooker Breakfast Recipes for 2

Cinnamon Berries Oatmeal

Preparation time: 10 minutes | *Cooking time:* 6 hours | *Servings:* 2

Ingredients:
- 1 cup old fashioned oats
- 3 cups almond milk
- 1 cup blackberries
- ½ cup Greek yogurt
- ½ teaspoon cinnamon powder
- ½ teaspoon vanilla extract

Directions:
In your slow cooker, mix the oats with the milk, berries and the other ingredients, toss, put the lid on and cook on Low for 6 hours. Divide into bowls and serve for breakfast.

Nutrition: calories 201, fat 3, fiber 6, carbs 12, protein 6

Sausage and Potato Mix

Preparation time: 10 minutes | *Cooking time:* 6 hours | *Servings:* 2

Ingredients:
- 2 sweet potatoes, peeled and roughly cubed
- 1 green bell pepper, minced
- ½ yellow onion, chopped
- 4 ounces smoked andouille sausage, sliced
- 1 cup cheddar cheese, shredded
- ¼ cup Greek yogurt
- ¼ teaspoon basil, dried
- 1 cup chicken stock
- Salt and black pepper to the taste
- 1 tablespoon parsley, chopped

Directions:
In your slow cooker, combine the potatoes with the bell pepper, sausage and the other ingredients, toss, put the lid on and cook on Low for 6 hours. Divide between plates and serve for breakfast.

Nutrition: calories 355, fat 14, fiber 4, carbs 20, protein 22

Coconut Quinoa

Preparation time: 10 minutes | *Cooking time:* 8 hours | *Servings:* 2

Ingredients:
- ½ cup quinoa
- 2 cups coconut milk
- 1 tablespoon maple syrup
- 1 teaspoon vanilla extract
- 2 tablespoons raisins
- ¼ cup blackberries

Directions:
In your slow cooker, mix the quinoa with the milk, maple syrup and the other ingredients, toss, put the lid on and cook on Low for 8 hours. Divide into 2 bowls and serve for breakfast.

Nutrition: calories 261, fat 5, fiber 7, carbs 12, protein 5

Veggie Hash Brown Mix

Preparation time: 10 minutes | Cooking time: 6 hours and 5 minutes | Servings: 2

Ingredients:
- 1 tablespoon olive oil
- ½ cup white mushrooms, chopped
- ½ yellow onion, chopped
- ¼ teaspoon garlic powder
- ¼ teaspoon onion powder
- ¼ cup sour cream
- 10 ounces hash browns
- ¼ cup cheddar cheese, shredded
- Salt and black pepper to the taste
- ½ tablespoon parsley, chopped

Directions:
Heat up a pan with the oil over medium heat, add the onion and mushrooms, stir and cook for 5 minutes. Transfer this to the slow cooker, add hash browns and the other ingredients, toss, put the lid on and cook on Low for 6 hours. Divide between plates and for breakfast.

Nutrition: calories 245, fat 4, fiber 7, carbs 7, protein 10

Hash Brown and Bacon Casserole

Preparation time: 10 minutes | Cooking time: 3 hours | Servings: 2

Ingredients:
- 5 ounces hash browns, shredded
- 2 bacon slices, cooked and chopped
- ¼ cup mozzarella cheese, shredded
- 2 eggs, whisked
- ¼ cup sour cream
- 1 tablespoon cilantro, chopped
- 1 tablespoon olive oil
- A pinch of salt and black pepper

Directions:
Grease your slow cooker with the oil, add the hash browns mixed with the eggs, sour cream and the other ingredients, toss, put the lid on and cook on High for 4 hours. Divide the casserole into bowls and serve.

Nutrition: calories 281, fat 4, fiber 6, carbs 12, protein 11

Cinnamon French Toast

Preparation time: 10 minutes | Cooking time: 4 hours | Servings: 2

Ingredients:
- ½ French baguette, sliced
- 2 ounces cream cheese
- 1 tablespoon brown sugar
- 1 egg, whisked
- 3 tablespoons almond milk
- 2 tablespoons honey
- ½ teaspoon cinnamon powder
- 1 tablespoon butter, melted
- Cooking spray

Directions:
Spread the cream cheese on all bread slices, grease your slow cooker with the cooking spray and arrange the slices in the pot. In a bowl, mix the egg with the cinnamon, almond milk and the remaining ingredients, whisk and pour over the bread slices. Put the lid on, cook on High for 4 hours, divide the mix between plates and serve for breakfast.

Nutrition: calories 251, fat 5, fiber 7, carbs 12, protein 4

Carrots Oatmeal

Preparation time: 10 minutes | Cooking time: 8 hours | Servings: 2

Ingredients:
- ½ cup old fashioned oats
- 1 cup almond milk
- 2 carrots, peeled and grated
- ½ teaspoon cinnamon powder
- 2 tablespoons brown sugar
- ¼ cup walnuts, chopped
- Cooking spray

Directions:
Grease your slow cooker with cooking spray, add the oats, milk, carrots and the other ingredients, toss, put the lid on and cook on Low for 8 hours. Divide the oatmeal into 2 bowls and serve.

Nutrition: calories 200, fat 4, fiber 8, carbs 11, protein 5

Thyme Hash Browns

Preparation time: 10 minutes | Cooking time: 4 hours | Servings: 2

Ingredients:
- Cooking spray
- 10 ounces hash browns
- 2 eggs, whisked
- ¼ cup heavy cream
- ¼ teaspoon thyme, dried
- ¼ teaspoon garlic powder
- A pinch of salt and black pepper
- ½ cup mozzarella, shredded
- 1 tablespoon chives, chopped
- 1 tablespoon parsley, chopped

Directions:
Grease your slow cooker with cooking spray, spread the hash browns on the bottom, add the eggs, cream and the other ingredients except the cheese and toss. Sprinkle the cheese on top, put the lid on and cook on High for 4 hours. Divide the mix between plates and serve for breakfast.

Nutrition: calories 231, fat 5, fiber 9, carbs 15, protein 11

Maple Banana Oatmeal

Preparation time: 10 minutes | Cooking time: 6 hours | Servings: 2

Ingredients:
- 1/2 cup old fashioned oats
- 1 banana, mashed
- ½ teaspoon cinnamon powder
- 2 tablespoons maple syrup
- 2 cups almond milk
- Cooking spray

Directions:
Grease your slow cooker with the cooking spray, add the oats, banana and the other ingredients, stir, put the lid on and cook on Low for 6 hours. Divide into 2 bowls and serve for breakfast.

Nutrition: calories 200, fat 4, fiber 5, carbs 8, protein 5

Chia Oatmeal

Preparation time: 10 minutes | Cooking time: 8 hours | Servings: 2

Ingredients:
- 2 cups almond milk
- 1 cup steel cut oats
- 2 tablespoons butter, soft
- ½ teaspoon almond extract
- 2 tablespoons chia seeds

Directions:
In your slow cooker, mix the oats with the chia seeds and the other ingredients, toss, put the lid on and cook on Low for 8 hours. Stir the oatmeal one more time, divide into 2 bowls and serve.

Nutrition: calories 222, fat 5, fiber 6, carbs 9, protein 11

Buttery Oatmeal

Preparation time: 10 minutes | Cooking time: 3 hours | Servings: 2

Ingredients:
- Cooking spray
- 2 cups coconut milk
- 1 cup old fashioned oats
- 1 pear, cubed
- 1 apple, cored and cubed
- 2 tablespoons butter, melted

Directions:
Grease your slow cooker with the cooking spray, add the milk, oats and the other ingredients, toss, put the lid on and cook on High for 3 hours. Divide the mix into bowls and serve for breakfast.

Nutrition: calories 182, fat 4, fiber 6, carbs 8, protein 10

Ginger Raisins Oatmeal

Preparation time: 10 minutes | Cooking time: 8 hours | Servings: 2

Ingredients:
- 1 cup almond milk
- ½ cup steel cut oats
- ¼ cup raisins
- ½ teaspoon ginger, ground
- 1 tablespoon orange zest, grated
- 1 tablespoon orange juice
- ½ teaspoon vanilla extract
- ½ tablespoon honey

Directions:
In your slow cooker, combine the milk with the oats, raisins and the other ingredients, toss, put the lid on and cook on Low for 8 hours. Divide into 2 bowls and serve for breakfast.

Nutrition: calories 200, fat 4, fiber 6, carbs 8, protein 8

Apple and Chia Mix

Preparation time: 10 minutes | Cooking time: 8 hours | Servings: 2

Ingredients:
- ¼ cup chia seeds
- 2 apples, cored and roughly cubed
- 1 cup almond milk
- 2 tablespoons maple syrup
- 1 teaspoon vanilla extract
- ½ tablespoon cinnamon powder
- Cooking spray

Directions:
Grease your slow cooker with the cooking spray, add the chia seeds, milk and the other ingredients, toss, put the lid on and cook on Low for 8 hours. Divide the mix into bowls and serve for breakfast.

Nutrition: calories 221, fat 4, fiber 6, carbs 8, protein 10

Pumpkin and Quinoa Mix

Preparation time: 10 minutes | Cooking time: 8 hours | Servings: 2

Ingredients:
- Cooking spray
- ½ cup quinoa
- 1 cup almond milk
- 1 tablespoon honey
- ¼ cup pumpkin puree
- ½ teaspoon vanilla extract
- ¼ teaspoon cinnamon powder

Directions:
Grease your slow cooker with the cooking spray, add the quinoa, milk, honey and the other ingredients, stir, put the lid on and cook on Low for 7 hours. Divide the mix into bowls and serve for breakfast.

Nutrition: calories 242, fat 3, fiber 8, carbs 20, protein 7

Cocoa and Berries Quinoa

Preparation time: 10 minutes | Cooking time: 8 hours | Servings: 2

Ingredients:
- Cooking spray
- 1 cup quinoa
- 2 cups almond milk
- ¼ cup heavy cream
- ¼ cup blueberries
- 2 tablespoons cocoa powder
- 1 tablespoon brown sugar

Directions:
Grease your slow cooker with the cooking spray, add the quinoa, berries and the other ingredients, toss, put the lid on and cook on Low for 8 hours. Divide into 2 bowls and serve for breakfast.

Nutrition: calories 200, fat 4, fiber 5, carbs 17, protein 5

Quinoa and Veggies Casserole

Preparation time: 10 minutes | *Cooking time:* 6 hours | *Servings:* 2

Ingredients:
- ¼ cup quinoa
- 1 cup almond milk
- 2 eggs, whisked
- 1 tablespoon parsley, chopped
- 1 tablespoon chives, chopped
- A pinch of salt and black pepper
- ¼ cup baby spinach
- ¼ cup cherry tomatoes, halved
- 2 tablespoons parmesan, shredded
- Cooking spray

Directions:
Grease your slow cooker with the cooking spray, add the quinoa mixed with he milk, eggs and the other ingredients except the parmesan, toss and spread into the pot. Sprinkle the parmesan on top, put the lid on and cook on Low for 6 hours. Divide between plates and serve.

Nutrition: calories 251, fat 5, fiber 7, carbs 19, protein 11

Cauliflower and Eggs Bowls

Preparation time: 10 minutes | *Cooking time:* 7 hours | *Servings:* 2

Ingredients:
- Cooking spray
- 4 eggs, whisked
- A pinch of salt and black pepper
- ¼ teaspoon thyme, dried
- ½ teaspoon turmeric powder
- 1 cup cauliflower florets
- ½ small yellow onion, chopped
- 3 ounces breakfast sausages, sliced
- ½ cup cheddar cheese, shredded

Directions:
Grease your slow cooker with cooking spray and spread the cauliflower florets on the bottom of the pot. Add the eggs mixed with salt, pepper and the other ingredients and toss. Put the lid on, cook on Low for 7 hours, divide between plates and serve for breakfast.

Nutrition: calories 261, fat 6, fiber 7, carbs 22, protein 6

Sausage and Eggs Mix

Preparation time: 10 minutes | *Cooking time:* 8 hours and 10 minutes | *Servings:* 2

Ingredients:
- 4 eggs, whisked
- 1 red onion, chopped
- ¼ teaspoon rosemary, dried
- ½ teaspoon turmeric powder
- ½ pound pork sausage, sliced
- ½ tablespoon garlic powder
- 1 teaspoon basil, dried
- A pinch of salt and black pepper
- Cooking spray

Directions:
Grease a pan with the cooking spray, heat it up over medium-high heat, add the onion and the pork sausage, toss and cook for 10 minutes. Transfer this to the slow cooker, also add the eggs mixed with the remaining ingredients, toss everything, put the lid on and cook on Low for 8 hours. Divide between plates and serve right away for breakfast.

Nutrition: calories 271, fat 7, fiber 8, carbs 20, protein 11

Parmesan Quinoa

Preparation time: 10 minutes | Cooking time: 6 hours | Servings: 2

Ingredients:
- 1 cup quinoa
- 2 cups veggie stock
- 1 tablespoon chives, chopped
- 1 carrot, peeled and grated
- ½ cup parmesan, grated
- ¼ cup heavy cream
- Salt and black pepper to the taste
- Cooking spray

Directions:
Grease your slow cooker with the cooking spray, add the quinoa mixed with the stock and the other ingredients except the parmesan and the cream, toss, put the lid on and cook on High for 3 hours. Add the remaining ingredients, toss the mix again, cook on High for 3 more hours, divide into bowls and serve for breakfast.

Nutrition: calories 261, fat 6, fiber 8, carbs 26, protein 11

Broccoli Casserole

Preparation time: 10 minutes | Cooking time: 6 hours | Servings: 2

Ingredients:
- 2 eggs, whisked
- 1 cup broccoli florets
- 2 cups hash browns
- ½ teaspoon coriander, ground
- ½ teaspoon rosemary, dried
- ½ teaspoon turmeric powder
- ½ teaspoon mustard powder
- A pinch of salt and black pepper
- 1 small red onion, chopped
- ½ red bell pepper, chopped
- 1 ounce cheddar cheese, shredded
- Cooking spray

Directions:
Grease your slow cooker with the cooking spray, and spread hash browns, broccoli, bell pepper and the onion on the bottom of the pan. In a bowl, mix the eggs with the coriander and the other ingredients, whisk and pour over the broccoli mix in the pot. Put the lid on, cook on Low for 6 hours, divide between plates and serve for breakfast.

Nutrition: calories 261, fat 7, fiber 8, carbs 20, protein 11

Creamy Shrimp Bowls

Preparation time: 10 minutes | Cooking time: 2 hours | Servings: 2

Ingredients:
- ½ cup chicken stock
- ½ pound shrimp, peeled and deveined
- 1 carrot, peeled and cubed
- ½ cup baby spinach
- ¼ cup heavy cream
- ¼ tablespoon garlic powder
- ¼ tablespoon onion powder
- ¼ teaspoon rosemary, dried
- A pinch of salt and black pepper
- ¼ cup cheddar cheese, shredded
- 1 ounce cream cheese
- 1 tablespoon chives, chopped

Directions:
In your slow cooker, mix the shrimp with the stock, cream and the other ingredients, toss, put the lid on and cook on Low for 2 hours. Divide into bowls, and serve for breakfast.

Nutrition: calories 300, fat 7, fiber 12, carbs 20, protein 10

Peach, Vanilla and Oats Mix

Preparation time: 10 minutes | *Cooking time: 8 hours* | *Servings: 2*

Ingredients:
- ½ cup steel cut oats
- 2 cups almond milk
- ½ cup peaches, pitted and roughly chopped
- ½ teaspoon vanilla extract
- 1 teaspoon cinnamon powder

Directions:
In your slow cooker, mix the oats with the almond milk, peaches and the other ingredients, toss, put the lid on and cook on Low for 8 hours. Divide into bowls and serve for breakfast right away.

Nutrition: calories 261, fat 5, fiber 8, carbs 18, protein 6

Hot Eggs Mix

Preparation time: 10 minutes | *Cooking time: 2 hours* | *Servings: 2*

Ingredients:
- Cooking spray
- 4 eggs, whisked
- ¼ cup sour cream
- A pinch of salt and black pepper
- ½ teaspoon chili powder
- ½ teaspoon hot paprika
- ½ red bell pepper, chopped
- ½ yellow onion, chopped
- 2 cherry tomatoes, cubed
- 1 tablespoon parsley, chopped

Directions:
In a bowl, mix the eggs with the cream, salt, pepper and the other ingredients except the cooking spray and whisk well. Grease your slow cooker with cooking spray, pour the eggs mix inside, spread, stir, put the lid on and cook on High for 2 hours. Divide the mix between plates and serve.

Nutrition: calories 162, fat 5, fiber 7, carbs 15, protein 4

Potato and Ham Mix

Preparation time: 10 minutes | *Cooking time: 6 hours* | *Servings: 2*

Ingredients:
- Cooking spray
- 4 eggs, whisked
- ½ cup red potatoes, peeled and grated
- ¼ cup heavy cream
- ¼ cup ham, chopped
- 1 tablespoon cilantro, chopped
- ½ teaspoon turmeric powder
- Salt and black pepper to the taste

Directions:
Grease your slow cooker with cooking spray, add the eggs, potatoes and the other ingredients, whisk, put the lid on and cook on High for 6 hours. Divide between plates and serve for breakfast.

Nutrition: calories 200, fat 4, fiber 6, carbs 12, protein 6

Spinach Frittata

Preparation time: 10 minutes | *Cooking time: 5 hours and 10 minutes* | *Servings: 2*

Ingredients:
- Cooking spray
- 1 cup baby spinach
- 1 cup cherry tomatoes, halved
- 3 spring onions, chopped
- 3 ounces roasted red peppers, drained and chopped
- 2 ounces mozzarella, shredded
- 4 eggs, whisked
- ½ teaspoon allspice, ground
- A pinch of salt and black pepper

Directions:
Grease a pan with the cooking spray, heat up over medium heat, add the spring onions and roasted peppers and cook for 10 minutes. Transfer the mix to the slow cooker, add the eggs mixed with the rest of the ingredients, toss, spread into the pot, put the lid on and cook on Low for 5 hours. Divide the frittata between plates and serve.

Nutrition: calories 251, fat 4, fiber 6, carbs 12, protein 5

Chili Eggs Mix

Preparation time: 10 minutes | Cooking time: 3 hours | Servings: 2

Ingredients:
- Cooking spray
- 3 spring onions, chopped
- 2 tablespoons sun dried tomatoes, chopped
- 1 ounce canned and roasted green chili pepper, chopped
- ½ teaspoon rosemary, dried
- Salt and black pepper to the taste
- 3 ounces cheddar cheese, shredded
- 4 eggs, whisked
- ¼ cup heavy cream
- 1 tablespoon chives, chopped

Directions:
Grease your slow cooker with cooking spray and mix the eggs with the chili peppers and the other ingredients except the cheese. Toss everything into the pot, sprinkle the cheese on top, put the lid on and cook on High for 3 hours. Divide between plates and serve.

Nutrition: calories 224, fat 4, fiber 7, carbs 18, protein 11

Cheesy Eggs

Preparation time: 10 minutes | Cooking time: 3 hours | Servings: 2

Ingredients:
- 4 eggs, whisked
- ¼ cup spring onions, chopped
- 1 tablespoon oregano, chopped
- 1 cup milk
- 2 ounces feta cheese, crumbled
- A pinch of salt and black pepper
- Cooking spray

Directions:
In a bowl, combine the eggs with the spring onions and the other ingredients except the cooking spray and whisk. Grease your slow cooker with cooking spray, add eggs mix, stir , put the lid on and cook on Low for 3 hours. Divide between plates and serve for breakfast.

Nutrition: calories 214, fat 4, fiber 7, carbs 18, protein 5

Tomato and Zucchini Eggs Mix

Preparation time: 10 minutes | Cooking time: 3 hours | Servings: 2

Ingredients:
- Cooking spray
- 4 eggs, whisked
- 2 spring onions, chopped
- 1 tablespoon basil, chopped
- ½ teaspoon turmeric powder
- ½ cup tomatoes, cubed
- 1 zucchini, grated
- ¼ teaspoon sweet paprika
- A pinch of salt and black pepper
- 1 tablespoon parsley, chopped
- 2 tablespoons parmesan, grated

Directions:
Grease your slow cooker with cooking spray, add the eggs mixed with the zucchini, tomatoes and the other ingredients except the cheese and stir well. Sprinkle the cheese, put the lid on and cook on High for 3 hours. Divide between plates and serve for breakfast right away.

Nutrition: calories 261, fat 5, fiber 7, carbs 19, protein 6

Chocolate Breakfast Bread

Preparation time: 10 minutes | Cooking time: 3 hours | Servings: 2

Ingredients:
- Cooking spray
- 1 cup almond flour
- ½ teaspoon baking soda
- ½ teaspoon cinnamon powder
- 1 tablespoon avocado oil
- 2 tablespoons maple syrup
- 2 eggs, whisked
- 1 tablespoon butter
- ½ tablespoon milk
- ½ teaspoon vanilla extract
- ½ cup dark chocolate, melted
- 2 tablespoons walnuts, chopped

Directions:
In a bowl, mix the flour with the baking soda, cinnamon, oil and the other ingredients except the cooking spray and stir well. Grease a loaf pan that fits the slow cooker with the cooking spray, pour the bread batter into the pan, put the pan in the slow cooker after you've lined it with tin foil, put the lid on and cook on High for 3 hours. Cool the sweet bread down, slice, divide between plates and serve for breakfast.

Nutrition: calories 200, fat 3, fiber 5, carbs 8, protein 4

Almond and Quinoa Bowls

Preparation time: 10 minutes | Cooking time: 5 hours | Servings: 2

Ingredients:
- 1 cup quinoa
- 2 cups almond milk
- 2 tablespoons butter, melted
- 2 tablespoons brown sugar
- A pinch of cinnamon powder
- A pinch of nutmeg, ground
- ¼ cup almonds, sliced
- Cooking spray

Directions:
Grease your slow cooker with the cooking spray, add the quinoa, milk, melted butter and the other ingredients, toss, put the lid on and cook on Low for 5 hours. Divide the mix into bowls and serve for breakfast.

Nutrition: calories 211, fat 3, fiber 6, carbs 12, protein 5

Carrots Casserole

Preparation time: 10 minutes | Cooking time: 3 hours | Servings: 2

Ingredients:
- 1 teaspoon ginger, ground
- ½ pound carrots, peeled and grated
- 2 eggs, whisked
- ½ teaspoon garlic powder
- ½ teaspoon rosemary, dried
- Salt and black pepper to the taste
- 1 red onion, chopped
- 1 tablespoons parsley, chopped
- 2 garlic cloves, minced
- ½ tablespoon olive oil

Directions:
Grease your slow cooker with the oil and mix the carrots with the eggs, ginger and the other ingredients inside. Toss, put the lid on, cook High for 3 hours, divide between plates and serve.

Nutrition: calories 218, fat 6, fiber 6, carbs 14, protein 5

Cranberry Maple Oatmeal

Preparation time: 10 minutes | Cooking time: 6 hours | Servings: 2

Ingredients:
- 1 cup almond milk
- ½ cup steel cut oats
- ½ cup cranberries
- ½ teaspoon vanilla extract
- 1 tablespoon maple syrup
- 1 tablespoon sugar

Directions:
In your slow cooker, mix the oats with the berries, milk and the other ingredients, toss, put the lid on and cook on Low for 6 hours. Divide into bowls and serve for breakfast.

Nutrition: calories 200, fat 5, fiber 7, carbs 14, protein 4

Mushroom Casserole

Preparation time: 10 minutes | Cooking time: 5 hours | Servings: 2

Ingredients:
- ½ cup mozzarella, shredded
- 2 eggs, whisked
- ½ tablespoon balsamic vinegar
- ½ tablespoon olive oil
- 4 ounces baby kale
- 1 red onion, chopped
- ¼ teaspoon oregano
- ½ pound white mushrooms, sliced
- Salt and black pepper to the taste
- Cooking spray

Directions:
In a bowl, mix the eggs with the kale, mushrooms and the other ingredients except the cheese and cooking spray and stir well. Grease your slow cooker with cooking spray, add the mushroom mix, spread, sprinkle the mozzarella all over, put the lid on and cook on Low for 5 hours. Divide between plates and serve for breakfast.

Nutrition: calories 216, fat 6, fiber 8, carbs 12, protein 4

Ginger Apple Bowls

Preparation time: 10 minutes | Cooking time: 6 hours | Servings: 2

Ingredients:
- 2 apples, cored, peeled and cut into medium chunks
- 1 tablespoon sugar
- 1 tablespoon ginger, grated
- 1 cup heavy cream
- ¼ teaspoon cinnamon powder
- ½ teaspoon vanilla extract
- ¼ teaspoon cardamom, ground

Directions:
In your slow cooker, combine the apples with the sugar, ginger and the other ingredients, toss, put the lid on and cook on Low for 6 hours. Divide into bowls and serve for breakfast.

Nutrition: calories 201, fat 3, fiber 7, carbs 19, protein 4

Granola Bowls

Preparation time: 10 minutes | Cooking time: 4 hours | Servings: 2

Ingredients:
- ½ cup granola
- ¼ cup coconut cream
- 2 tablespoons brown sugar
- 2 tablespoons cashew butter
- 1 teaspoon cinnamon powder
- ½ teaspoon nutmeg, ground

Directions:
In your slow cooker, mix the granola with the cream, sugar and the other ingredients, toss, put the lid on and cook on Low for 4 hours. Divide into bowls and serve for breakfast.

Nutrition: calories 218, fat 6, fiber 9, carbs 17, protein 6

Squash Bowls

Preparation time: 10 minutes | Cooking time: 6 hours | Servings: 2

Ingredients:
- 2 tablespoons walnuts, chopped
- 2 cups squash, peeled and cubed
- ½ cup coconut cream
- ½ teaspoon cinnamon powder
- ½ tablespoon sugar

Directions:
In your slow cooker, mix the squash with the nuts and the other ingredients, toss, put the lid on and cook on Low for 6 hours. Divide into bowls and serve.

Nutrition: calories 140, fat 1, fiber 2, carbs 2, protein 5

Lamb and Eggs Mix

Preparation time: 10 minutes | *Cooking time:* 6 hours | *Servings:* 2

Ingredients:
- 1 pound lamb meat, ground
- 4 eggs, whisked
- 1 tablespoon basil, chopped
- ½ teaspoon cumin powder
- 1 tablespoon chili powder
- 1 red onion, chopped
- 1 tablespoon olive oil
- A pinch of salt and black pepper

Directions:
Grease the slow cooker with the oil and mix the lamb with the eggs, basil and the other ingredients inside Toss, put the lid on, cook on Low for 6 hours, divide into bowls and serve for breakfast.

Nutrition: calories 220, fat 2, fiber 2, carbs 6, protein 2

Cauliflower Casserole

Preparation time: 10 minutes | *Cooking time:* 5 hours | *Servings:* 2

Ingredients:
- 1 pound cauliflower florets
- 3 eggs, whisked
- 1 red onion, sliced
- ½ teaspoon sweet paprika
- ½ teaspoon turmeric powder
- 1 garlic clove, minced
- A pinch of salt and black pepper
- Cooking spray

Directions:
Spray your slow cooker with the cooking spray, and mix the cauliflower with the eggs, onion and the other ingredients inside. Put the lid on, cook on Low for 5 hours, divide between 2 plates and serve for breakfast.

Nutrition: calories 200, fat 3, fiber 6, carbs 13, protein 8

Beef Meatloaf

Preparation time: 10 minutes | *Cooking time:* 4 hours | *Servings:* 2

Ingredients:
- 1 red onion, chopped
- 1 pound beef stew meat, ground
- ½ teaspoon chili powder
- 1 egg, whisked
- ½ teaspoon olive oil
- ½ teaspoon sweet paprika
- 2 tablespoons white flour
- ½ teaspoon oregano, chopped
- ½ tablespoon basil, chopped
- A pinch of salt and black pepper
- ½ teaspoon marjoram, dried

Directions:
In a bowl, mix the beef with the onion, chili powder and the other ingredients except the oil, stir well and shape your meatloaf. Grease a loaf pan that fits your slow cooker with the oil, add meatloaf mix into the pan, put it in your slow cooker, put the lid on and cook on Low for 4 hours. Slice and serve for breakfast.

Nutrition: calories 200, fat 6, fiber 12, carbs 17, protein 10

Leek Casserole

Preparation time: 10 minutes | *Cooking time:* 4 hours | *Servings:* 2

Ingredients:
- 1 cup leek, chopped
- Cooking spray
- ½ cup mozzarella, shredded
- 1 garlic clove, minced
- 4 eggs, whisked
- 1 cup beef sausage, chopped
- 1 tablespoon cilantro, chopped

Directions:
Grease the slow cooker with the cooking spray and mix the leek with the mozzarella and the other ingredients inside. Toss, spread into the pot, put the lid on and cook on Low for 4 hours. Divide between plates and serve for breakfast.

Nutrition: calories 232, fat 4, fiber 8, carbs 17, protein 4

Eggs and Sweet Potato Mix
Preparation time: 10 minutes | Cooking time: 6 hours | Servings: 2

Ingredients:
- ½ red onion, chopped
- ½ green bell pepper, chopped
- 2 sweet potatoes, peeled and grated
- ½ red bell pepper, chopped
- 1 garlic clove, minced
- ½ teaspoon olive oil
- 4 eggs, whisked
- 1 tablespoon chives, chopped
- A pinch of red pepper, crushed
- A pinch of salt and black pepper

Directions:
In a bowl, mix the eggs with the onion, bell peppers and the other ingredients except the oil and whisk well. Grease your slow cooker with the oil, add the eggs and potato mix, spread, put the lid on and cook on Low for 6 hours. Divide everything between plates and serve.

Nutrition: calories 261, fat 6, fiber 6, carbs 16, protein 4

Pork and Eggplant Casserole
Preparation time: 10 minutes | Cooking time: 6 hours | Servings: 2

Ingredients:
- 1 red onion, chopped
- 1 eggplant, cubed
- ½ pound pork stew meat, ground
- 3 eggs, whisked
- ½ teaspoon chili powder
- ½ teaspoon garam masala
- 1 tablespoon sweet paprika
- 1 teaspoon olive oil

Directions:
In a bowl, mix the eggs with the meat, onion, eggplant and the other ingredients except the oil and stir well. Grease your slow cooker with oil, add the pork and eggplant mix, spread into the pot, put the lid on and cook on Low for 6 hours. Divide the mix between plates and serve for breakfast.

Nutrition: calories 261, fat 7, fiber 6, carbs 16, protein 7

Apple Spread
Preparation time: 10 minutes | Cooking time: 4 hours | Servings: 2

Ingredients:
- 2 apples, cored, peeled and pureed
- ½ cup coconut cream
- 2 tablespoons apple cider
- 2 tablespoons sugar
- ¼ teaspoon cinnamon powder
- ½ teaspoon lemon juice
- ¼ teaspoon ginger, grated

Directions:
In your slow cooker, mix the apple puree with the cream, sugar and the other ingredients, whisk, put the lid on and cook on High for 4 hours. Blend using an immersion blender, cool down and serve for breakfast.

Nutrition: calories 172, fat 3, fiber 3, carbs 8, protein 3

Cherries and Cocoa Oats
Preparation time: 10 minutes | Cooking time: 7 hours | Servings: 2

Ingredients:
- 1 cup almond milk
- ½ cup steel cut oats
- 1 tablespoon cocoa powder
- ½ cup cherries, pitted
- 2 tablespoons sugar
- ¼ teaspoon vanilla extract

Directions:
In your slow cooker, mix the almond milk with the cherries and the other ingredients, toss, put the lid on and cook on Low for 7 hours. Divide into 2 bowls and serve for breakfast.

Nutrition: calories 150, fat 1, fiber 2, carbs 6, protein 5

Beans Salad

Preparation time: 10 minutes | Cooking time: 6 hours | Servings: 2

Ingredients:
- 1 cup canned black beans, drained
- 1 cup canned red kidney beans, drained
- 1 cup baby spinach
- 2 spring onions, chopped
- ½ red bell pepper, chopped
- ¼ teaspoon turmeric powder
- ½ teaspoon garam masala
- ¼ cup veggie stock
- A pinch of cumin, ground
- A pinch of chili powder
- A pinch of salt and black pepper
- ½ cup salsa

Directions:
In your slow cooker, mix the beans with the spinach, onions and the other ingredients, toss, put the lid on and cook on High for 6 hours Divide the mix into bowls and serve for breakfast.

Nutrition: calories 130, fat 4, fiber 2, carbs 5, protein 4

Peppers Rice Mix

Preparation time: 10 minutes | Cooking time: 3 hours | Servings: 2

Ingredients:
- ½ cup brown rice
- 1 cup chicken stock
- 2 spring onions, chopped
- ½ orange bell pepper, chopped
- ½ red bell pepper, chopped
- ½ green bell pepper, chopped
- 2 ounces canned green chilies, chopped
- ½ cup canned black beans, drained
- ½ cup mild salsa
- ½ teaspoon sweet paprika
- ½ teaspoon lime zest, grated
- A pinch of salt and black pepper

Directions:
In your slow cooker, mix the rice with the stock, spring onions and the other ingredients, toss, put the lid on and cook on High for 3 hours. Divide the mix into bowls and serve for breakfast.

Nutrition: calories 140, fat 2, fiber 2, carbs 5, protein 5

Cashew Butter

Preparation time: 10 minutes | Cooking time: 4 hours | Servings: 2

Ingredients:
- 1 cup cashews, soaked overnight, drained and blended
- ½ cup coconut cream
- ¼ teaspoon cinnamon powder
- 1 teaspoon lemon zest, grated
- 2 tablespoons sugar
- A pinch of ginger, ground

Directions:
In your slow cooker, mix the cashews with the cream and the other ingredients, whisk, put the lid on and cook on High for 4 hours. Blend using an immersion blender, divide into jars, and serve for breakfast cold.

Nutrition: calories 143, fat 2, fiber 3, carbs 3, protein 4

Pumpkin and Berries Bowls

Preparation time: 10 minutes | Cooking time: 4 hours | Servings: 2

Ingredients:
- ½ cup coconut cream
- 1 and ½ cups pumpkin, peeled and cubed
- 1 cup blackberries
- 2 tablespoons maple syrup
- ¼ teaspoon nutmeg, ground
- ½ teaspoon vanilla extract

Directions:
In your slow cooker, combine the pumpkin with the berries, cream and the other ingredients, toss, put the lid on and cook on Low for 4 hours. Divide into bowls and serve for breakfast!

Nutrition: calories 120, fat 2, fiber 2, carbs 4, protein 2

Quinoa and Chia Pudding

Preparation time: 10 minutes | Cooking time: 6 hours | Servings: 2

Ingredients:

- 1 cup coconut cream
- 2 tablespoons chia seeds
- ½ cup almond milk
- 1 tablespoon sugar
- ½ cup quinoa, rinsed
- ½ teaspoon vanilla extract

Directions:

In your slow cooker, mix the cream with the chia seeds and the other ingredients, toss, put the lid on and cook on Low for 6 hours. Divide into 2 bowls and serve for breakfast.

Nutrition: calories 120, fat 2, fiber 1, carbs 6, protein 4

Beans Breakfast Bowls

Preparation time: 10 minutes | Cooking time: 3 hours and 10 minutes | Servings: 2

Ingredients:

- 2 spring onions, chopped
- ½ green bell pepper, chopped
- ½ red bell pepper, chopped
- ½ yellow onion, chopped
- 5 ounces canned black beans, drained
- 5 ounces canned red kidney beans, drained
- 5 ounces canned pinto beans, drained
- ½ cup corn
- ½ teaspoon turmeric powder
- 1 teaspoons chili powder
- ½ teaspoon hot sauce
- A pinch of salt and black pepper
- 1 tablespoon olive oil

Directions:

Heat up a pan with the oil over medium-high heat, add the spring onions, bell peppers and the onion, sauté for 10 minutes and transfer to the slow cooker. Add the beans and the other ingredients, toss, put the lid on and cook on High for 3 hours. Divide the mix into bowls and serve for breakfast.

Nutrition: calories 240, fat 4, fiber 2, carbs 6, protein 9

Basil Sausage and Broccoli Mix

Preparation time: 10 minutes | Cooking time: 8 hours and 10 minutes | Servings: 2

Ingredients:

- 4 eggs, whisked
- 1 yellow onion, chopped
- 2 spring onions, chopped
- 1 cup pork sausage, chopped
- 1 cup broccoli florets
- 2 teaspoons basil, dried
- A pinch of salt and black pepper
- A drizzle of olive oil

Directions:

Heat up a pan with the oil over medium-high heat, add the yellow onion and the sausage, toss, cook for 10 minutes and transfer to the slow cooker. Add the eggs and the other ingredients, toss, put the lid on and cook on Low for 8 hours. Divide between plates and serve for breakfast.

Nutrition: calories 251, fat 4, fiber 4, carbs 6, protein 7

Zucchini and Cauliflower Eggs Mix

Preparation time: 10 minutes | Cooking time: 6 hours | Servings: 2

Ingredients:
- 2 spring onions, chopped
- A pinch of salt and black pepper
- 4 eggs, whisked
- ½ cup cauliflower florets
- 1 zucchini, grated
- ¼ cup cheddar cheese, shredded
- ¼ cup whipping cream
- 1 tablespoon chives, chopped
- Cooking spray

Directions:
Grease the slow cooker with the cooking spray and mix the eggs with the spring onions, cauliflower and the other ingredients inside. Put the lid on and cook on Low for 6 hours. Divide the mix between plates and serve for breakfast.

Nutrition: calories 211, fat 7, fiber 4, carbs 5, protein 5

Mushroom Quiche

Preparation time: 10 minutes | Cooking time: 6 hours | Servings: 2

Ingredients:
- 2 cups baby Bella mushrooms, chopped
- ½ cup cheddar cheese, shredded
- 4 eggs, whisked
- ½ cup heavy cream
- 1 tablespoon basil, chopped
- 2 tablespoons chives, chopped
- A pinch of salt and black pepper
- ½ cup almond flour
- ¼ teaspoons baking soda
- Cooking spray

Directions:
In a bowl, mix the eggs with the cream, flour and the other ingredients except the cooking spray and stir well. Grease the slow cooker with the cooking spray, pour the quiche mix, spread well, put the lid on and cook on High for 6 hours. Slice the quiche, divide between plates and serve for breakfast.

Nutrition: calories 211, fat 6, fiber 6, carbs 6, protein 10

Scallions Quinoa and Carrots Bowls

Preparation time: 10 minutes | Cooking time: 4 hours | Servings: 2

Ingredients:
- 1 cup quinoa
- 2 cups veggie stock
- 4 scallions, chopped
- 2 carrots, peeled and grated
- 1 tablespoon olive oil
- A pinch of salt and black pepper
- 3 eggs, whisked
- 2 tablespoons cheddar cheese, grated
- 2 tablespoons heavy cream

Directions:
In a bowl mix the eggs with the cream, cheddar, salt and pepper and whisk. Grease the slow cooker with the oil, add the quinoa, scallions, carrots and the stock, stir, put the lid on and cook on Low for 2 hours. Add the eggs mix, stir the whole thing, cook on Low for 2 more hours, divide into bowls and serve for breakfast.

Nutrition: calories 172, fat 5, fiber 4, carbs 6, protein 8

Ham Omelet

Preparation time: 10 minutes | Cooking time: 3 hours | Servings: 2

Ingredients:

- Cooking spray
- 4 eggs, whisked
- 1 tablespoon sour cream
- 2 spring onions, chopped
- 1 small yellow onion, chopped
- ½ cup ham, chopped
- ½ cup cheddar cheese, shredded
- 1 tablespoon chives, chopped
- A pinch of salt and black pepper

Directions:

Grease your slow cooker with the cooking spray and mix the eggs with the sour cream, spring onions and the other ingredients inside. Toss the mix, spread into the pot, put the lid on and cook on High for 3 hours. Divide the mix between plates and serve for breakfast right away.

Nutrition: calories 192, fat 6, fiber 5, carbs 6, protein 12

Peppers and Eggs Mix

Preparation time: 10 minutes | Cooking time: 4 hours | Servings: 2

Ingredients:

- 4 eggs, whisked
- ½ teaspoon coriander, ground
- ½ teaspoon rosemary, dried
- 2 spring onions, chopped
- 1 red bell pepper, cut into strips
- 1 green bell pepper, cut into strips
- 1 yellow bell pepper, cut into strips
- ¼ cup heavy cream
- ½ teaspoon garlic powder
- A pinch of salt and black pepper
- 1 teaspoon sweet paprika
- Cooking spray

Directions:

Grease your slow cooker with the cooking spray, and mix the eggs with the coriander, rosemary and the other ingredients into the pot. Put the lid on, cook on Low for 4 hours, divide between plates and serve for breakfast.

Nutrition: calories 172, fat 6, fiber 3, carbs 6, protein 7

Baby Spinach Rice Mix

Preparation time: 10 minutes | Cooking time: 6 hours | Servings: 4

Ingredients:

- ¼ cup mozzarella, shredded
- ½ cup baby spinach
- ½ cup wild rice
- 1 and ½ cups chicken stock
- ½ teaspoon turmeric powder
- ½ teaspoon oregano, dried
- A pinch of salt and black pepper
- 3 scallions, minced
- ¾ cup goat cheese, crumbled

Directions:

In your slow cooker, mix the rice with the stock, turmeric and the other ingredients, toss, put the lid on and cook on Low for 6 hours. Divide the mix into bowls and serve for breakfast.

Nutrition: calories 199, fat 3, fiber 6, carbs 6, protein 4

Herbed Egg Scramble

Preparation time: 10 minutes | Cooking time: 6 hours | Servings: 2

Ingredients:

- 4 eggs, whisked
- ¼ cup heavy cream
- ¼ cup mozzarella, shredded
- 1 tablespoon chives, chopped
- 1 tablespoon oregano, chopped
- 1 tablespoon rosemary, chopped
- A pinch of salt and black pepper
- Cooking spray

Directions:

Grease your slow cooker with the cooking spray, and mix the eggs with the cream, herbs and the other ingredients inside. Stir well, put the lid on, cook for 6 hours on Low, stir once again, divide between plates and serve.

Nutrition: calories 177, fat 4, fiber 5, carbs 6, protein 9

Peas and Rice Bowls

Preparation time: 10 minutes | Cooking time: 6 hours | Servings: 2

Ingredients:

- ¼ cup peas
- 1 cup wild rice
- 2 cups veggie stock
- ¼ cup heavy cream
- 1 tablespoon dill, chopped
- 3 spring onions, chopped
- ½ teaspoon coriander, ground
- ½ teaspoon allspice, ground
- A pinch of salt and black pepper
- ¼ cup cheddar cheese, shredded
- 1 teaspoon olive oil

Directions:

Grease the slow cooker with the oil, add the rice, peas, stock and the other ingredients except the dill and heavy cream, stir, put the lid on and cook on Low for 3 hours. Add the remaining ingredients, stir the mix, put the lid back on, cook on Low for 3 more hours, divide into bowls and serve for breakfast.

Nutrition: calories 241, fat 5, fiber 4, carbs 5, protein 12

Asparagus Casserole

Preparation time: 10 minutes | Cooking time: 5 hours | Servings: 2

Ingredients:

- 1 pound asparagus spears, cut into medium pieces
- 1 red onion, sliced
- 4 eggs, whisked
- ½ cup cheddar cheese, shredded
- ¼ cup heavy cream
- 1 tablespoon chives, chopped
- A drizzle of olive oil
- A pinch of salt and black pepper

Directions:

Grease your slow cooker with the oil, and mix the eggs with the asparagus, onion and the other ingredients except the cheese into the pot. Sprinkle the cheese all over, put the lid on and cook on Low for 5 hours. Divide between plates and serve right away for breakfast.

Nutrition: calories 211, fat 4, fiber 4, carbs 6, protein 5

Slow Cooker Lunch Recipes for 2

Seafood Soup

Preparation time: 10 minutes | Cooking time: 8 hours | Servings: 2

Ingredients:
- 2 cups chicken stock
- 1 cup coconut milk
- 1 sweet potato, cubed
- ½ yellow onion, chopped
- 1 bay leaf
- 1 carrot, peeled and sliced
- ½ tablespoon thyme, dried
- Salt and black pepper to the taste
- ½ pounds salmon fillets, skinless, boneless cubed
- 12 shrimp, peeled and deveined
- 1 tablespoon chives, chopped

Directions:
In your slow cooker, mix the carrot with the sweet potato, onion and the other ingredients except the salmon, shrimp and chives, toss, put the lid on and cook on Low for 6 hours. Add the rest of the ingredients, toss, put the lid on and cook on Low for 2 more hours. Divide the soup into bowls and serve for lunch.

Nutrition: calories 354, fat 10, fiber 4, carbs 17, protein 12

Sesame Salmon Bowls

Preparation time: 10 minutes | Cooking time: 3 hours | Servings: 2

Ingredients:
- 2 salmon fillets, boneless and roughly cubed
- 1 cup cherry tomatoes, halved
- 3 spring onions, chopped
- 1 cup baby spinach
- ½ cup chicken stock
- Salt and black pepper to the taste
- 2 tablespoons balsamic vinegar
- 2 tablespoons lemon juice
- 1 teaspoon sesame seeds

Directions:
In your slow cooker, mix the salmon with the cherry tomatoes, spring onions and the other ingredients, toss gently, put the lid on and cook on Low for 3 hours. Divide everything into bowls and serve.

Nutrition: calories 230, fat 4, fiber 2, carbs 7, protein 6

Shrimp Stew

Preparation time: 10 minutes | Cooking time: 3 hours | Servings: 2

Ingredients:
- 1 garlic clove, minced
- 1 red onion, chopped
- 1 cup canned tomatoes, crushed
- 1 cup veggie stock
- ½ teaspoon turmeric powder
- 1 pound shrimp, peeled and deveined
- ½ teaspoon coriander, ground
- ½ teaspoon thyme, dried
- ½ teaspoon basil, dried
- A pinch of salt and black pepper
- A pinch of red pepper flakes

Directions:
In your slow cooker, mix the onion with the garlic, shrimp and the other ingredients, toss, put the lid on and cook on High for 3 hours. Divide the stew into bowls and serve.

Nutrition: calories 230, fat 3, fiber 5, carbs 17, protein 6

Garlic Shrimp and Spinach

Preparation time: 10 minutes | Cooking time: 2 hours | Servings: 2

Ingredients:

- 1 pound shrimp, peeled and deveined
- 1 cup baby spinach
- ½ teaspoon sweet paprika
- ½ cup chicken stock
- 1 garlic clove, minced
- 2 jalapeno peppers, chopped
- Cooking spray
- 1 teaspoon coriander, ground
- ½ teaspoon rosemary, dried
- A pinch of sea salt and black pepper

Directions:

Grease the slow cooker with the oil, add the shrimp, spinach and the other ingredients, toss, put the lid on and cook on High for 2 hours. Divide everything between plates and serve for lunch.

Nutrition: calories 200, fat 4, fiber 6, carbs 16, protein 4

Ginger Salmon

Preparation time: 10 minutes | Cooking time: 3 hours | Servings: 2

Ingredients:

- 2 salmon fillets, boneless
- 1 tablespoon olive oil
- 1 tablespoon balsamic vinegar
- 1 tablespoon ginger, grated
- A pinch of nutmeg, ground
- A pinch of cloves, ground
- A pinch of salt and black pepper
- 1 teaspoon onion powder
- ½ teaspoon cayenne pepper
- ¼ cup chicken stock

Directions:

Grease the slow cooker with the oil and arrange the salmon fillets inside. Add the vinegar, ginger and the other ingredients, rub gently, put the lid on and cook on Low for 3 hours. Divide the fish between plates and serve with a side salad for lunch.

Nutrition: calories 220, fat 13, fiber 6, carbs 16, protein 4

Creamy Cod Stew

Preparation time: 10 minutes | Cooking time: 3 hours | Servings: 2

Ingredients:

- ½ pound cod fillets, boneless and cubed
- 2 spring onions, chopped
- ¼ cup heavy cream
- 1 carrot, sliced
- 1 zucchini, cubed
- 1 tomato, cubed
- 1 cup chicken stock
- 1 tablespoon olive oil
- 1 green bell pepper, chopped
- 1 tablespoon chives, chopped
- A pinch of salt and black pepper

Directions:

In your slow cooker, combine the fish with the spring onions, carrot and the other ingredients except the cream, toss gently, put the lid on and cook on High for 2 hours and 30 minutes. Add the cream, toss gently, put the lid back on, cook the stew on Low for 30 minutes more, divide into bowls and serve.

Nutrition: calories 270, fat 4, fiber 7, carbs 13, protein 7

Sweet Potato and Clam Chowder

Preparation time: 10 minutes | Cooking time: 3 hours and 30 minutes | Servings: 2

Ingredients:

- 1 small yellow onion, chopped
- 1 carrot, chopped
- 1 red bell pepper, cubed
- 6 ounces canned clams, chopped
- 1 sweet potato, chopped
- 2 cups chicken stock
- ½ cup coconut milk
- 1 teaspoon Worcestershire sauce

Directions:

In your slow cooker, mix the onion with the carrot, clams and the other ingredients, toss, put the lid on and cook on High for 3 hours. Divide the chowder into bowls and serve for lunch.

Nutrition: calories 230, fat 10, fiber 7, carbs 18, protein 10

Maple Chicken Mix

Preparation time: 10 minutes | Cooking time: 6 hours | Servings: 2

Ingredients:

- 2 spring onions, chopped
- 1 pound chicken breast, skinless and boneless
- 2 garlic cloves, minced
- 1 tablespoon maple syrup
- A pinch of salt and black pepper
- ½ cup chicken stock
- ½ cup tomato sauce
- 1 tablespoon chives, chopped
- 1 teaspoon basil, dried

Directions:

In your slow cooker mix the chicken with the garlic, maple syrup and the other ingredients, toss, put the lid on and cook on Low for 6 hours. Divide the mix between plates and serve for lunch.

Nutrition: calories 200, fat 3, fiber 3, carbs 17, protein 6

Salsa Chicken

Preparation time: 10 minutes | Cooking time: 8 hours | Servings: 2

Ingredients:

- 7 ounces mild salsa
- 1 pound chicken breast, skinless, boneless and cubed
- 1 small yellow onion, chopped
- ½ teaspoon coriander, ground
- ½ teaspoon rosemary, dried
- 1 green bell pepper, chopped
- Cooking spray
- 1 tablespoon cilantro, chopped
- 1 red bell pepper, chopped
- 1 tablespoon chili powder

Directions:

Grease the slow cooker with the cooking spray and mix the chicken with the salsa, onion and the other ingredients inside. Put the lid on, cook on Low for 8 hours, divide into bowls and serve for lunch.

Nutrition: calories 240, fat 3, fiber 7, carbs 17, protein 8

Turkey and Mushrooms

Preparation time: 10 minutes | Cooking time: 7 hours and 10 minutes | Servings: 2

Ingredients:

- 1 red onion, sliced
- 2 garlic cloves, minced
- 1 pound turkey breast, skinless, boneless and cubed
- 1 tablespoon olive oil
- 1 teaspoon oregano, dried
- 1 teaspoon basil, dried
- A pinch of red pepper flakes
- 1 cup mushrooms, sliced
- ¼ cup chicken stock
- ½ cup canned tomatoes, chopped
- A pinch of salt and black pepper

Directions:

Heat up a pan with the oil over medium-high heat, add the onion, garlic and the meat, brown for 10 minutes and transfer to the slow cooker. Add the oregano, basil and the other ingredients, toss, put the lid on and cook on Low for 7 hours. Divide into bowls and serve for lunch.

Nutrition: calories 240, fat 4, fiber 6, carbs 18, protein 10

Indian Chicken and Tomato Mix

Preparation time: 10 minutes | Cooking time: 6 hours | Servings: 2

Ingredients:

- 1 cup cherry tomatoes, halved
- 1 pound chicken breast, skinless, boneless and cubed
- 1 red onion, sliced
- 1 tablespoons garam masala
- 1 garlic clove, minced
- ½ small yellow onion, chopped
- ½ teaspoon ginger powder
- A pinch of salt and cayenne pepper
- ½ teaspoon sweet paprika
- 2 tablespoons chives, chopped

Directions:

In your slow cooker, mix the chicken with the tomatoes, onion and the other ingredients, toss, put the lid on and cook on Low for 6 hours. Divide into bowls and serve right away.

Nutrition: calories 259, fat 3, fiber 7, carbs 17, protein 14

Turkey and Figs

Preparation time: 10 minutes | Cooking time: 8 hours | Servings: 2

Ingredients:

- 1 pound turkey breast, boneless, skinless and sliced
- ½ cup black figs, halved
- 1 red onion, sliced
- ½ cup tomato sauce
- ½ teaspoon onion powder
- ¼ teaspoon garlic powder
- 1 tablespoon basil, chopped
- ½ teaspoon chili powder
- ¼ cup white wine
- ½ teaspoon thyme, dried
- ¼ teaspoon sage, dried
- ½ teaspoon paprika, dried
- A pinch of salt and black pepper

Directions:

In your slow cooker, mix the turkey breast with the figs, onion and the other ingredients, toss, put the lid on and cook on Low for 8 hours. Divide between plates and serve.

Nutrition: calories 220, fat 5, fiber 8, carbs 18, protein 15

Turkey and Walnuts

Preparation time: 10 minutes | Cooking time: 8 hours | Servings: 2

Ingredients:
- 1 pound turkey breast, skinless, boneless and sliced
- ½ cup scallions, chopped
- 2 tablespoons walnuts, chopped
- 1 tablespoon lemon juice
- ¼ cup veggie stock
- ½ teaspoon chili powder
- 1 tablespoon olive oil
- 1 tablespoon rosemary, chopped
- Salt and black pepper to the taste

Directions:
In your slow cooker, mix the turkey with the scallions, walnuts and the other ingredients, toss, put the lid on and cook on Low for 8 hours. Divide everything between plates and serve.

Nutrition: calories 264, fat 4, fiber 6, carbs 15, protein 15

Slow Cooked Thyme Chicken

Preparation time: 10 minutes | Cooking time: 7 hours | Servings: 2

Ingredients:
- 1 pound chicken legs
- 1 tablespoon thyme, chopped
- 2 garlic cloves, minced
- ½ cup chicken stock
- 1 carrot, chopped
- ½ yellow onion, chopped
- A pinch of salt and white pepper
- Juice of ½ lemon

Directions:
In your slow cooker, mix the chicken legs with the thyme, garlic and the other ingredients, toss, put the lid on and cook on Low for 7 hours. Divide between plates and serve.

Nutrition: calories 320, fat 4, fiber 7, carbs 16, protein 6

Roasted Beef and Cauliflower

Preparation time: 10 minutes | Cooking time: 8 hours | Servings: 2

Ingredients:
- 1 pound beef chuck roast, sliced
- 1 cup cauliflower florets
- ½ cup tomato sauce
- ½ cup veggie stock
- ½ tablespoon olive oil
- 2 garlic cloves, minced
- ½ carrot, roughly chopped
- 1 celery rib, roughly chopped
- A pinch of salt and black pepper to the taste
- 1 tablespoon parsley, chopped

Directions:
In your slow cooker, mix the roast with the cauliflower, tomato sauce and the other ingredients, toss, put the lid on and cook on Low for 8 hours. Divide between plates and serve.

Nutrition: calories 340, fat 5, fiber 7, carbs 18, protein 22

Soy Pork Chops

Preparation time: 10 minutes | Cooking time: 7 hours | Servings: 2

Ingredients:
- 1 pound pork chops
- 2 tablespoons sugar
- 2 tablespoons soy sauce
- ½ cup beef stock
- 1 tablespoon balsamic vinegar
- 1 tablespoon cilantro, chopped

Directions:
In your slow cooker, mix the pork chops with the soy sauce and the other ingredients, toss, put the lid on and cook on Low for 7 hours. Divide everything between plates and serve.

Nutrition: calories 345, fat 5, fiber 7, carbs 17, protein 14

Pork and Cranberries

Preparation time: 10 minutes | Cooking time: 8 hours | Servings: 2

Ingredients:
- 1 pound pork tenderloin, roughly cubed
- ½ cup cranberries
- ½ cup red wine
- ½ teaspoon sweet paprika
- ½ teaspoon chili powder
- 1 tablespoon maple syrup

Directions:
In your slow cooker, mix the pork with the cranberries, wine and the other ingredients, toss, put the lid on and cook on Low for 8 hours Divide between plates and serve.

Nutrition: calories 400, fat 12, fiber 8, carbs 18, protein 20

Lamb and Onion Stew

Preparation time: 10 minutes | Cooking time: 8 hours | Servings: 2

Ingredients:
- 1 pound lamb meat, cubed
- 1 red onion, sliced
- 3 spring onions, sliced
- Salt and black pepper to the taste
- 1 tablespoon olive oil
- ½ teaspoon rosemary, dried
- ¼ teaspoon thyme, dried
- 1 cup water
- ½ cup baby carrots, peeled
- ½ cup tomato sauce
- 1 tablespoon cilantro, chopped

Directions:
In your slow cooker, mix the lamb with the onion, spring onions and the other ingredients, toss, put the lid on and cook on Low for 8 hours Divide the stew between plates and serve hot.

Nutrition: calories 350, fat 8, fiber 3, carbs 14, protein 16

Pork Roast and Olives

Preparation time: 10 minutes | Cooking time: 6 hours | Servings: 2

Ingredients:
- 1 pound pork roast, sliced
- ½ cup black olives, pitted and halved
- ½ cup kalamata olives, pitted and halved
- 2 medium carrots, chopped
- ½ cup tomato sauce
- 1 small yellow onion, chopped
- 2 garlic cloves, minced
- 1 bay leaf
- Salt and black pepper to the taste

Directions:
In your slow cooker, mix the pork roast with the olives and the other ingredients, toss, put the lid on and cook on High for 6 hours Divide everything between plates and serve.

Nutrition: calories 360, fat 4, fiber 3, carbs 17, protein 27

Beef Stew

Preparation time: 10 minutes | Cooking time: 6 hours and 10 minutes | Servings: 2

Ingredients:
- 1 tablespoon olive oil
- 1 red onion, chopped
- 1 carrot, peeled and sliced
- 1 pound beef meat, cubed
- ½ cup beef stock
- ½ cup canned tomatoes, chopped
- 2 tablespoons tomato sauce
- 2 tablespoons balsamic vinegar
- 2 garlic cloves, minced
- ½ cup black olives, pitted and sliced
- 1 tablespoon rosemary, chopped
- Salt and black pepper to the taste

Directions:
Heat up a pan with the oil over medium-high heat, add the meat, brown for 10 minutes and transfer to your slow cooker Add the rest of the ingredients, toss, put the lid on and cook on High for 6 hours Divide between plates and serve right away!

Nutrition: calories 370, fat 14, fiber 6, carbs 26, protein 38

Beef and Celery Stew

Preparation time: 10 minutes | Cooking time: 8 hours | Servings: 2

Ingredients:

- ½ cup beef stock
- 1 pound beef stew meat, cubed
- 1 cup celery, cubed
- ½ cup tomato sauce
- 2 carrots, chopped
- ½ cup mushrooms, halved
- ½ red onion, roughly chopped
- ½ tablespoon olive oil
- Salt and black pepper to the taste
- ¼ cup red wine
- 1 tablespoon parsley, chopped

Directions:

In your slow cooker, mix the beef with the stock, celery and the other ingredients, toss, put the lid on and cook on Low for 8 hours. Divide the stew into bowls and serve.

Nutrition: calories 433, fat 20, fiber 4, carbs 14, protein 39

Tomato Pasta Mix

Preparation time: 10 minutes | Cooking time: 6 hours | Servings: 2

Ingredients:

- ½ pound beef stew meat, ground
- 1 red onion, chopped
- ½ teaspoon sweet paprika
- ½ teaspoon chili powder
- Salt and black pepper to the taste
- ½ teaspoon basil, dried
- ½ teaspoon parsley, dried
- 14 ounces canned tomatoes, chopped
- 1 cup chicken stock
- 1 cup short pasta

Directions:

In your slow cooker, mix the beef with the onion, paprika and the other ingredients except the pasta, toss, put the lid on and cook on Low for 5 hours and 30 minutes. Add the pasta, stir, put the lid on again and cook on Low for 30 minutes more. Divide everything between plates and serve.

Nutrition: calories 300, fat 6, fiber 8, carbs 18, protein 17

Honey Lamb Roast

Preparation time: 10 minutes | Cooking time: 7 hours | Servings: 2

Ingredients:

- 1 pound lamb roast, sliced
- 3 tablespoons honey
- ½ tablespoon basil, dried
- ½ tablespoons oregano, dried
- 1 tablespoon garlic, minced
- 1 tablespoon olive oil
- Salt and black pepper to the taste
- ½ cup beef stock

Directions:

In your slow cooker, mix the lamb roast with the honey, basil and the other ingredients, toss well, put the lid on and cook on Low for 7 hours. Divide everything between plates and serve.

Nutrition: calories 374, fat 6, fiber 8, carbs 29, protein 6

Worcestershire Beef Mix

Preparation time: 10 minutes | Cooking time: 8 hours | Servings: 2

Ingredients:

- 1 pound beef stew meat, cubed
- 1 teaspoon chili powder
- Salt and black pepper to the taste
- 1 cup beef stock
- 1 and ½ tablespoons Worcestershire sauce
- 1 teaspoon garlic, minced
- 2 ounces cream cheese, soft
- Cooking spray

Directions:

Grease your slow cooker with the cooking spray, and mix the beef with the stock and the other ingredients inside. Put the lid on, cook on Low for 8 hours, divide between plates and serve.

Nutrition: calories 372, fat 6, fiber 9, carbs 18, protein 22

Chickpeas Stew

Preparation time: 10 minutes | Cooking time: 6 hours | Servings: 2

Ingredients:
- ½ tablespoon olive oil
- 1 red onion, chopped
- 2 garlic cloves, minced
- 1 red chili pepper, chopped
- ¼ cup carrots, chopped
- 6 ounces canned tomatoes, chopped
- 6 ounces canned chickpeas, drained
- ½ cup chicken stock
- 1 bay leaf
- ½ teaspoon coriander, ground
- A pinch of red pepper flakes
- ½ tablespoon parsley, chopped
- Salt and black pepper to the taste

Directions:
In your slow cooker, mix the chickpeas with the onion, garlic and the other ingredients, toss, put the lid on and cook on Low for 6 hours. Divide into bowls and serve.

Nutrition: calories 462, fat 7, fiber 9, carbs 30, protein 17

Lentils Soup

Preparation time: 10 minutes | Cooking time: 4 hours | Servings: 2

Ingredients:
- 2 garlic cloves, minced
- 1 carrot, chopped
- 1 red onion, chopped
- 3 cups veggie stock
- 1 cup brown lentils
- ½ teaspoon cumin, ground
- 1 bay leaf
- 1 tablespoon lime juice
- 1 tablespoon cilantro, chopped
- Salt and black pepper to the taste

Directions:
In your slow cooker, mix the lentils with the garlic, carrot and the other ingredients, toss, put the lid on and cook on High for 4 hours. Ladle the soup into bowls and serve.

Nutrition: calories 361, fat 7, fiber 7, carbs 16, protein 5

Chicken Soup

Preparation time: 10 minutes | Cooking time: 7 hours | Servings: 2

Ingredients:
- ½ pound chicken breast, skinless, boneless and cubed
- 3 cups chicken stock
- 1 red onion, chopped
- 1 garlic clove, minced
- ½ celery stalk, chopped
- ¼ teaspoon chili powder
- ¼ teaspoon sweet paprika
- A pinch of salt and black pepper
- A pinch of cayenne pepper
- 1 tablespoon lemon juice
- ½ tablespoon chives, chopped

Directions:
In your slow cooker, mix the chicken with the stock, onion and the other ingredients, toss, put the lid on and cook on Low for 7 hours. Divide into bowls and serve right away.

Nutrition: calories 351, fat 6, fiber 7, carbs 17, protein 16

Lime and Thyme Chicken

Preparation time: 10 minutes | Cooking time: 6 hours | Servings: 2

Ingredients:

- 1 pound chicken thighs, boneless and skinless
- Juice of 1 lime
- 1 tablespoon lime zest, grated
- 2 teaspoons olive oil
- ½ cup tomato sauce
- 2 garlic cloves, minced
- 1 tablespoon thyme, chopped
- Salt and black pepper to the taste

Directions:

In your slow cooker, mix the chicken with the lime juice, zest and the other ingredients, toss, put the lid on and cook on High for 6 hours. Divide between plates and serve right away.

Nutrition: calories 324, fat 7, fiber 8, carbs 20, protein 17

Shrimp Gumbo

Preparation time: 10 minutes | Cooking time: 2 hours | Servings: 2

Ingredients:

- 1 pound shrimp, peeled and deveined
- ½ pound pork sausage, sliced
- 1 red onion, chopped
- ½ green bell pepper, chopped
- 1 red chili pepper, minced
- ½ teaspoon cumin, ground
- ½ teaspoon coriander, ground
- Salt and black pepper to the taste
- 1 cup tomato sauce
- ½ cup chicken stock
- ½ tablespoon Cajun seasoning
- ½ teaspoon oregano, dried

Directions:

In your slow cooker, mix the shrimp with the sausage, onion and the other ingredients, toss, put the lid on and cook on High for 2 hours. Divide into bowls and serve.

Nutrition: calories 361, fat 6, fiber 8, carbs 14, protein 5

Squash and Chicken Soup

Preparation time: 10 minutes | Cooking time: 6 hours | Servings: 2

Ingredients:

- ½ pound chicken thighs, skinless, boneless and cubed
- ½ small yellow onion, chopped
- ½ red bell pepper, chopped
- ½ green bell pepper, chopped
- 3 cups chicken stock
- ½ cup butternut squash, peeled and cubed
- 2 ounces canned green chilies, chopped
- ½ teaspoon oregano, dried
- A pinch of salt and black pepper
- ½ tablespoon lime juice
- 1 tablespoon cilantro, chopped

Directions:

In your slow cooker, mix the chicken with the onion, bell pepper and the other ingredients, toss, put the lid on and cook on High for 6 hours. Ladle the soup into bowls and serve.

Nutrition: calories 254, fat 6, fiber 6, carbs 18, protein 22

Pork Soup

Preparation time: 10 minutes | Cooking time: 6 hours | Servings: 2

Ingredients:
- ½ cup canned black beans, drained and rinsed
- 1 pound pork stew meat, cubed
- 3 cups beef stock
- 1 small red bell pepper, chopped
- 1 yellow onion, chopped
- 1 teaspoon Italian seasoning
- ½ tablespoon olive oil
- Salt and black pepper to the taste
- ½ cup canned tomatoes, crushed
- 1 tablespoon basil, chopped

Directions:
In your slow cooker, mix the pork with the beans, stock and the other ingredients, toss, put the lid on and cook on Low for 6 hours. Divide into bowls and serve.

Nutrition: calories 385, fat 12, fiber 5, carbs 18, protein 40

Mushroom Stew

Preparation time: 10 minutes | Cooking time: 6 hours | Servings: 2

Ingredients:
- 1 pound white mushrooms, sliced
- 2 carrots, peeled and cubed
- 1 red onion, chopped
- 1 tablespoon olive oil
- 1 tablespoon balsamic vinegar
- ½ cup tomato sauce
- Salt and black pepper to the taste
- 1 cup veggie stock
- 1 tablespoon basil, chopped

Directions:
In your slow cooker, mix the mushrooms with the onion and the other ingredients, toss, put the lid on and cook on Low for 6 hours. Divide the stew into bowls and serve.

Nutrition: calories 400, fat 15, fiber 4, carbs 25, protein 14

Beans Chili

Preparation time: 10 minutes | Cooking time: 3 hours | Servings: 2

Ingredients:
- ½ red bell pepper, chopped
- ½ green bell pepper, chopped
- 1 garlic clove, minced
- ½ cup yellow onion, chopped
- ½ cup roasted tomatoes, crushed
- 1 cup canned red kidney beans, drained
- 1 cup canned white beans, drained
- 1 cup canned black beans, drained
- ½ cup corn
- Salt and black pepper to the taste
- 1 tablespoon chili powder
- 1 cup veggie stock

Directions:
In your slow cooker, mix the peppers with the beans and the other ingredients, toss, put the lid on and cook on High for 3 hours. Divide into bowls and serve right away.

Nutrition: calories 400, fat 14, fiber 5, carbs 29, protein 22

Parsley Chicken Stew

Preparation time: 10 minutes | Cooking time: 4 hours | Servings: 2

Ingredients:
- 1 tablespoon olive oil
- Salt and black pepper to the taste
- 2 spring onions, chopped
- 1 carrot, peeled and sliced
- ¼ cup chicken stock
- 1 pound chicken breast, skinless, boneless sand cubed
- ½ cup tomato sauce
- 1 tablespoon parsley, chopped

Directions:
In your slow cooker, mix the chicken with the spring onions and the other ingredients, toss, put the lid on and cook on High for 4 hours. Divide into bowls and serve.

Nutrition: calories 453, fat 15, fiber 5, carbs 20, protein 20

Mustard Short Ribs

Preparation time: 10 minutes | Cooking time: 8 hours | Servings: 2

Ingredients:
- 2 beef short ribs, bone in and cut into individual ribs
- Salt and black pepper to the taste
- ½ cup BBQ sauce
- 1 tablespoon mustard
- 1 tablespoon green onions, chopped

Directions:
In your slow cooker, mix the ribs with the sauce and the other ingredients, toss, put the lid on and cook on Low for 8 hours. Divide the mix between plates and serve.

Nutrition: calories 284, fat 7, 4, carbs 18, protein 20

Creamy Brisket

Preparation time: 10 minutes | Cooking time: 8 hours | Servings: 2

Ingredients:
- 1 tablespoon olive oil
- 1 shallot, chopped
- 2 garlic cloves, mined
- 1 pound beef brisket
- Salt and black pepper to the taste
- ¼ cup beef stock
- 3 tablespoons heavy cream
- 1 tablespoon parsley, chopped

Directions:
In your slow cooker, mix the brisket with the oil and the other ingredients, toss, put the lid on and cook on Low for 8 hours. Transfer the beef to a cutting board, slice, divide between plates and serve with the sauce drizzled all over.

Nutrition: calories 400, fat 10, fiber 4, carbs 15, protein 20

Mushroom Soup

Preparation time: 10 minutes | Cooking time: 4 hours | Servings: 2

Ingredients:
- 1 small yellow onion, chopped
- 1 carrot, chopped
- 1 small red bell pepper, chopped
- 1 green bell pepper, chopped
- 1 pound mushrooms, sliced
- 1 garlic clove, minced
- ½ teaspoon Italian seasoning
- Salt and black pepper to the taste
- 3 cups chicken stock
- ½ cup half and half
- 1 tablespoon chives, chopped

Directions:
In your slow cooker, mix the mushrooms with the onion, carrot and the other ingredients, toss, put the lid on and cook on High for 4 hours. Divide into bowls and serve.

Nutrition: calories 453, fat 14, fiber 6, carbs 28, protein 33

Creamy Potato Soup

Preparation time: 10 minutes | Cooking time: 5 hours | Servings: 2

Ingredients:
- 1 small yellow onion, chopped
- 3 cups chicken stock
- ½ pound red potatoes, peeled and cubed
- 1 teaspoon turmeric powder
- ½ cup heavy whipping cream
- 2 ounces cream cheese, cubed
- 1 tablespoon chives, chopped

Directions:
In your slow cooker, mix the potatoes with the stock, onion and the other ingredients, toss, put the lid on and cook on High for 5 hours. Divide into bowls and serve.

Nutrition: calories 372, fat 15, fiber 4, carbs 20, protein 22

Chicken with Corn and Wild Rice

Preparation time: 10 minutes | Cooking time: 6 hours | Servings: 2

Ingredients:
- 1 pound chicken breast, skinless, boneless and cubed
- 1 cup wild rice
- 1 cup chicken stock
- 1 tablespoon tomato paste
- Salt and black pepper to the taste
- ¼ teaspoon cumin, ground
- 3 ounces canned roasted tomatoes, chopped
- ¼ cup corn
- 2 tablespoons cilantro, chopped

Directions:
In your slow cooker, mix the chicken with the rice, stock and the other ingredients, toss, put the lid on and cook on Low for 6 hours. Divide everything between plates and serve.

Nutrition: calories 372, fat 12, fiber 5, carbs 20, protein 25

Mixed Pork and Beans

Preparation time: 10 minutes | Cooking time: 8 hours | Servings: 2

Ingredients:
- 1 cup canned black beans, drained
- 1 cup green beans, trimmed and halved
- ½ pound pork shoulder, cubed
- Salt and black pepper to the taste
- 3 garlic cloves, minced
- ½ yellow onion, chopped
- ½ cup beef stock
- ¼ tablespoon balsamic vinegar
- 1 tablespoon olive oil

Directions:
In your slow cooker, mix the beans with the pork and the other ingredients, toss, put the lid on and cook on Low for 8 hours. Divide everything between plates and serve.

Nutrition: calories 453, fat 10, fiber 12, carbs 20, protein 36

Pork Chops and Butter Sauce

Preparation time: 10 minutes | Cooking time: 7 hours | Servings: 2

Ingredients:
- ½ pound pork loin chops
- 2 tablespoons butter
- 2 scallions, chopped
- 1 cup beef stock
- 1 garlic clove, minced
- ¼ teaspoon thyme, dried
- Salt and black pepper to the taste
- ¼ cup heavy cream
- ¼ tablespoon cornstarch
- ½ teaspoon basil, dried

Directions:
In your slow cooker, mix the pork chops with the butter, scallions and the other ingredients, toss, put the lid on and cook on Low for 7 hours. Divide everything between plates and serve.

Nutrition: calories 453, fat 16, fiber 8, carbs 7, protein 27

Chicken and Peach Mix

Preparation time: 10 minutes | Cooking time: 6 hours | Servings: 2

Ingredients:

- 1 pound chicken breast, skinless and boneless
- 1 cup peaches, cubed
- ½ tablespoon avocado oil
- ½ cup chicken stock
- 1 tablespoon balsamic vinegar
- ½ teaspoon garlic, minced
- ¼ cup cherry tomatoes, halved
- 1 tablespoon basil, chopped

Directions:

In your slow cooker, mix the chicken with the peaches, oil and the other ingredients, toss, put the lid on and cook on Low for 6 hours. Divide everything between plates and serve.

Nutrition: calories 300, fat 7, fiber 8, carbs 20, protein 39

Chicken Drumsticks and Buffalo Sauce

Preparation time: 10 minutes | Cooking time: 8 hours | Servings: 2

Ingredients:

- 1 pound chicken drumsticks
- 2 tablespoons buffalo wing sauce
- ½ cup chicken stock
- 2 tablespoons honey
- 1 teaspoon lemon juice
- Salt and black pepper to the taste

Directions:

In your slow cooker, mix the chicken with the sauce and the other ingredients, toss, put the lid on and cook on Low for 8 hours. Divide everything between plates and serve.

Nutrition: calories 361, fat 7, fiber 8, carbs 18, protein 22

Mustard Pork Chops and Carrots

Preparation time: 10 minutes | Cooking time: 4 hours | Servings: 2

Ingredients:

- 1 tablespoon butter
- 1 pound pork chops, bone in
- 2 carrots, sliced
- 1 cup beef stock
- ½ tablespoon honey
- ½ tablespoon lime juice
- 1 tablespoon lime zest, grated

Directions:

In your slow cooker, mix the pork chops with the butter and the other ingredients, toss, put the lid on and cook on High for 4 hours. Divide between plate sand serve.

Nutrition: calories 300, fat 8, fiber 10, carbs 16, protein 16

Fennel Soup

Preparation time: 10 minutes | Cooking time: 4 hours | Servings: 2

Ingredients:

- 2 fennel bulbs, sliced
- ½ cup tomatoes, crushed
- 1 red onion, sliced
- 1 leek, chopped
- 2 cups veggie stock
- ½ teaspoon cumin, ground
- 1 tablespoon dill, chopped
- ½ tablespoon olive oil
- Salt and black pepper to the taste

Directions:

In your slow cooker, mix the fennel with the tomatoes, onion and the other ingredients, toss, put the lid on and cook on High for 4 hours. Ladle into bowls and serve hot.

Nutrition: calories 132, fat 2, fiber 5, carbs 11, protein 3

Artichoke Soup

Preparation time: 10 minutes | Cooking time: 5 hours | Servings: 2

Ingredients:

- 2 cups canned artichoke hearts, drained and halved
- 1 small carrot, chopped
- 1 small yellow onion, chopped
- 1 garlic clove, minced
- ¼ teaspoon oregano, dried
- ¼ teaspoon rosemary, dried
- A pinch of red pepper flakes
- A pinch of garlic powder
- A pinch of salt and black pepper
- 3 cups chicken stock
- 1 tablespoon tomato paste
- 1 tablespoon cilantro, chopped

Directions:

In your slow cooker, mix the artichokes with the carrot, onion and the other ingredients, toss, put the lid on and cook on Low for 5 hours. Ladle into bowls and serve.

Nutrition: calories 362, fat 3, fiber 5, carbs 16, protein 5

Beans and Mushroom Stew

Preparation time: 10 minutes | Cooking time: 8 hours | Servings: 2

Ingredients:

- Cooking spray
- ½ green bell pepper, chopped
- ½ red bell pepper, chopped
- ½ red onion, chopped
- 2 garlic cloves, minced
- 1 cup tomatoes, cubed
- 1 cup veggie stock
- Salt and black pepper to the taste
- 1 cup white mushrooms, sliced
- 1 cup canned kidney beans, drained
- ½ teaspoon turmeric powder
- ½ teaspoon coriander, ground
- 1 tablespoon parsley, chopped
- ½ tablespoon Cajun seasoning

Directions:

Grease the slow cooker with the cooking spray and mix the bell peppers with the onion, garlic and the other ingredients into the pot. Put the lid on, cook on Low for 8 hours, divide into bowls and serve.

Nutrition: calories 272, fat 4, fiber 7, carbs 19, protein 7

Chicken and Eggplant Stew

Preparation time: 10 minutes | Cooking time: 8 hours | Servings: 2

Ingredients:

- 1 cup tomato paste
- ½ cup chicken stock
- 1 pound chicken breast, skinless, boneless and cubed
- 2 eggplants, cubed
- 1 small red onion, chopped
- 1 red bell pepper, chopped
- ½ teaspoon rosemary, dried
- ½ tablespoon smoked paprika
- 1 teaspoon cumin, ground
- Cooking spray
- Salt and black pepper to the taste
- Juice of ½ lemon
- ½ tablespoon parsley, chopped

Directions:

In your slow cooker, mix the chicken with the stock, tomato paste and the other ingredients, toss, put the lid on and cook on Low for 8 hours. Divide into bowls and serve for lunch.

Nutrition: calories 261, fat 4, fiber 6, carbs 14, protein 7

Turmeric Lentils Stew

Preparation time: 10 minutes | Cooking time: 5 hours | Servings: 2

Ingredients:

- 2 cups veggie stock
- ½ cup canned red lentils, drained
- 1 carrot, sliced
- 1 eggplant, cubed
- ½ cup tomatoes, chopped
- 1 red onion, chopped
- 1 garlic clove, minced
- 1 teaspoon turmeric powder
- ¼ tablespoons ginger, grated
- ½ teaspoons mustard seeds
- ¼ teaspoon sweet paprika
- ½ cup tomato paste
- 1 tablespoon dill, chopped
- Salt and black pepper to the taste

Directions:

In your slow cooker, combine the lentils with the stock, tomatoes, eggplant and the other ingredients, toss, put the lid on, cook on High for 5 hours, divide into bowls and serve.

Nutrition: calories 303, fat 4, fiber 8, carbs 12, protein 4

Pork Chili

Preparation time: 10 minutes | Cooking time: 10 hours | Servings: 2

Ingredients:

- 1 pound pork stew meat, cubed
- 1 red onion, sliced
- 1 carrot, sliced
- 1 teaspoon sweet paprika
- ½ teaspoon cumin, ground
- 1 cup tomato paste
- 1 cup veggie stock
- 2 tablespoons chili powder
- 2 teaspoons cayenne pepper
- 1 tablespoon red pepper flakes
- A pinch of salt and black pepper
- 1 red bell pepper, chopped
- 1 yellow bell pepper, chopped
- 1 tablespoon chives, chopped

Directions:

In your slow cooker, mix the pork meat with the onion, carrot and the other ingredients, toss, put the lid on and cook on Low for 10 hours. Divide the mix into bowls and serve.

Nutrition: calories 261, fat 7, fiber 4, carbs 8, protein 18

Cinnamon Pork Ribs

Preparation time: 10 minutes | Cooking time: 8 hours | Servings: 2

Ingredients:

- 2 pounds baby back pork ribs
- 1 tablespoon cinnamon powder
- 2 tablespoons olive oil
- ½ teaspoon allspice, ground
- A pinch of salt and black pepper
- ½ teaspoon garlic powder
- 1 tablespoon balsamic vinegar
- ½ cup beef stock
- 1 tablespoon tomato paste

Directions:

In your slow cooker, mix the pork ribs with the cinnamon, the oil and the other ingredients, toss, put the lid on and cook on Low for 8 hours. Divide ribs between plates and serve for lunch with a side salad.

Nutrition: calories 312, fat 7, fiber 7, carbs 8, protein 18

Pork and Mushroom Stew

Preparation time: 10 minutes | Cooking time: 7 hours | Servings: 2

Ingredients:
- 2 tablespoons olive oil
- 1 garlic clove, minced
- 1 red onion, sliced
- 2 pounds pork stew meat, cubed
- 1 cup mushrooms, sliced
- 1 cup tomato paste
- A pinch of salt and black pepper
- 1 teaspoon oregano, dried
- 1 teaspoon rosemary, dried
- ½ teaspoon nutmeg, ground
- 1 and ½ cups veggie stock
- 1 tablespoon chives, chopped

Directions:
Grease the slow cooker with the oil, add the meat, onion, garlic and the other ingredients, toss, put the lid on and cook on Low for 7 hours. Divide into bowls and serve for lunch.

Nutrition: calories 345, fat 7, fiber 5, carbs 14, protein 32

Pork and Tomatoes Mix

Preparation time: 10 minutes | Cooking time: 8 hours | Servings: 2

Ingredients:
- 1 and ½ pounds pork stew meat, cubed
- 1 cup cherry tomatoes, halved
- 1 cup tomato paste
- 1 tablespoon rosemary, chopped
- ½ teaspoon sweet paprika
- ½ teaspoon coriander, ground
- A pinch of salt and black pepper
- 1 tablespoon chives, chopped

Directions:
In your Crockpot, combine the meat with the tomatoes, tomato paste and the other ingredients, toss, put the lid on and cook on Low for 8 hours. Divide between plates and serve for lunch.

Nutrition: calories 352, fat 8, fiber 4, carbs 10, protein 27

Pesto Pork Shanks

Preparation time: 10 minutes | Cooking time: 7 hours | Servings: 2

Ingredients:
- 1 and ½ pounds pork shanks
- 1 tablespoon olive oil
- 2 tablespoons basil pesto
- 1 red onion, sliced
- 1 cup beef stock
- ½ cup tomato paste
- 4 garlic cloves, minced
- 1 tablespoon oregano, chopped
- Zest and juice of 1 lemon
- A pinch of salt and black pepper

Directions:
In your slow cooker, mix the pork shanks with the oil, pesto and the other ingredients, toss, put the lid on and cook on Low for 7 hours. Divide everything between plates and serve for lunch.

Nutrition: calories 372, fat 7, fiber 5, carbs 12, protein 37

Potato Stew

Preparation time: 10 minutes | Cooking time: 5 hours and 5 minutes | Servings: 4

Ingredients:
- ½ tablespoon olive oil
- 1 pound gold potatoes, peeled and cut into wedges
- 1 red onion, sliced
- 1 cup tomato paste
- ½ cup beef stock
- 1 carrot, sliced
- 1 red bell pepper, cubed
- 4 garlic cloves, minced
- 1 teaspoon sweet paprika
- 1 tablespoon chives, chopped

Directions:
Heat up a pan with the oil over medium-high heat, add the onion and garlic, sauté for 5 minutes and transfer to the slow cooker. Add the potatoes and the other ingredients, toss, put the lid on and cook on Low for 5 hours. Divide the stew into bowls and serve for lunch.

Nutrition: calories 273, fat 6, fiber 7, carbs 10, protein 17

Chicken and Rice

Preparation time: 10 minutes | Cooking time: 6 hours | Servings: 2

Ingredients:
- 1 pound chicken breast, skinless, boneless and cubed
- 1 red onion, sliced
- 2 spring onions, chopped
- Cooking spray
- 1 cup wild rice
- 2 cups chicken stock
- ½ teaspoon garam masala
- ½ teaspoon turmeric powder
- 1 tablespoon cilantro, chopped
- A pinch of salt and black pepper

Directions:
Grease the slow cooker with the cooking spray, add the chicken, rice, onion and the other ingredients, toss, put the lid on and cook on Low for 6 hours. Divide the mix into bowls and serve for lunch.

Nutrition: calories 362, fat 8, fiber 8, carbs 10, protein 26

Salmon Stew

Preparation time: 10 minutes | Cooking time: 2 hours | Servings: 4

Ingredients:
- 1 pound salmon fillets, boneless and roughly cubed
- 1 cup chicken stock
- ½ cup tomato paste
- ½ red onion, sliced
- 1 carrot, sliced
- 1 sweet potato, peeled and cubed
- 1 tablespoon cilantro, chopped
- Cooking spray
- ½ cup mild salsa
- 2 garlic cloves, minced
- A pinch of salt and black pepper

Directions:
In your slow cooker, mix the fish with the stock, tomato paste, onion and the other ingredients, toss gently, put the lid on and cook on Low for 2 hours Divide the mix into bowls and serve for lunch.

Nutrition: calories 292, fat 6, fiber 7, carbs 12, protein 22

Paprika Pork and Chickpeas

Preparation time: 10 minutes | Cooking time: 10 hours | Servings: 2

Ingredients:
- 1 red onion, sliced
- 1 pound pork stew meat, cubed
- 1 cup canned chickpeas, drained
- 1 cup beef stock
- 1 cup tomato paste
- ½ teaspoon sweet paprika
- ½ teaspoon turmeric powder
- A pinch of salt and black pepper
- 1 tablespoon hives, chopped

Directions:
In your slow cooker, mix the onion with the meat, chickpeas, stock and the other ingredients, toss, put the lid on and cook on Low for 10 hours. Divide the mix between plates and serve for lunch.

Nutrition: calories 322, fat 6, fiber 6, carbs 9, protein 22

Beef and Cabbage

Preparation time: 10 minutes | Cooking time: 8 hours | Servings: 2

Ingredients:
- 1 pound beef stew meat, cubed
- 1 cup green cabbage, shredded
- 1 cup red cabbage, shredded
- 1 carrot, grated
- ½ cup water
- 1 cup tomato paste
- ½ teaspoon sweet paprika
- 1 tablespoon chives, chopped
- A pinch of salt and black pepper

Directions:
In your slow cooker, mix the beef with the cabbage, carrot and the other ingredients, toss, put the lid on and cook on Low for 8 hours. Divide the mix between plates and serve for lunch.

Nutrition: calories 251, fat 6, fiber 7, carbs 12, protein 6

Balsamic Beef Stew

Preparation time: 10 minutes | Cooking time: 6 hours | Servings: 2

Ingredients:
- 1 pound beef stew meat, cubed
- 1 teaspoon sweet paprika
- 1 red onion, sliced
- ½ cup mushrooms, sliced
- 1 carrot, peeled and cubed
- ½ cup tomatoes, cubed
- 1 tablespoon balsamic vinegar
- A pinch of salt and black pepper
- 1 teaspoon onion powder
- 1 teaspoon thyme, dried
- 1 cup beef stock
- 1 tablespoon cilantro, chopped

Directions:
In your slow cooker, mix the beef with the paprika, onion, mushrooms and the other ingredients except the cilantro, toss, put the lid on and cook on Low for 6 hours. Divide into bowls and serve with the cilantro, sprinkled on top.

Nutrition: calories 322, fat 5, fiber 7, carbs 9, protein 16

Beef Curry

Preparation time: 10 minutes | Cooking time: 6 hours | Servings: 2

Ingredients:
- 1 pound beef stew meat
- 4 garlic cloves, minced
- 1 red onion, sliced
- 2 carrots, grated
- 1 tablespoon ginger, grated
- 2 tablespoons yellow curry paste
- 2 cups coconut milk
- A pinch of salt and black pepper

Directions:
In your slow cooker, mix the beef with the garlic, onion and the other ingredients, toss, put the lid on and cook on Low for 6 hours. Divide the curry into bowls and serve for lunch.

Nutrition: calories 352, fat 6, fiber 7, carbs 9, protein 18

Chicken and Brussels Sprouts Mix

Preparation time: 10 minutes | Cooking time: 6 hours | Servings: 2

Ingredients:
- 1 pound chicken breast, skinless, boneless and cubed
- 1 red onion, sliced
- 1 cup Brussels sprouts, trimmed and halved
- 1 cup chicken stock
- ½ cup tomato paste
- A pinch of salt and black pepper
- 1 garlic clove, crushed
- 1 tablespoon thyme, chopped
- 1 tablespoon rosemary, chopped

Directions:
In your slow cooker, mix the chicken with the onion, sprouts and the other ingredients, toss, put the lid on and cook on Low for 6 hours. Divide the mix between plates and serve for lunch.

Nutrition: calories 261, fat 7, fiber 6, carbs 8, protein 26

Chickpeas Stew

Preparation time: 10 minutes | Cooking time: 3 hours | Servings: 4

Ingredients:
- 2 cups canned chickpeas, drained and rinsed
- 1 cup tomato sauce
- ½ cup chicken stock
- 1 red onion, sliced
- 2 garlic cloves, minced
- 1 tablespoon thyme, chopped
- ½ teaspoon turmeric powder
- ½ teaspoon garam masala
- 2 carrots, chopped
- 3 celery stalks, chopped
- 2 tablespoons parsley, chopped
- A pinch of salt and black pepper

Directions:
In your slow cooker, mix the chickpeas with the tomato sauce, chicken stock and the other ingredients, toss, put the lid on and cook on High for 3 hours. Divide into bowls and serve for lunch.

Nutrition: calories 300, fat 4, fiber 7, carbs 9, protein 22

Eggplant Curry

Preparation time: 10 minutes | Cooking time: 3 hours | Servings: 2

Ingredients:
- 2 tablespoons olive oil
- 1 pound eggplant, cubed
- 2 tablespoons red curry paste
- 1 cup coconut milk
- ½ cup veggie stock
- 1 teaspoon turmeric powder
- ½ teaspoon rosemary, dried
- 4 kaffir lime leaves

Directions:
In your slow cooker, mix the eggplant with the oil, curry paste and the other ingredients, toss, put the lid on and cook on High for 3 hours. Discard lime leaves, divide the curry into bowls and serve for lunch.

Nutrition: calories 281, fat 7, fiber 6, carbs 8, protein 22

Beef and Artichokes Stew

Preparation time: 10 minutes | Cooking time: 4 hours | Servings: 2

Ingredients:
- 1 pound beef stew meat, cubed
- 1 cup canned artichoke hearts, halved
- 1 cup beef stock
- 1 red onion, sliced
- 1 cup tomato sauce
- ½ teaspoon rosemary, dried
- ½ teaspoon coriander, ground
- 1 teaspoon garlic powder
- A drizzle of olive oil
- A pinch of salt and black pepper
- 1 tablespoon chives, chopped

Directions:
Grease the slow cooker with the oil and mix the beef with the artichokes, stock and the other ingredients inside. Toss, put the lid on and cook on High for 4 hours. Divide the stew into bowls and serve.

Nutrition: calories 322, fat 5, fiber 4, carbs 12, protein 22

Beef Soup

Preparation time: 10 minutes | Cooking time: 5 hours | Servings: 2

Ingredients:
- 1 pound beef stew meat, cubed
- 3 cups beef stock
- ½ cup tomatoes, cubed
- 1 red onion, chopped
- 1 green bell pepper, chopped
- 1 carrot, cubed
- A pinch of salt and black pepper
- ½ tablespoon oregano, dried
- ¼ teaspoon chili pepper
- 2 tablespoon tomato paste
- 1 jalapeno, chopped
- 1 tablespoon cilantro, chopped

Directions:
In your slow cooker, mix the beef with the stock, tomatoes and the other ingredients, toss, put the lid on and cook on Low for 5 hours. Divide the soup into bowls and serve for lunch.

Nutrition: calories 391, fat 6, fiber 7, carbs 8, protein 27

Veggie Soup

Preparation time: 10 minutes | Cooking time: 4 hours | Servings: 2

Ingredients:
- ½ pound gold potatoes, peeled and roughly cubed
- 1 carrot, sliced
- 1 zucchini, cubed
- 1 eggplant, cubed
- 1 cup tomatoes, cubed
- 4 cups veggie stock
- A pinch of salt and black pepper
- 3 tablespoons tomato paste
- 1 sweet onion, chopped
- 1 tablespoon lemon juice
- 1 tablespoon chives, chopped

Directions:
In your slow cooker, mix the potatoes with the carrot, zucchini and the other ingredients, toss, put the lid on and cook on Low for 4 hours. Divide the soup into bowls and serve.

Nutrition: calories 392, fat 7, fiber 8, carbs 12, protein 28

Oregano Turkey Stew

Preparation time: 10 minutes | Cooking time: 8 hours | Servings: 2

Ingredients:
- 1 pound turkey breast, skinless, boneless and cubed
- 1 carrot, peeled and sliced
- 3 tomatoes, cubed
- 1 red onion, chopped
- 2 garlic cloves, minced
- ½ teaspoon sweet paprika
- ½ teaspoon chili powder
- 1 cup chicken stock
- 2 tablespoons tomato paste
- 1 teaspoon cumin powder
- 1 teaspoon oregano, dried
- A pinch of salt and black pepper

Directions:
In your slow cooker, mix the turkey with the carrot, tomatoes, onion and the other ingredients, toss, put the lid on and cook on Low for 8 hours. Divide the stew into bowls and serve for lunch.

Nutrition: calories 328, fat 6, fiber 8, carbs 12, protein 28

Masala Beef Mix

Preparation time: 10 minutes | Cooking time: 5 hours | Servings: 2

Ingredients:
- 1 pound beef roast meat, cubed
- 1 red onion, sliced
- 1 eggplant, cubed
- 2 tablespoons olive oil
- 1 teaspoon black mustard seeds
- A pinch of salt and black pepper
- 1 tablespoon lemon zest, grated
- 2 tablespoons lemon juice
- 1 tablespoon garam masala
- 1 tablespoons coriander powder
- 1 teaspoon turmeric powder
- ½ teaspoon black peppercorns, ground
- ½ cup beef stock

Directions:
In your slow cooker, mix the meat with the onion, eggplant, oil, mustard seeds and the other ingredients, toss, put the lid on and cook on High for 5 hours. Divide the mix between plates and serve for lunch with a side salad.

Nutrition: calories 300, fat 4, fiber 6, carbs 9, protein 22

Slow Cooker Side Dish Recipes for 2

Cheddar Potatoes Mix

Preparation time: 10 minutes | Cooking time: 3 hours | Servings: 2

Ingredients:

- ½ pound gold potatoes, peeled and cut into wedges
- 2 ounces heavy cream
- ½ teaspoon turmeric powder
- ½ teaspoon rosemary, dried
- ¼ cup cheddar cheese, shredded
- 1 tablespoon butter, melted
- Cooking spray
- A pinch of salt and black pepper

Directions:

Grease your slow cooker with the cooking spray, add the potatoes, cream, turmeric and the other ingredients, toss, put the lid on and cook on High for 3 hours. Divide between plates and serve as a side dish.

Nutrition: calories 300, fat 14, fiber 6, carbs 22, protein 6

Balsamic Cauliflower

Preparation time: 10 minutes | Cooking time: 5 hours | Servings: 2

Ingredients:

- 2 cups cauliflower florets
- ½ cup veggie stock
- 1 tablespoon balsamic vinegar
- 1 tablespoon lemon zest, grated
- 2 spring onions, chopped
- ¼ teaspoon sweet paprika
- Salt and black pepper to the taste
- 1 tablespoon dill, chopped

Directions:

In your slow cooker, mix the cauliflower with the stock, vinegar and the other ingredients, toss, put the lid on and cook on Low for 5 hours. Divide the cauliflower mix between plates and serve.

Nutrition: calories 162, fat 11, fiber 2, carbs 11, protein 5

Italian Black Beans Mix

Preparation time: 10 minutes | Cooking time: 5 hours | Servings: 2

Ingredients:

- 2 tablespoons tomato paste
- Cooking spray
- 2 cups black beans
- ¼ cup veggie stock
- 1 red onion, sliced
- Cooking spray
- 1 teaspoon Italian seasoning
- ½ celery rib, chopped
- ½ red bell pepper, chopped
- ½ sweet red pepper, chopped
- ¼ teaspoon mustard seeds
- Salt and black pepper to the taste
- 2 ounces canned corn, drained
- 1 tablespoon cilantro, chopped

Directions:

Grease the slow cooker with the cooking spray, and mix the beans with the stock, onion and the other ingredients inside. Put the lid on, cook on Low for 5 hours, divide between plates and serve as a side dish.

Nutrition: calories 255, fat 6, fiber 7, carbs 38, protein 7

Butter Green Beans

Preparation time: 10 minutes | Cooking time: 2 hours | Servings: 2

Ingredients:
- 1 pound green beans, trimmed and halved
- 2 tablespoons butter, melted
- ½ cup veggie stock
- 1 teaspoon rosemary, dried
- 1 tablespoon chives, chopped
- Salt and black pepper to the taste
- ¼ teaspoon soy sauce

Directions:
In your slow cooker, combine the green beans with the melted butter, stock and the other ingredients, toss, put the lid on and cook on Low for 2 hours. Divide between plates and serve as a side dish.

Nutrition: calories 236, fat 6, fiber 8, carbs 10, protein 6

Corn Sauté

Preparation time: 10 minutes | Cooking time: 2 hours | Servings: 2

Ingredients:
- 3 cups corn
- 2 tablespoon whipping cream
- 1 carrot, peeled and grated
- 1 tablespoon chives, chopped
- 2 tablespoons butter, melted
- Salt and black pepper to the taste
- 2 bacon strips, cooked and crumbled
- 1 tablespoon green onions, chopped

Directions:
In your slow cooker, combine the corn with the cream, carrot and the other ingredients, toss, put the lid on and cook on Low for 2 hours. Divide between plates, and serve.

Nutrition: calories 261, fat 11, fiber 3, carbs 17, protein 6

Sage Peas

Preparation time: 10 minutes | Cooking time: 2 hours | Servings: 2

Ingredients:
- 1 pound peas
- 1 red onion, sliced
- ½ cup veggie stock
- ½ cup tomato sauce
- 2 garlic cloves, minced
- ¼ teaspoon sage, dried
- Salt and black pepper to the taste
- 1 tablespoon dill, chopped

Directions:
In your slow cooker, combine the peas with the onion, stock and the other ingredients, toss, put the lid on and cook on Low for 2 hours. Divide between plates and serve as a side dish.

Nutrition: calories 100, fat 4, fiber 3, carbs 15, protein 4

Tomato and Corn Mix

Preparation time: 10 minutes | Cooking time: 4 hours | Servings: 2

Ingredients:
- 1 red onion, sliced
- 2 spring onions, chopped
- 1 cup corn
- 1 cup tomatoes, cubed
- 1 tablespoon olive oil
- ½ red bell pepper, chopped
- ½ cup tomato sauce
- ¼ teaspoon sweet paprika
- ½ teaspoon cumin, ground
- 1 tablespoon chives, chopped
- Salt and black pepper to the taste

Directions:
Heat up a pan with the oil over medium-high heat, add the onion, spring onions and bell pepper and cook for 10 minutes. Transfer the mix to the slow cooker, add the corn and the other ingredients, toss, put the lid on and cook on Low for 4 hours. Divide the mix between plates and serve as a side dish.

Nutrition: calories 312, fat 4, fiber 6, carbs 12, protein 6

Dill Mushroom Sauté

Preparation time: 10 minutes | Cooking time: 3 hours | Servings: 2

Ingredients:
- 1 pound white mushrooms, halved
- 1 tablespoon olive oil
- 1 red onion, sliced
- 1 carrot, peeled and grated
- 2 green onions, chopped
- 1 garlic clove, minced
- 1 cup beef stock
- ½ cup tomato sauce
- 1 tablespoon dill, chopped

Directions:
Grease the slow cooker with the oil and mix the mushrooms with the onion, carrot and the other ingredients inside. Put the lid on, cook on Low for 3 hours, divide between plates and serve as a side dish.

Nutrition: calories 200, fat 6, fiber 4, carbs 28, protein 5

Hot Zucchini Mix

Preparation time: 10 minutes | Cooking time: 2 hours | Servings: 2

Ingredients:
- ¼ cup carrots, grated
- 1 pound zucchinis, roughly cubed
- 1 teaspoon hot paprika
- ½ teaspoon chili powder
- 2 spring onions, chopped
- ½ tablespoon olive oil
- ½ teaspoon curry powder
- 1 garlic clove, minced
- ½ teaspoon ginger powder
- A pinch of salt and black pepper
- 1 tablespoon cilantro, chopped

Directions:
In your slow cooker, mix the carrots with the zucchinis, paprika and the other ingredients, toss, put the lid on and cook on Low for 2 hours. Divide between plates and serve as a side dish.

Nutrition: calories 200, fat 5, fiber 7, carbs 28, protein 4

Butternut Squash and Eggplant Mix

Preparation time: 10 minutes | Cooking time: 4 hours | Servings: 2

Ingredients:
- 1 butternut squash, peeled and roughly cubed
- 1 eggplant, roughly cubed
- 1 red onion, chopped
- Cooking spray
- ½ cup veggie stock
- ¼ cup tomato paste
- ½ tablespoon parsley, chopped
- Salt and black pepper to the taste
- 2 garlic cloves, minced

Directions:
Grease the slow cooker with the cooking spray and mix the squash with the eggplant, onion and the other ingredients inside. Put the lid on and cook on Low for 4 hours. Divide between plates and serve as a side dish.

Nutrition: calories 114, fat 4, fiber 4, carbs 18, protein 4

Carrots and Spinach Mix

Preparation time: 10 minutes | Cooking time: 2 hours | Servings: 2

Ingredients:
- 2 carrots, sliced
- 1 small yellow onion, chopped
- Salt and black pepper to the taste
- ¼ teaspoon oregano, dried
- ½ teaspoon sweet paprika
- 2 ounces baby spinach
- 1 cup veggie stock
- 1 tablespoons lemon juice
- 2 tablespoons pistachios, chopped

Directions:
In your slow cooker, mix the spinach with the carrots, onion and the other ingredients, toss, put the lid on and cook on Low for 2 hours. Divide everything between plates and serve.

Nutrition: calories 219, fat 8, fiber 14, carbs 15, protein 17

Creamy Coconut Potatoes

Preparation time: 10 minutes | Cooking time: 4 hours | Servings: 2

Ingredients:
- ½ pound gold potatoes, halved and sliced
- 2 scallions, chopped
- 1 tablespoon avocado oil
- 2 ounces coconut milk
- ¼ cup veggie stock
- Salt and black pepper to the taste
- 1 tablespoons parsley, chopped

Directions:
In your slow cooker, mix the potatoes with the scallions and the other ingredients, toss, put the lid on and cook on High for 4 hours. Divide the mix between plates and serve.

Nutrition: calories 306, fat 14, fiber 4, carbs 15, protein 12

Sage Sweet Potatoes

Preparation time: 10 minutes | Cooking time: 3 hours | Servings: 2

Ingredients:
- ½ pound sweet potatoes, thinly sliced
- 1 tablespoon sage, chopped
- 2 tablespoons orange juice
- A pinch of salt and black pepper
- ½ cup veggie stock
- ½ tablespoon olive oil

Directions:
In your slow cooker, mix the potatoes with the sage and the other ingredients, toss, put the lid on and cook on High for 3 hours. Divide between plates and serve as a side dish.

Nutrition: calories 189, fat 4, fiber 4, carbs 17, protein 4

Cauliflower and Almonds Mix

Preparation time: 10 minutes | Cooking time: 3 hours | Servings: 2

Ingredients:
- 2 cups cauliflower florets
- 2 ounces tomato paste
- 1 small yellow onion, chopped
- 1 tablespoon chives, chopped
- Salt and black pepper to the taste
- 1 tablespoon almonds, sliced

Directions:
In your slow cooker, mix the cauliflower with the tomato paste and the other ingredients, toss, put the lid on and cook on High for 3 hours. Divide between plates and serve as a side dish.

Nutrition: calories 177, fat 12, fiber 7, carbs 20, protein 7

Garlic Risotto

Preparation time: 10 minutes | Cooking time: 2 hours | Servings: 2

Ingredients:
- 1 small shallot, chopped
- 1 cup wild rice
- 1 cup chicken stock
- 1 tablespoons olive oil
- 2 garlic cloves, minced
- Salt and black pepper to the taste
- 2 tablespoons cilantro, chopped

Directions:
In your slow cooker, mix the rice with the stock, shallot and the other ingredients, toss, put the lid on and cook on High for 2 hours Divide between plates and serve as a side dish.

Nutrition: calories 204, fat 7, fiber 3, carbs 17, protein 7

Red Curry Veggie Mix

Preparation time: 10 minutes | Cooking time: 3 hours | Servings: 2

Ingredients:
- 2 zucchinis, cubed
- 1 eggplant, cubed
- ½ cup button mushrooms, quartered
- 1 small red sweet potato, chopped
- ½ cup veggie stock
- 1 garlic cloves, minced
- ¼ tablespoon Thai red curry paste
- ¼ tablespoon ginger, grated
- Salt and black pepper to the taste
- 2 tablespoons coconut milk

Directions:
In your slow cooker, mix the zucchinis with the eggplant and the other ingredients, toss, put the lid on and cook on Low for 3 hours. Divide between plates and serve as a side dish.

Nutrition: calories 169, fat 2, fiber 2, carbs 15, protein 6

Rosemary Leeks

Preparation time: 10 minutes | Cooking time: 3 hours | Servings: 2

Ingredients:
- ½ tablespoon olive oil
- ½ leeks, sliced
- ½ cup tomato sauce
- 2 garlic cloves, minced
- Salt and black pepper to the taste
- ¼ tablespoon rosemary, chopped

Directions:
In your slow cooker, mix the leeks with the oil, sauce and the other ingredients, toss, put the lid on, cook on High for 3 hours, divide between plates and serve as a side dish.

Nutrition: calories 202, fat 2, fiber 6, carbs 18, protein 8

Mustard Brussels Sprouts

Preparation time: 10 minutes | Cooking time: 3 hours | Servings: 2

Ingredients:
- ½ pounds Brussels sprouts, trimmed and halved
- A pinch of salt and black pepper
- 2 tablespoons mustard
- ½ cup veggie stock
- 1 tablespoons olive oil
- 2 tablespoons maple syrup
- 1 tablespoon thyme, chopped

Directions:
In your slow cooker, mix the sprouts with the mustard and the other ingredients, toss, put the lid on and cook on Low for 3 hours. Divide between plates and serve as a side dish.

Nutrition: calories 170, fat 4, fiber 4, carbs 14, protein 6

Potatoes and Leeks Mix

Preparation time: 10 minutes | Cooking time: 4 hours | Servings: 2

Ingredients:
- 2 leeks, sliced
- ½ pound sweet potatoes, cut into medium wedges
- ½ cup veggie stock
- ½ tablespoon balsamic vinegar
- 1 tablespoon chives, chopped
- ½ teaspoon pumpkin pie spice

Directions:

In your slow cooker, mix the leeks with the potatoes and the other ingredients, toss, put the lid on and cook on High for 4 hours. Divide between plates and serve as a side dish.

Nutrition: calories 351, fat 8, fiber 5, carbs 48, protein 7

Black Beans Mix

Preparation time: 10 minutes | Cooking time: 6 hours | Servings: 2

Ingredients:
- ½ pound black beans, soaked overnight and drained
- A pinch of salt and black pepper
- ½ cup veggie stock
- ½ tablespoon lime juice
- 2 tablespoons cilantro, chopped
- 2 tablespoons pine nuts

Directions:

In your slow cooker, mix the beans with the stock and the other ingredients, toss, put the lid on and cook on Low for 6 hours. Divide everything between plates and serve.

Nutrition: calories 200, fat 3, fiber 4, carbs 7, protein 5

Orange Carrots Mix

Preparation time: 10 minutes | Cooking time: 6 hours | Servings: 2

Ingredients:
- ½ pound carrots, sliced
- A pinch of salt and black pepper
- ½ tablespoon olive oil
- ½ cup orange juice
- ½ teaspoon orange rind, grated

Directions:

In your slow cooker, mix the carrots with the oil and the other ingredients, toss, put the lid on and cook on Low for 6 hours. Divide between plates and serve as a side dish.

Nutrition: calories 140, fat 2, fiber 2, carbs 7, protein 6

Hot Lentils

Preparation time: 10 minutes | Cooking time: 6 hours | Servings: 2

Ingredients:
- 1 tablespoon thyme, chopped
- ½ tablespoon olive oil
- 1 cup canned lentils, drained
- ½ cup veggie stock
- 2 garlic cloves, minced
- 1 tablespoon cider vinegar
- 2 tablespoons tomato paste
- 1 tablespoon rosemary, chopped

Directions:

In your slow cooker, mix the lentils with the thyme and the other ingredients, toss, put the lid on and cook on Low for 6 hours. Divide between plates and serve as a side dish.

Nutrition: calories 200, fat 2, fiber 4, carbs 7, protein 8

Marjoram Rice Mix

Preparation time: 10 minutes | Cooking time: 6 hours | Servings: 2

Ingredients:
- 1 cup wild rice
- 2 cups chicken stock
- 1 carrot, peeled and grated
- 2 tablespoons marjoram, chopped
- 1 tablespoon olive oil
- A pinch of salt and black pepper
- 1 tablespoon green onions, chopped

Directions:
In your slow cooker, mix the rice with the stock and the other ingredients, toss, put the lid on and cook on Low for 6 hours. Divide between plates and serve.

Nutrition: calories 200, fat 2, fiber 3, carbs 7, protein 5

Mashed Potatoes

Preparation time: 10 minutes | Cooking time: 6 hours | Servings: 2

Ingredients:
- 1 pound gold potatoes, peeled and cubed
- 2 garlic cloves, chopped
- 1 cup milk
- 1 cup water
- 2 tablespoons butter
- A pinch of salt and white pepper

Directions:
In your slow cooker, mix the potatoes with the water, salt and pepper, put the lid on and cook on Low for 6 hours. Mash the potatoes, add the rest of the ingredients, whisk and serve.

Nutrition: calories 135, fat 4, fiber 2, carbs 10, protein 4

Barley Mix

Preparation time: 10 minutes | Cooking time: 6 hours | Servings: 2

Ingredients:
- 1 red onion, sliced
- ½ teaspoon sweet paprika
- ½ teaspoon turmeric powder
- 1 cup barley
- 1 cup veggie stock
- A pinch of salt and black pepper
- 1 garlic clove, minced

Directions:
In your slow cooker, mix the barley with the onion, paprika and the other ingredients, toss, put the lid on and cook on Low for 6 hours. Divide between plates and serve as a side dish.

Nutrition: calories 160, fat 3, fiber 7, carbs 13, protein 7

Lime Beans Mix

Preparation time: 10 minutes | Cooking time: 8 hours | Servings: 2

Ingredients:
- ½ pound lima beans, soaked for 6 hours and drained
- 1 tablespoon olive oil
- 2 scallions, chopped
- 1 carrot, chopped
- 2 tablespoons tomato paste
- 1 garlic cloves, minced
- A pinch of salt and black pepper to the taste
- 3 cups water
- A pinch of red pepper, crushed
- 2 tablespoons parsley, chopped

Directions:
In your slow cooker, mix the beans with the scallions, oil and the other ingredients, toss, put the lid on and cook on Low for 8 hours Divide between plates and serve as a side dish/

Nutrition: calories 160, fat 3, fiber 7, carbs 9, protein 12

Creamy Beans

Preparation time: 10 minutes | Cooking time: 2 hours | Servings: 2

Ingredients:
- 2 ounces green beans, trimmed and halved
- 2 tablespoons hot sauce
- 2 tablespoons heavy cream
- ½ cup coconut milk
- ¼ teaspoon cumin, ground
- ¼ tablespoon chili powder

Directions:
In your slow cooker, mix the beans with the hot sauce and the other ingredients, toss, put the lid on and cook on Low for 2 hours Divide between plates and serve right away as a side dish.

Nutrition: calories 230, fat 4, fiber 6, carbs 8, protein 10

Spinach Mix

Preparation time: 10 minutes | Cooking time: 1 hour | Servings: 2

Ingredients:
- 1 pound baby spinach
- ½ cup cherry tomatoes, halved
- ½ tablespoon olive oil
- ½ cup veggie stock
- 1 small yellow onion, chopped
- ¼ teaspoon coriander, ground
- ¼ teaspoon cumin, ground
- ¼ teaspoon garam masala
- ¼ teaspoon chili powder
- Salt and black pepper to the taste

Directions:
In your slow cooker, mix the spinach with the tomatoes, oil and the other ingredients, toss, put the lid on and cook on High for 1 hour. Divide between plates and serve as a side dish.,

Nutrition: calories 270, fat 4, fiber 6, carbs 8, protein 12

Bbq Beans

Preparation time: 10 minutes | Cooking time: 8 hours | Servings: 2

Ingredients:
- ¼ pound navy beans, soaked overnight and drained
- 1 cup bbq sauce
- 1 tablespoon sugar
- 1 tablespoon ketchup
- 1 tablespoon water
- 1 tablespoon apple cider vinegar
- 1 tablespoon olive oil
- 1 tablespoon soy sauce

Directions:
In your slow cooker, mix the beans with the sauce, sugar and the other ingredients, toss, put the lid on and cook on Low for 8 hours Divide between plates and serve as a side dish.

Nutrition: calories 430, fat 7, fiber 8, carbs 15, protein 19

White Beans Mix

Preparation time: 10 minutes | Cooking time: 6 hours | Servings: 4

Ingredients:
- 1 celery stalk, chopped
- 2 garlic cloves, minced
- 1 carrot, chopped
- 1 cup veggie stock
- ½ cup canned tomatoes, crushed
- ½ teaspoon chili powder
- ½ tablespoon Italian seasoning
- 15 ounces canned white beans, drained
- 1 tablespoon parsley, chopped

Directions:
In your slow cooker, mix the beans with the celery, garlic and the other ingredients, toss, put the lid on and cook on Low for 6 hours Divide the mix between plates and serve.

Nutrition: calories 223, fat 3, fiber 7, carbs 10, protein 7

Sweet Potato and Cauliflower Mix

***Preparation time:** 10 minutes | **Cooking time:** 4 hours | **Servings:** 2*

Ingredients:
- 2 sweet potatoes, peeled and cubed
- 1 cup cauliflower florets
- ½ cup coconut milk
- 1 teaspoons sriracha sauce
- A pinch of salt and black pepper
- ½ tablespoon sugar
- 1 tablespoon red curry paste
- 3 ounces white mushrooms, roughly chopped
- 2 tablespoons cilantro, chopped

Directions:
In your slow cooker, mix the sweet potatoes with the cauliflower and the other ingredients, toss, put the lid on and cook on Low for 4 hours Divide between plates and serve as a side dish.

Nutrition: calories 200, fat 3, fiber 5, carbs 15, protein 12

Cabbage Mix

***Preparation time:** 10 minutes | **Cooking time:** 6 hours | **Servings:** 2*

Ingredients:
- 1 pound red cabbage, shredded
- 1 apple, peeled, cored and roughly chopped
- A pinch of salt and black pepper to the taste
- ¼ cup chicken stock
- 1 tablespoon mustard
- ½ tablespoon olive oil

Directions:
In your slow cooker, mix the cabbage with the apple and the other ingredients, toss, put the lid on and cook on Low for 6 hours Divide between plates and serve as a side dish.

Nutrition: calories 200, fat 4, fiber 2, carbs 8, protein 6

Parsley Mushroom Mix

***Preparation time:** 10 minutes | **Cooking time:** 4 hours | **Servings:** 2*

Ingredients:
- 1 pound brown mushrooms, halved
- 2 garlic cloves, minced
- A pinch of basil, dried
- A pinch of oregano, dried
- ½ cup veggie stock
- Salt and black pepper to the taste
- 1 tablespoon olive oil
- 1 tablespoon parsley, chopped

Directions:
In your slow cooker, mix the mushrooms with the garlic, basil and the other ingredients, toss, put the lid on and cook on Low for 4 hours Divide everything between plates and serve.

Nutrition: calories 122, fat 6, fiber 1, carbs 8, protein 5

Cinnamon Squash

***Preparation time:** 10 minutes | **Cooking time:** 4 hours | **Servings:** 2*

Ingredients:
- 1 acorn squash, peeled and cut into medium wedges
- 1 cup coconut cream
- A pinch of cinnamon powder
- A pinch of salt and black pepper

Directions:
In your slow cooker, mix the squash with the cream and the other ingredients, toss, put the lid on and cook on Low for 4 hours. Divide between plates and serve as a side dish.

Nutrition: calories 230, fat 3, fiber 3, carbs 10, protein 2

Zucchini Mix

Preparation time: 10 minutes | Cooking time: 6 hours | Servings: 2

Ingredients:
- 1 pound zucchinis, sliced
- ½ teaspoon Italian seasoning
- ½ teaspoon sweet paprika
- Salt and black pepper
- ½ cup heavy cream
- ½ teaspoon garlic powder
- 1 tablespoon olive oil

Directions:
In your slow cooker, mix the zucchinis with the seasoning, paprika and the other ingredients, toss, put the lid on and cook on Low for 6 hours. Divide between plates and serve as a side dish.

Nutrition: calories 170, fat 2, fiber 4, carbs 8, protein 5

Kale Mix

Preparation time: 10 minutes | Cooking time: 2 hours | Servings: 2

Ingredients:
- 1 pound baby kale
- ½ tablespoon tomato paste
- ½ cup chicken stock
- ½ teaspoon chili powder
- A pinch of salt and black pepper
- 1 tablespoon olive oil
- 1 small yellow onion, chopped
- 1 tablespoon apple cider vinegar

Directions:
In your slow cooker, mix the kale with the tomato paste, stock and the other ingredients, toss, put the lid on and cook on Low for 2 hours. Divide between plates and serve as a side dish.

Nutrition: calories 200, fat 4, fiber 7, carbs 10, protein 3

Buttery Spinach

Preparation time: 10 minutes | Cooking time: 2 hours | Servings: 2

Ingredients:
- 1 pound baby spinach
- 1 cup heavy cream
- ½ teaspoon turmeric powder
- A pinch of salt and black pepper
- ½ teaspoon garam masala
- 2 tablespoons butter, melted

Directions:
In your slow cooker, mix the spinach with the cream and the other ingredients, toss, put the lid on and cook on Low for 2 hours. Divide between plates and serve as a side dish.

Nutrition: calories 230, fat 12, fiber 2, carbs 9, protein 12

Bacon Potatoes Mix

Preparation time: 10 minutes | Cooking time: 6 hours | Servings: 2

Ingredients:
- 2 sweet potatoes, peeled and cut into wedges
- 1 tablespoon balsamic vinegar
- ½ tablespoon sugar
- A pinch of salt and black pepper
- ¼ teaspoon sage, dried
- A pinch of thyme, dried
- 1 tablespoon olive oil
- ½ cup veggie stock
- 2 bacon slices, cooked and crumbled

Directions:
In your slow cooker, mix the potatoes with the vinegar, sugar and the other ingredients, toss, put the lid on and cook on Low for 6 hours Divide between plates and serve as a side dish.

Nutrition: calories 209, fat 4, fiber 4, carbs 29, protein 4

Cauliflower Mash

Preparation time: 10 minutes | Cooking time: 5 hours | Servings: 2

Ingredients:
- 1 pound cauliflower florets
- ½ cup heavy cream
- 1 tablespoon dill, chopped
- 2 garlic cloves, minced
- 1 tablespoons butter, melted
- A pinch of salt and black pepper

Directions:
In your slow cooker, mix the cauliflower with the cream and the other ingredients, toss, put the lid on and cook on High for 5 hours. Mash the mix, whisk, divide between plates and serve.

Nutrition: calories 187, fat 4, fiber 5, carbs 7, protein 3

Veggie Mix

Preparation time: 10 minutes | Cooking time: 5 hours | Servings: 2

Ingredients:
- 1 eggplant, cubed
- 1 cup cherry tomatoes, halved
- 1 small zucchini, halved and sliced
- ½ red bell pepper, chopped
- ½ cup tomato sauce
- 1 carrot, peeled and cubed
- 1 sweet potato, peeled and cubed
- A pinch of red pepper flakes, crushed
- 1 tablespoon basil, chopped
- 1 tablespoon parsley, chopped
- A pinch of salt and black pepper
- ½ cup veggie stock
- 1 tablespoon capers
- 1 tablespoon red wine vinegar

Directions:
In your slow cooker, mix the eggplant with the tomatoes, zucchini and the other ingredients, toss, put the lid on and cook on Low for 5 hours. Divide between plates and serve as a side dish.

Nutrition: calories 100, fat 1, fiber 2, carbs 7, protein 5

Farro Mix

Preparation time: 10 minutes | Cooking time: 4 hours | Servings: 2

Ingredients:
- 2 scallions, chopped
- 2 garlic cloves, minced
- 1 tablespoon olive oil
- 1 cup whole grain farro
- 2 cups chicken stock
- Salt and black pepper to the taste
- ½ tablespoon parsley, chopped
- 1 tablespoon cherries, dried

Directions:
In your slow cooker, mix the farro with the scallions, garlic and the other ingredients, toss, put the lid on and cook on Low for 4 hours Divide between plates and serve as a side dish.

Nutrition: calories 152, fat 4, fiber 5, carbs 20, protein 4

Cumin Quinoa Pilaf

Preparation time: 10 minutes | Cooking time: 2 hours | Servings: 2

Ingredients:
- 1 cup quinoa
- 2 teaspoons butter, melted
- Salt and black pepper to the taste
- 1 teaspoon turmeric powder
- 2 cups chicken stock
- 1 teaspoon cumin, ground

Directions:
Grease your slow cooker with the butter, add the quinoa and the other ingredients, toss, put the lid on and cook on High for 2 hour Divide between plates and serve as a side dish.

Nutrition: calories 152, fat 3, fiber 6, carbs 8, protein 4

Saffron Risotto

Preparation time: 10 minutes | Cooking time: 2 hours | Servings: 2

Ingredients:
- ½ tablespoon olive oil
- ¼ teaspoon saffron powder
- 1 cup Arborio rice
- 2 cups veggie stock
- A pinch of salt and black pepper
- A pinch of cinnamon powder
- 1 tablespoon almonds, chopped

Directions:
In your slow cooker, mix the rice with the stock and the other ingredients, toss, put the lid on and cook on High for 2 hours. Divide between plates and serve as a side dish.

Nutrition: calories 251, fat 4, fiber 7, carbs 29, protein 4

Mint Farro Pilaf

Preparation time: 10 minutes | Cooking time: 4 hours | Servings: 2

Ingredients:
- ½ tablespoon balsamic vinegar
- ½ cup whole grain farro
- A pinch of salt and black pepper
- 1 cup chicken stock
- ½ tablespoon olive oil
- 1 tablespoon green onions, chopped
- 1 tablespoon mint, chopped

Directions:
In your slow cooker, mix the farro with the vinegar and the other ingredients, toss, put the lid on and cook on Low for 4 hours Divide between plates and serve.

Nutrition: calories 162, fat 3, fiber 6, carbs 9, protein 4

Parmesan Rice

Preparation time: 10 minutes | Cooking time: 2 hours and 30 minutes | Servings: 2

Ingredients:
- 1 cup rice
- 2 cups chicken stock
- 1 tablespoon olive oil
- 1 red onion, chopped
- 1 tablespoon lemon juice
- Salt and black pepper to the taste
- 1 tablespoon parmesan, grated

Directions:
In your slow cooker, mix the rice with the stock, oil and the other ingredients, toss, put the lid on and cook on High for 2 hours and 30 minutes Divide between plates and serve as a side dish.

Nutrition: calories 162, fat 4, fiber 6, carbs 29, protein 6

Spinach Rice

Preparation time: 10 minutes | Cooking time: 2 hours | Servings: 2

Ingredients:
- 2 scallions, chopped
- 1 tablespoon olive oil
- 1 cup Arborio rice
- 1 cup chicken stock
- 6 ounces spinach, chopped
- Salt and black pepper to the taste
- 2 ounces goat cheese, crumbled

Directions:
In your slow cooker, mix the rice with the stock and the other ingredients, toss, put the lid on and cook on High for 2 hours Divide between plates and serve as a side dish.

Nutrition: calories 300, fat 10, fiber 6, carbs 20, protein 14

Mango Rice

Preparation time: 10 minutes | Cooking time: 2 hours | Servings: 2

Ingredients:
- 1 cup rice
- 2 cups chicken stock
- ½ cup mango, peeled and cubed
- Salt and black pepper to the taste
- 1 teaspoon olive oil

Directions:
In your slow cooker, mix the rice with the stock and the other ingredients, toss, put the lid on and cook on High for 2 hours. Divide between plates and serve as a side dish.

Nutrition: calories 152, fat 4, fiber 5, carbs 18, protein 4

Lemon Artichokes

Preparation time: 10 minutes | Cooking time: 3 hours | Servings: 2

Ingredients:
- 1 cup veggie stock
- 2 medium artichokes, trimmed
- 1 tablespoon lemon juice
- 1 tablespoon lemon zest, grated
- Salt to the taste

Directions:
In your slow cooker, mix the artichokes with the stock and the other ingredients, toss, put the lid on and cook on Low for 3 hours. Divide artichokes between plates and serve as a side dish.

Nutrition: calories 100, fat 2, fiber 5, carbs 10, protein 4

Coconut Bok Choy

Preparation time: 10 minutes | Cooking time: 1 hour | Servings: 2

Ingredients:
- 1 pound bok choy, torn
- ½ cup chicken stock
- ½ teaspoon chili powder
- 1 garlic clove, minced
- 1 teaspoon ginger, grated
- 1 tablespoon coconut oil
- Salt to the taste

Directions:
In your slow cooker, mix the bok choy with the stock and the other ingredients, toss, put the lid on and cook on High for 1 hour. Divide between plates and serve as a side dish.

Nutrition: calories 100, fat 1, fiber 2, carbs 7, protein 4

Italian Eggplant

Preparation time: 10 minutes | Cooking time: 2 hours | Servings: 2

Ingredients:
- 2 small eggplants, roughly cubed
- ½ cup heavy cream
- Salt and black pepper to the taste
- 1 tablespoon olive oil
- A pinch of hot pepper flakes
- 2 tablespoons oregano, chopped

Directions:
In your slow cooker, mix the eggplants with the cream and the other ingredients, toss, put the lid on and cook on High for 2 hours. Divide between plates and serve as a side dish.

Nutrition: calories 132, fat 4, fiber 6, carbs 12, protein 3

Cabbage and Onion Mix

Preparation time: 10 minutes | Cooking time: 2 hours | Servings: 2

Ingredients:

- 1 and ½ cups green cabbage, shredded
- 1 cup red cabbage, shredded
- 1 tablespoon olive oil
- 1 red onion, sliced
- 2 spring onions, chopped
- ½ cup tomato paste
- ¼ cup veggie stock
- 2 tomatoes, chopped
- 2 jalapenos, chopped
- 1 tablespoon chili powder
- 1 tablespoon chives, chopped
- A pinch of salt and black pepper

Directions:

Grease your slow cooker with the oil and mix the cabbage with the onion, spring onions and the other ingredients inside. Toss, put the lid on and cook on High for 2 hours. Divide between plates and serve as a side dish.

Nutrition: calories 211, fat 3, fiber 3, carbs 6, protein 8

Balsamic Okra Mix

Preparation time: 10 minutes | Cooking time: 2 hours | Servings: 4

Ingredients:

- 2 cups okra, sliced
- 1 cup cherry tomatoes, halved
- 1 tablespoon olive oil
- ½ teaspoon turmeric powder
- ½ cup canned tomatoes, crushed
- 2 tablespoons balsamic vinegar
- 2 tablespoons basil, chopped
- 1 tablespoon thyme, chopped

Directions:

In your slow cooker, mix the okra with the tomatoes, crushed tomatoes and the other ingredients, toss, put the lid on and cook on High for 2 hours. Divide between plates and serve as a side dish.

Nutrition: calories 233, fat 12, fiber 4, carbs 8, protein 4

Garlic Carrots Mix

Preparation time: 10 minutes | Cooking time: 4 hours | Servings: 2

Ingredients:

- 1 pound carrots, sliced
- 2 garlic cloves, minced
- 1 red onion, chopped
- 1 tablespoon olive oil
- ½ cup tomato sauce
- A pinch of salt and black pepper
- ½ teaspoon oregano, dried
- 2 teaspoons lemon zest, grated
- 1 tablespoon lemon juice
- 1 tablespoon chives, chopped

Directions:

In your slow cooker, mix the carrots with the garlic, onion and the other ingredients, toss, put the lid on and cook on Low for 4 hours Divide the mix between plates and serve.

Nutrition: calories 219, fat 8, fiber 4, carbs 8, protein 17

Curry Broccoli Mix

Preparation time: 10 minutes | Cooking time: 3 hours | Servings: 2

Ingredients:

- 1 pound broccoli florets
- 1 cup tomato paste
- 1 tablespoon red curry paste
- 1 red onion, sliced
- ½ teaspoon Italian seasoning
- 1 teaspoon thyme, dried
- Salt and black pepper to the taste
- ½ tablespoon cilantro, chopped

Directions:

In your slow cooker, mix the broccoli with the curry paste, tomato paste and the other ingredients, toss, put the lid on and cook on Low for 3 hours Divide the mix between plates and serve as a side dish.

Nutrition: calories 177, fat 12, fiber 2, carbs 7, protein 7

Rice and Corn

Preparation time: 10 minutes | *Cooking time:* 6 hours | *Servings:* 2

Ingredients:
- 2 cups veggie stock
- 1 cup wild rice
- 1 cup corn
- 3 spring onions, chopped
- 1 tablespoon olive oil
- 2 teaspoons rosemary, dried
- ½ teaspoon garam masala
- Salt and black pepper to the taste
- 1 tablespoon cilantro, chopped

Directions:
In your slow cooker, mix the stock with the rice, corn and the other ingredients, toss, put the lid on and cook on Low for 6 hours. Divide between plates and serve as a side dish.

Nutrition: calories 169, fat 5, fiber 3, carbs 8, protein 5

Cauliflower and Potatoes Mix

Preparation time: 10 minutes | *Cooking time:* 4 hours | *Servings:* 2

Ingredients:
- 1 cup cauliflower florets
- ½ pound sweet potatoes, peeled and cubed
- 1 cup veggie stock
- ½ cup tomato sauce
- 1 tablespoon chives, chopped
- Salt and black pepper to the taste
- 1 teaspoon sweet paprika

Directions:
In your slow cooker, mix the cauliflower with the potatoes, stock and the other ingredients, toss, put the lid on and cook on High for 4 hours. Divide between plates and serve as a side dish.

Nutrition: calories 135, fat 5, fiber 1, carbs 7, protein 3

Asparagus Mix

Preparation time: 10 minutes | *Cooking time:* 2 hours | *Servings:* 2

Ingredients:
- 1 pound asparagus, trimmed and halved
- 1 red onion, sliced
- 2 garlic cloves, minced
- 1 cup veggie stock
- 1 tablespoon lemon juice
- A pinch of salt and black pepper
- ¼ cup parsley, chopped

Directions:
In your slow cooker, mix the asparagus with the onion, garlic and the other ingredients, toss, put the lid on and cook on High for 2 hours. Divide between plates and serve as a side dish.

Nutrition: calories 159, fat 4, fiber 4, carbs 6, protein 2

Garlic Squash Mix

Preparation time: 10 minutes | *Cooking time:* 3 hours | *Servings:* 2

Ingredients:
- 1 pound butternut squash, peeled and cubed
- 2 spring onions, chopped
- 1 cup veggie stock
- ½ teaspoon red pepper flakes, crushed
- ½ teaspoon turmeric powder
- A pinch of salt and black pepper
- 3 garlic cloves, minced

Directions:
In your slow cooker, mix the squash with the garlic, stock and the other ingredients, toss, put the lid on and cook on Low for 3 hours. Divide squash mix between plates and serve as a side dish.

Nutrition: calories 196, fat 3, fiber 7, carbs 8, protein 7

Baby Carrots and Parsnips Mix

Preparation time: 10 minutes | Cooking time: 6 hours | Servings: 2

Ingredients:

- 1 tablespoon avocado oil
- 1 pound baby carrots, peeled
- ½ pound parsnips, peeled and cut into sticks
- 1 teaspoon sweet paprika
- ½ cup tomato paste
- ½ cup veggie stock
- ½ teaspoon chili powder
- A pinch of salt and black pepper
- 2 garlic cloves, minced
- 1 tablespoon dill, chopped

Directions:

Grease the slow cooker with the oil and mix the carrots with the parsnips, paprika and the other ingredients inside. Toss, put the lid on and cook on Low for 6 hours. Divide everything between plates and serve as a side dish.

Nutrition: calories 273, fat 7, fiber 5, carbs 8, protein 12

Lemon Kale Mix

Preparation time: 10 minutes | Cooking time: 2 hours | Servings: 2

Ingredients:

- 1 yellow bell pepper, chopped
- 1 red bell pepper, chopped
- 1 tablespoon olive oil
- 1 red onion, sliced
- 4 cups baby kale
- 1 teaspoon lemon zest, grated
- 1 tablespoon lemon juice
- ½ cup veggie stock
- 1 garlic clove, minced
- A pinch of salt and black pepper
- 1 tablespoon basil, chopped

Directions:

In your slow cooker, mix the kale with the oil, onion, bell peppers and the other ingredients, toss, put the lid on and cook on Low for 2 hours. Divide the mix between plates and serve as a side dish.

Nutrition: calories 251, fat 9, fiber 6, carbs 7, protein 8

Brussels Sprouts and Cauliflower

Preparation time: 10 minutes | Cooking time: 4 hours | Servings: 2

Ingredients:

- 1 cup Brussels sprouts, trimmed and halved
- 1 cup cauliflower florets
- 1 tablespoon olive oil
- 1 cup veggie stock
- 2 tablespoons tomato paste
- 1 teaspoon chili powder
- ½ teaspoon ginger powder
- A pinch of salt and black pepper
- 1 tablespoon thyme, chopped

Directions:

In your slow cooker, mix the Brussels sprouts with the cauliflower, oil, stock and the other ingredients, toss, put the lid on and cook on Low for 4 hours. Divide the mix between plates and serve as a side dish.

Nutrition: calories 100, fat 4, fiber 4, carbs 8, protein 3

Cabbage and Kale Mix

Preparation time: 10 minutes | Cooking time: 2 hours | Servings: 2

Ingredients:
- 1 red onion, sliced
- 1 cup green cabbage, shredded
- 1 cup baby kale
- ½ cup canned tomatoes, crushed
- ½ teaspoon hot paprika
- ½ teaspoon Italian seasoning
- A pinch of salt and black pepper
- 1 tablespoon dill, chopped

Directions:
In your slow cooker, mix the cabbage with the kale, onion and the other ingredients, toss, put the lid on and cook on High for 2 hours. Divide between plates and serve right away as a side dish.

Nutrition: calories 200, fat 4, fiber 2, carbs 8, protein 6

Thyme Mushrooms and Corn

Preparation time: 10 minutes | Cooking time: 4 hours | Servings: 2

Ingredients:
- 4 garlic cloves, minced
- 1 tablespoon olive oil
- 1 pound white mushroom caps, halved
- 1 cup corn
- 1 cup canned tomatoes, crushed
- ¼ teaspoon thyme, dried
- ½ cup veggie stock
- A pinch of salt and black pepper
- 2 tablespoons parsley, chopped

Directions:
Grease your slow cooker with the oil, and mix the garlic with the mushrooms, corn and the other ingredients inside Toss, put the lid on and cook on Low for 4 hours Divide between plates and serve as a side dish.

Nutrition: calories 122, fat 6, fiber 1, carbs 8, protein 5

Veggie Medley

Preparation time: 10 minutes | Cooking time: 3 hours | Servings: 2

Ingredients:
- 1 zucchini, cubed
- 1 eggplant, cubed
- ½ cup baby carrots, peeled
- ½ cup baby kale
- 1 cup cherry tomatoes, halved
- 1 teaspoon sweet paprika
- 1 tablespoon olive oil
- 1 cup tomato sauce
- 1 teaspoon Italian seasoning
- A pinch of salt and black pepper
- 1 cup yellow squash, peeled and cut into wedges
- 1 teaspoon garlic powder
- 1 tablespoon cilantro, chopped
- A pinch of salt and black pepper

Directions:
Grease your Crockpot with the oil, and mix the zucchini with the eggplant, carrots and the other ingredients inside. Toss, put the lid on and cook on Low for 3 hours. Divide the mix between plates and serve as a side dish.

Nutrition: calories 100, fat 2, fiber 4, carbs 8, protein 5

Paprika Green Beans and Zucchinis

Preparation time: 10 minutes | Cooking time: 3 hours | Servings: 2

Ingredients:
- 1 pound green beans, trimmed and halved
- 1 cup zucchinis, cubed
- 1 cup tomato sauce
- 1 teaspoon smoked paprika
- ½ teaspoon cumin, ground
- Salt and black pepper to the taste
- ½ teaspoon garlic powder
- ¼ tablespoon chives, chopped

Directions:
In your slow cooker, mix the green beans with the zucchinis, tomato sauce and the other ingredients, toss, put the lid on and cook on Low for 3 hours. Divide the mix between plates and serve as a side dish.

Nutrition: calories 114, fat 5, fiber 6, carbs 8, protein 9

Tarragon Sweet Potatoes

Preparation time: 10 minutes | Cooking time: 3 hours | Servings: 4

Ingredients:
- 1 pound sweet potatoes, peeled and cut into wedges
- 1 cup veggie stock
- ½ teaspoon chili powder
- ½ teaspoon cumin, ground
- Salt and black pepper to the taste
- 1 tablespoon olive oil
- 1 tablespoon tarragon, dried
- 2 tablespoons balsamic vinegar

Directions:
In your slow cooker, mix the sweet potatoes with the stock, chili powder and the other ingredients, toss, put the lid on and cook on High for 3 hours. Divide the mix between plates and serve as a side dish.

Nutrition: calories 80, fat 4, fiber 4, carbs 8, protein 4

Mustard Brussels Sprouts

Preparation time: 10 minutes | Cooking time: 3 hours | Servings: 2

Ingredients:
- 1 pound Brussels sprouts, trimmed and halved
- 1 tablespoon olive oil
- 1 tablespoon mustard
- 1 tablespoon balsamic vinegar
- Salt and black pepper to the taste
- ¼ cup veggie stock
- A pinch of red pepper, crushed
- 2 tablespoons chives, chopped

Directions:
In your slow cooker, mix the Brussels sprouts with the oil, mustard and the other ingredients, toss, put the lid on and cook on High for 3 hours. Divide the mix between plates and serve as a side dish.

Nutrition: calories 256, fat 12, fiber 6, carbs 8, protein 15

Parmesan Spinach Mix

Preparation time: 10 minutes | Cooking time: 2 hours | Servings: 2

Ingredients:
- 2 garlic cloves, minced
- 1 pound baby spinach
- ¼ cup veggie stock
- A drizzle of olive oil
- Salt and black pepper to the taste
- 4 tablespoons heavy cream
- 2 tablespoons parmesan cheese, grated

Directions:
Grease your Crockpot with the oil, and mix the spinach with the garlic and the other ingredients inside. Toss, put the lid on and cook on Low for 2 hours. Divide the mix between plates and serve as a side dish.

Nutrition: calories 133, fat 10, fiber 4, carbs 4, protein 2

Minty Peas and Tomatoes

Preparation time: 10 minutes | Cooking time: 3 hours | Servings: 2

Ingredients:
- 1 pound okra, sliced
- ½ pound tomatoes, cut into wedges
- 1 tablespoon olive oil
- ½ cup veggie stock
- ½ teaspoon chili powder
- Salt and black pepper to the taste
- 1 tablespoon mint, chopped
- 3 green onions, chopped
- 1 tablespoon chives, chopped

Directions:
Grease your slow cooker with the oil, and mix the okra with the tomatoes and the other ingredients inside. Put the lid on, cook on Low for 3 hours, divide between plates and serve as a side dish.

Nutrition: calories 70, fat 1, fiber 1, carbs 4, protein 6

Savoy Cabbage Mix

Preparation time: 10 minutes | Cooking time: 2 hours | Servings: 2

Ingredients:
- 1 pound Savoy cabbage, shredded
- 1 red onion, sliced
- 1 tablespoon olive oil
- ½ cup veggie stock
- A pinch of salt and black pepper
- 1 carrot, grated
- ½ cup tomatoes, cubed
- ½ teaspoon sweet paprika
- ½ inch ginger, grated

Directions:
In your slow cooker, mix the cabbage with the onion, oil and the other ingredients, toss, put the lid on and cook on High for 2 hours. Divide the mix between plates and serve as a side dish.

Nutrition: calories 100, fat 3, fiber 4, carbs 5, protein 2

Slow Cooker Snack Recipes for 2

Spinach Spread

Preparation time: 10 minutes | Cooking time: 2 hours | Servings: 2

Ingredients:
- 4 ounces baby spinach
- 2 tablespoons mayonnaise
- 2 ounces heavy cream
- ½ teaspoon turmeric powder
- A pinch of salt and black pepper
- 1 ounce Swiss cheese, shredded

Directions:
In your slow cooker, mix the spinach with the cream, mayo and the other ingredients, toss, put the lid on and cook on Low for 2 hours. Divide into bowls and serve as a party spread.

Nutrition: calories 132, fat 4, fiber 3, carbs 10, protein 4

Artichoke Dip

Preparation time: 10 minutes | Cooking time: 2 hours | Servings: 2

Ingredients:
- 2 ounces canned artichoke hearts, drained and chopped
- 2 ounces heavy cream
- 2 tablespoons mayonnaise
- ¼ cup mozzarella, shredded
- 2 green onions, chopped
- ½ teaspoon garam masala
- Cooking spray

Directions:
Grease your slow cooker with the cooking spray, and mix the artichokes with the cream, mayo and the other ingredients inside. Stir, cover, cook on Low for 2 hours, divide into bowls and serve as a party dip.

Nutrition: calories 100, fat 3, fiber 2, carbs 7, protein 3

Crab Dip

Preparation time: 10 minutes | Cooking time: 1 hour | Servings: 2

Ingredients:
- 2 ounces crabmeat
- 1 tablespoon lime zest, grated
- ½ tablespoon lime juice
- 2 tablespoons mayonnaise
- 2 green onions, chopped
- 2 ounces cream cheese, cubed
- Cooking spray

Directions:
Grease your slow cooker with the cooking spray, and mix the crabmeat with the lime zest, juice and the other ingredients inside. Put the lid on, cook on Low for 1 hour, divide into bowls and serve as a party dip.

Nutrition: calories 100, fat 3, fiber 2, carbs 9, protein 4

Lemon Shrimp Dip

Preparation time: 10 minutes | Cooking time: 2 hours | Servings: 2

Ingredients:
- 3 ounces cream cheese, soft
- ½ cup heavy cream
- 1 pound shrimp, peeled, deveined and chopped
- ½ tablespoon balsamic vinegar
- 2 tablespoons mayonnaise
- ½ tablespoon lemon juice
- A pinch of salt and black pepper
- 2 ounces mozzarella, shredded
- 1 tablespoon parsley, chopped

Directions:
In your slow cooker, mix the cream cheese with the shrimp, heavy cream and the other ingredients, whisk, put the lid on and cook on Low for 2 hours. Divide into bowls and serve as a dip.

Nutrition: calories 342, fat 4, fiber 3, carbs 7, protein 10

Squash Salsa

Preparation time: 10 minutes | Cooking time: 3 hours | Servings: 2

Ingredients:
- 1 cup butternut squash, peeled and cubed
- 1 cup cherry tomatoes, cubed
- 1 cup avocado, peeled, pitted and cubed
- ½ tablespoon balsamic vinegar
- ½ tablespoon lemon juice
- 1 tablespoon lemon zest, grated
- ¼ cup veggie stock
- 1 tablespoon chives, chopped
- A pinch of rosemary, dried
- A pinch of sage, dried
- A pinch of salt and black pepper

Directions:
In your slow cooker, mix the squash with the tomatoes, avocado and the other ingredients, toss, put the lid on and cook on Low for 3 hours. Divide into bowls and serve as a snack.

Nutrition: calories 182, fat 5, fiber 7, carbs 12, protein 5

Beans Spread

Preparation time: 10 minutes | Cooking time: 6 hours | Servings: 2

Ingredients:
- 1 cup canned black beans, drained
- 2 tablespoons tahini paste
- ½ teaspoon balsamic vinegar
- ¼ cup veggie stock
- ½ tablespoon olive oil

Directions:
In your slow cooker, mix the beans with the tahini paste and the other ingredients, toss, put the lid on and cook on Low for 6 hours. Transfer to your food processor, blend well, divide into bowls and serve.

Nutrition: calories 221, fat 6, fiber 5, carbs 19, protein 3

Rice Snack Bowls

Preparation time: 10 minutes | Cooking time: 6 hours | Servings: 2

Ingredients:
- ½ cup wild rice
- 1 red onion, sliced
- ½ cup brown rice
- 2 cups veggie stock
- ½ cup baby spinach
- ½ cup cherry tomatoes, halved
- 2 tablespoons pine nuts, toasted
- 1 tablespoon raisins
- 1 tablespoon chives, chopped
- 1 tablespoon dill, chopped
- ½ tablespoon olive oil
- A pinch of salt and black pepper

Directions:
In your slow cooker, mix the rice with the onion, stock and the other ingredients, toss, put the lid on and cook on Low for 6 hours. Divide in to bowls and serve as a snack.

Nutrition: calories 301, fat 6, fiber 6, carbs 12, protein 3

Cauliflower Spread

Preparation time: 10 minutes | Cooking time: 7 hours | Servings: 2

Ingredients:
- 1 cup cauliflower florets
- 1 tablespoon mayonnaise
- ½ cup heavy cream
- 1 tablespoon lemon juice
- ½ teaspoon garlic powder
- ¼ teaspoon smoked paprika
- ¼ teaspoon mustard powder
- A pinch of salt and black pepper

Directions:
In your slow cooker, combine the cauliflower with the cream, mayonnaise and the other ingredients, toss, put the lid on and cook on Low for 7 hours. Transfer to a blender, pulse well, into bowls and serve as a spread.

Nutrition: calories 301, fat 7, fiber 4, carbs 14, protein 3

Mushroom Dip

Preparation time: 10 minutes | Cooking time: 5 hours | Servings: 2

Ingredients:
- 4 ounces white mushrooms, chopped
- 1 eggplant, cubed
- ½ cup heavy cream
- ½ tablespoon tahini paste
- 2 garlic cloves, minced
- A pinch of salt and black pepper
- 1 tablespoon balsamic vinegar
- ½ tablespoon basil, chopped
- ½ tablespoon oregano, chopped

Directions:
In your slow cooker, mix the mushrooms with the eggplant, cream and the other ingredients, toss, put the lid on and cook on High for 5 hours. Divide the mushroom mix into bowls and serve as a dip.

Nutrition: calories 261, fat 7, fiber 6, carbs 10, protein 6

Chickpeas Spread

Preparation time: 10 minutes | Cooking time: 8 hours | Servings: 2

Ingredients:
- ½ cup chickpeas, dried
- 1 tablespoons olive oil
- 1 tablespoon lemon juice
- 1 cup veggie stock
- 1 tablespoon tahini
- A pinch of salt and black pepper
- 1 garlic clove, minced
- ½ tablespoon chives, chopped

Directions:
In your slow cooker, combine the chickpeas with the stock, salt, pepper and the garlic, stir, put the lid on and cook on Low for 8 hours. Drain chickpeas, transfer them to a blender, add the rest of the ingredients, pulse well, divide into bowls and serve as a party spread.

Nutrition: calories 211, fat 6, fiber 7, carbs 8, protein 4

Spinach Dip

Preparation time: 10 minutes | Cooking time: 1 hour | Servings: 2

Ingredients:
- 2 tablespoons heavy cream
- ½ cup Greek yogurt
- ½ pound baby spinach
- 2 garlic cloves, minced
- Salt and black pepper to the taste

Directions:
In your slow cooker, mix the spinach with the cream and the other ingredients, toss, put the lid on and cook on High for 1 hour. Blend using an immersion blender, divide into bowls and serve as a party dip.

Nutrition: calories 221, fat 5, fiber 7, carbs 12, protein 5

Dill Potato Salad

Preparation time: 10 minutes | Cooking time: 8 hours | Servings: 2

Ingredients:
- 1 red onion, sliced
- 1 pound gold potatoes, peeled and roughly cubed
- 2 tablespoons balsamic vinegar
- ½ cup heavy cream
- 1 tablespoons mustard
- A pinch of salt and black pepper
- 1 tablespoon dill, chopped
- ½ cup celery, chopped

Directions:
In your slow cooker, mix the potatoes with the cream, mustard and the other ingredients, toss, put the lid on and cook on Low for 8 hours. Divide salad into bowls, and serve as an appetizer.

Nutrition: calories 251, fat 6, fiber 7, carbs 8, protein 7

Stuffed Peppers Platter

Preparation time: 10 minutes | Cooking time: 4 hours | Servings: 2

Ingredients:
- 1 red onion, chopped
- 1 teaspoons olive oil
- ½ teaspoon sweet paprika
- ½ tablespoon chili powder
- 1 garlic clove, minced
- 1 cup white rice, cooked
- ½ cup corn
- A pinch of salt and black pepper
- 2 colored bell peppers, tops and insides scooped out
- ½ cup tomato sauce

Directions:
In a bowl, mix the onion with the oil, paprika and the other ingredients except the peppers and tomato sauce, stir well and stuff the peppers the with this mix. Put the peppers in the slow cooker, add the sauce, put the lid on and cook on Low for 4 hours. Transfer the peppers on a platter and serve as an appetizer.

Nutrition: calories 253, fat 5, fiber 4, carbs 12, protein 3

Corn Dip

Preparation time: 10 minutes | Cooking time: 2 hours | Servings: 2

Ingredients:
- 1 cup corn
- 1 tablespoon chives, chopped
- ½ cup heavy cream
- 2 ounces cream cheese, cubed
- ¼ teaspoon chili powder

Directions:
In your slow cooker, mix the corn with the chives and the other ingredients, whisk, put the lid on and cook on Low for 2 hours. Divide into bowls and serve as a dip.

Nutrition: calories 272, fat 5, fiber 10, carbs 12, protein 4

Tomato and Mushroom Salsa

Preparation time: 10 minutes | Cooking time: 4 hours | Servings: 2

Ingredients:
- 1 cup cherry tomatoes, halved
- 1 cup mushrooms, sliced
- 1 small yellow onion, chopped
- 1 garlic clove, minced
- 12 ounces tomato sauce
- ¼ cup cream cheese, cubed
- 1 tablespoon chives, chopped
- Salt and black pepper to the taste

Directions:
In your slow cooker, mix the tomatoes with the mushrooms and the other ingredients, toss, put the lid on and cook on Low for 4 hours. Divide into bowls and serve as a party salsa

Nutrition: calories 285, fat 4, fiber 7, carbs 12, protein 4

Salsa Beans Dip

Preparation time: 10 minutes | Cooking time: 1 hour | Servings: 2

Ingredients:
- ¼ cup salsa
- 1 cup canned red kidney beans, drained and rinsed
- ½ cup mozzarella, shredded
- 1 tablespoon green onions, chopped

Directions:
In your slow cooker, mix the salsa with the beans and the other ingredients, toss, put the lid on cook on High for 1 hour. Divide into bowls and serve as a party dip

Nutrition: calories 302, fat 5, fiber 10, carbs 16, protein 6

Pineapple and Tofu Salsa

Preparation time: 10 minutes | Cooking time: 6 hours | Servings: 2

Ingredients:
- ½ cup firm tofu, cubed
- 1 cup pineapple, peeled and cubed
- 1 cup cherry tomatoes, halved
- ½ tablespoons sesame oil
- 1 tablespoon soy sauce
- ½ cup pineapple juice
- ½ tablespoon ginger, grated
- 1 garlic clove, minced

Directions:
In your slow cooker, mix the tofu with the pineapple and the other ingredients, toss, put the lid on and cook on Low for 6 hours. Divide into bowls and serve as an appetizer.

Nutrition: calories 201, fat 5, fiber 7, carbs 15, protein 4

Chickpeas Salsa

Preparation time: 10 minutes | Cooking time: 6 hours | Servings: 2

Ingredients:
- 1 cup canned chickpeas, drained
- 1 cup veggie stock
- ½ cup black olives, pitted and halved
- 1 small yellow onion, chopped
- ¼ tablespoon ginger, grated
- 4 garlic cloves, minced
- ¼ tablespoons coriander, ground
- ¼ tablespoons red chili powder
- ¼ tablespoons garam masala
- 1 tablespoon lemon juice

Directions:
In your slow cooker, mix the chickpeas with the stock, olives and the other ingredients, toss, put the lid on and cook on Low for 6 hours. Divide into bowls and serve as an appetizer.

Nutrition: calories 355, fat 5, fiber 14, carbs 16, protein 11

Creamy Mushroom Spread

Preparation time: 10 minutes | Cooking time: 4 hours | Servings: 2

Ingredients:
- 1 pound mushrooms, sliced
- 3 garlic cloves, minced
- 1 cup heavy cream
- 2 teaspoons smoked paprika
- Salt and black pepper to the taste
- 2 tablespoons parsley, chopped

Directions:
In your slow cooker, mix the mushrooms with the garlic and the other ingredients, whisk, put the lid on and cook on Low for 4 hours. Whisk, divide into bowls and serve as a party spread.

Nutrition: calories 300, fat 6, fiber 12, carbs 16, protein 6

Bulgur and Beans Salsa

Preparation time: 10 minutes | Cooking time: 8 hours | Servings: 2

Ingredients:
- 1 cup veggie stock
- ½ cup bulgur
- 1 small yellow onion, chopped
- 1 red bell pepper, chopped
- 1 garlic clove, minced
- 5 ounces canned kidney beans, drained
- ½ cup salsa
- 1 tablespoon chili powder
- ¼ teaspoon oregano, dried
- Salt and black pepper to the taste

Directions:
In your slow cooker, mix the bulgur with the stock and the other ingredients, toss, put the lid on and cook on Low for 8 hours. Divide into bowls and serve cold as an appetizer.

Nutrition: calories 351, fat 4, fiber 6, carbs 12, protein 4

Beets Salad

Preparation time: 10 minutes | Cooking time: 6 hours | Servings: 2

Ingredients:
- 2 cups beets, cubed
- ¼ cup carrots, grated
- 2 ounces tempeh, rinsed and cubed
- 1 cup cherry tomatoes, halved
- ¼ cup veggie stock
- 3 ounces canned black beans, drained
- Salt and black pepper to the taste
- ½ teaspoon nutmeg, ground
- ½ teaspoon sweet paprika
- ½ cup parsley, chopped

Directions:
In your slow cooker, mix the beets with the carrots, tempeh and the other ingredients, toss, put the lid on and cook on Low for 6 hours. Divide into bowls and serve cold as an appetizer.

Nutrition: calories 300, fat 6, fiber 6, carbs 16, protein 6

Lentils Salsa

Preparation time: 10 minutes | Cooking time: 3 hours | Servings: 2

Ingredients:
- 1 cup canned lentils, drained
- 1 cup mild salsa
- 3 ounces tomato paste
- 2 tablespoons balsamic vinegar
- 1 small sweet onion, chopped
- 1 garlic clove, minced
- ½ tablespoon sugar
- A pinch of red pepper flakes
- A pinch of salt and black pepper
- 1 tablespoon chives, chopped

Directions:
In your slow cooker, mix the lentils with the salsa and the other ingredients, toss, put the lid on and cook on High for 3 hours. Divide into bowls and serve as a party salsa.

Nutrition: calories 260, fat 3, fiber 4, carbs 6, protein 7

Tacos

Preparation time: 10 minutes | Cooking time: 4 hours | Servings: 2

Ingredients:
- 13 ounces canned pinto beans, drained
- ¼ cup chili sauce
- 2 ounces chipotle pepper in adobo sauce, chopped
- ½ tablespoon cocoa powder
- ¼ teaspoon cinnamon powder
- 4 taco shells

Directions:
In your slow cooker, mix the beans with the chili sauce and the other ingredients except the taco shells, toss, put the lid on and cook on Low for 4 hours Divide the mix into the taco shells and serve them as an appetizer.

Nutrition: calories 352, fat 3, fiber 6, carbs 12, protein 10

Almond Bowls

Preparation time: 10 minutes | Cooking time: 4 hours | Servings: 2

Ingredients:
- 1 tablespoon cinnamon powder
- 1 cup sugar
- 2 cups almonds
- ½ cup water
- ½ teaspoons vanilla extract

Directions:
In your slow cooker, mix the almonds with the cinnamon and the other ingredients, toss, put the lid on and cook on Low for 4 hours. Divide into bowls and serve as a snack.

Nutrition: calories 260, fat 3, fiber 4, carbs 12, protein 8

Eggplant Salsa

Preparation time: 10 minutes | Cooking time: 7 hours | Servings: 2

Ingredients:
- 2 cups eggplant, chopped
- 1 teaspoon capers, drained
- 1 cup black olives, pitted and halved
- ½ cup mild salsa
- 2 garlic cloves, minced
- ½ tablespoon basil, chopped
- 1 teaspoon balsamic vinegar
- A pinch of salt and black pepper

Directions:
In your slow cooker, mix the eggplant with the capers and the other ingredients, toss, put the lid on and cook on Low for 7 hours. Divide into bowls and serve as an appetizer.

Nutrition: calories 170, fat 3, fiber 5, carbs 10, protein 5

Almond Spread

Preparation time: 10 minutes | Cooking time: 8 hours | Servings: 2

Ingredients:
- ¼ cup almonds
- 1 cup heavy cream
- ½ teaspoon nutritional yeast flakes
- A pinch of salt and black pepper

Directions:
In your slow cooker, mix the almonds with the cream and the other ingredients, toss, put the lid on and cook on Low for 8 hours. Transfer to a blender, pulse well, divide into bowls and serve.

Nutrition: calories 270, fat 4, fiber 4, carbs 8, protein 10

Onion Dip

Preparation time: 10 minutes | Cooking time: 8 hours | Servings: 2

Ingredients:
- 2 cups yellow onions, chopped
- A pinch of salt and black pepper
- 1 tablespoon olive oil
- ½ cup heavy cream
- 2 tablespoons mayonnaise

Directions:
In your slow cooker, mix the onions with the cream and the other ingredients, whisk, put the lid on and cook on Low for 8 hours. Divide into bowls and serve as a party dip.

Nutrition: calories 240, fat 4, fiber 4, carbs 9, protein 7

Nuts Bowls

Preparation time: 10 minutes | Cooking time: 2 hours | Servings: 2

Ingredients:
- 2 tablespoons almonds, toasted
- 2 tablespoons pecans, halved and toasted
- 2 tablespoons hazelnuts, toasted and peeled
- 2 tablespoons sugar
- ½ cup coconut cream
- 2 tablespoons butter, melted
- A pinch of cinnamon powder
- A pinch of cayenne pepper

Directions:
In your slow cooker, mix the nuts with the sugar and the other ingredients, toss, put the lid on, cook on Low for 2 hours, divide into bowls and serve as a snack.

Nutrition: calories 125, fat 3, fiber 2, carbs 5, protein 5

Eggplant Salad

Preparation time: 10 minutes | Cooking time: 8 hours | Servings: 2

Ingredients:
- 2 eggplants, cubed
- 2 scallions, chopped
- 1 red bell pepper, chopped
- ½ teaspoon coriander, ground
- ½ cup mild salsa
- 1 teaspoon cumin, ground
- A pinch of salt and black pepper
- 1 tablespoon lemon juice

Directions:
In your slow cooker, combine the eggplants with the scallions, pepper and the other ingredients, toss, put the lid on, cook on Low for 8 hours, divide into bowls and serve cold as an appetizer salad.

Nutrition: calories 203, fat 2, fiber 3, carbs 7, protein 8

Lentils Dip

Preparation time: 10 minutes | Cooking time: 6 hours | Servings: 2

Ingredients:
- 2 carrots, peeled and grated
- 2 garlic cloves, minced
- A pinch of cayenne pepper
- 2 tablespoons tahini paste
- ¼ cup lemon juice
- 1 cup canned lentils, drained and rinsed
- A pinch of sea salt and black pepper
- ½ tablespoon rosemary, chopped

Directions:
In your slow cooker, mix the lentils with the carrots, garlic and the other ingredients, toss, put the lid on and cook on Low for 6 hours. Transfer to a blender, pulse well, divide into bowls and serve.

Nutrition: calories 200, fat 2, fiber 5, carbs 8, protein 6

Turkey Meatballs

Preparation time: 10 minutes | Cooking time: 7 hours | Servings: 2

Ingredients:
- 1 pound turkey breast, skinless, boneless and ground
- 1 egg, whisked
- 6 ounces canned tomato puree
- 2 tablespoons parsley, chopped
- 1 tablespoon oregano, chopped
- 1 garlic clove, minced
- 1 small yellow onion, chopped
- Salt and black pepper to the taste

Directions:
In a bowl, mix the meat with the egg, parsley and the other ingredients except the tomato puree, stir well and shape medium meatballs out of it. Put the meatballs in the slow cooker, add the tomato puree, put the lid on and cook on Low for 7 hours Arrange the meatballs on a platter and serve as an appetizer.

Nutrition: calories 170, fat 5, fiber 3, carbs 10, protein 7

Stuffed Mushrooms

Preparation time: 10 minutes | Cooking time: 3 hours | Servings: 2

Ingredients:
- ¼ pound chorizo, chopped
- 4 Portobello mushroom caps
- 1 red onion, chopped
- Salt and black pepper to the taste
- ¼ teaspoon garlic powder
- ¼ cup tomato sauce

Directions:
In a bowl, mix the chorizo with the onion, garlic powder, salt and pepper, stir and stuff the mushroom caps with this mix. Put the mushroom caps in the slow cooker, add the tomato sauce, put the lid on and cook on High for 3 hours. Arrange the stuffed mushrooms on a platter and serve.

Nutrition: calories 170, fat 2, fiber 3, carbs 8, protein 3

Paprika Cod Sticks

Preparation time: 10 minutes | Cooking time: 2 hours | Servings: 2

Ingredients:
- 1 eggs whisked
- ½ pound cod fillets, cut into medium strips
- ½ cup almond flour
- ½ teaspoon cumin, ground
- ½ teaspoon coriander, ground
- ½ teaspoon turmeric powder
- A pinch of salt and black pepper
- ¼ teaspoon sweet paprika
- Cooking spray

Directions:
In a bowl, mix the flour with cumin, coriander and the other ingredients except the fish, eggs and cooking spray. Put the egg in another bowl and whisk it. Dip the fish sticks in the egg and then dredge them in the flour mix. Grease the slow cooker with cooking spray, add fish sticks, put the lid on, cook on High for 2 hours, arrange on a platter and serve.

Nutrition: calories 200, fat 2, fiber 4, carbs 13, protein 12

Macadamia Nuts Snack

Preparation time: 10 minutes | Cooking time: 2 hours | Servings: 2

Ingredients:
- ½ pound macadamia nuts
- 1 tablespoon avocado oil
- ¼ cup water
- ½ tablespoon chili powder
- ½ teaspoon oregano, dried
- ½ teaspoon onion powder

Directions:
In your slow cooker, mix the macadamia nuts with the oil and the other ingredients, toss, put the lid on, cook on Low for 2 hours, divide into bowls and serve as a snack.

Nutrition: calories 108, fat 3, fiber 2, carbs 9, protein 2

Salmon Bites

Preparation time: 10 minutes | Cooking time: 2 hours | Servings: 2

Ingredients:
- 1 pound salmon fillets, boneless
- ¼ cup chili sauce
- A pinch of salt and black pepper
- ½ teaspoon turmeric powder
- 2 tablespoons grape jelly

Directions:
In your slow cooker, mix the salmon with the chili sauce and the other ingredients, toss gently, put the lid on and cook on High for 2 hours Serve as an appetizer.

Nutrition: calories 200, fat 6, fiber 3, carbs 15, protein 12

Spinach and Walnuts Dip

Preparation time: 10 minutes | Cooking time: 2 hours | Servings: 2

Ingredients:
- ½ cup heavy cream
- ½ cup walnuts, chopped
- 1 cup baby spinach
- 1 garlic clove, chopped
- 1 tablespoon mayonnaise
- Salt and black pepper to the taste

Directions:
In your slow cooker, mix the spinach with the walnuts and the other ingredients, toss, put the lid on and cook on High for 2 hours. Blend using an immersion blender, divide into bowls and serve as a party dip.

Nutrition: calories 260, fat 4, fiber 2, carbs 12, protein 5

Curry Pork Meatballs

Preparation time: 10 minutes | Cooking time: 4 hours | Servings: 2

Ingredients:
- ½ pound pork stew meat, ground
- 1 red onion, chopped
- 1 egg, whisked
- Salt and black pepper to the taste
- 1 tablespoon cilantro, chopped
- 5 ounces coconut milk
- ¼ tablespoon green curry paste

Directions:
In a bowl, mix the meat with the onion and the other ingredients except the coconut milk, stir well and shape medium meatballs out of this mix. Put the meatballs in your slow cooker, add the coconut milk, put the lid on and cook on High for 4 hours. Arrange the meatballs on a platter and serve them as an appetizer

Nutrition: calories 225, fat 6, fiber 2, carbs 8, protein 4

Calamari Rings Bowls

Preparation time: 10 minutes | Cooking time: 6 hours | Servings: 2

Ingredients:
- ½ pound calamari rings
- 1 tablespoon balsamic vinegar
- ½ tablespoon soy sauce
- 1 tablespoon sugar
- 1 cup veggie stock
- ½ teaspoon turmeric powder
- ½ teaspoon sweet paprika
- ½ cup chicken stock

Directions:
In your slow cooker, mix the calamari rings with the vinegar, soy sauce and the other ingredients, toss, put the lid on and cook on High for 6 hours. Divide into bowls and serve right away as an appetizer.

Nutrition: calories 230, fat 2, fiber 4, carbs 7, protein 5

Shrimp Salad

Preparation time: 10 minutes | Cooking time: 2 hours | Servings: 2

Ingredients:
- ½ pound shrimp, peeled and deveined
- 1 green bell pepper, chopped
- ½ cup kalamata olives, pitted and halved
- 4 spring onions, chopped
- 1 red bell pepper, chopped
- ½ cup mild salsa
- 1 tablespoon olive oil
- 1 garlic clove, minced
- ¼ teaspoon oregano, dried
- ¼ teaspoon basil, dried
- Salt and black pepper to the taste
- A pinch of red pepper, crushed
- 1 tablespoon parsley, chopped

Directions:
In your slow cooker, mix the shrimp with the peppers and the other ingredients, toss, put the lid on and cook on High for 2 hours. Divide into bowls and serve as an appetizer.

Nutrition: calories 240, fat 2, fiber 5, carbs 7, protein 2

Chicken Salad

Preparation time: 10 minutes | Cooking time: 6 hours | Servings: 2

Ingredients:

- 2 chicken breasts, skinless, boneless and cubed
- ½ cup mild salsa
- ½ tablespoon olive oil
- 1 red onion, chopped
- ½ cup mushrooms, sliced
- ½ cup kalamata olives, pitted and halved
- ½ cup cherry tomatoes, halved
- 1 chili pepper, chopped
- 2 ounces baby spinach
- 1 teaspoon oregano, chopped
- ½ tablespoon lemon juice
- ½ cup veggie stock
- A pinch of salt and black pepper

Directions:

In your slow cooker, mix the chicken with the salsa, oil and the other ingredients except the spinach, toss, put the lid on and cook on High for 5 hours. Add the spinach, cook on High for 1 more hour, divide into bowls and serve as an appetizer.

Nutrition: calories 245, fat 4, fiber 3, carbs 10, protein 6

Apple and Carrot Dip

Preparation time: 10 minutes | Cooking time: 6 hours | Servings: 2

Ingredients:

- 2 cups apples, peeled, cored and chopped
- 1 cup carrots, peeled and grated
- ¼ teaspoon cloves, ground
- ¼ teaspoon ginger powder
- 1 tablespoon lemon juice
- ½ tablespoon lemon zest, grated
- ½ cup coconut cream
- ¼ teaspoon nutmeg, ground

Directions:

In your slow cooker, mix the apples with the carrots, cloves and the other ingredients, toss, put the lid on and cook on Low for 6 hours. Bend using an immersion blender, divide into bowls and serve.

Nutrition: calories 212, fat 4, fiber 6, carbs 12, protein 3

Sweet Potato Dip

Preparation time: 10 minutes | Cooking time: 4 hours | Servings: 2

Ingredients:

- 2 sweet potatoes, peeled and cubed
- ½ cup coconut cream
- ½ teaspoon turmeric powder
- ½ teaspoon garam masala
- 2 garlic cloves, minced
- ½ cup veggie stock
- 1 cup basil leaves
- 2 tablespoons olive oil
- 1 tablespoon lemon juice
- A pinch of salt and black pepper

Directions:

In your slow cooker, mix the sweet potatoes with the cream, turmeric and the other ingredients, toss, put the lid on and cook on High for 4 hours. Blend using an immersion blender, divide into bowls and serve as a party dip.

Nutrition: calories 253, fat 5, fiber 6, carbs 13, protein 4

Spinach, Walnuts and Calamari Salad

***Preparation time:** 10 minutes | **Cooking time:** 4 hours and 30 minutes | **Servings:** 2*

Ingredients:
- 2 cups baby spinach
- ½ cup walnuts, chopped
- ½ cup mild salsa
- 1 cup calamari rings
- ½ cup kalamata olives, pitted and halved
- ½ teaspoons thyme, chopped
- 2 garlic cloves, minced
- 1 cup tomatoes, cubed
- A pinch of salt and black pepper
- ¼ cup veggie stock

Directions:

In your slow cooker, mix the salsa with the calamari rings and the other ingredients except the spinach, toss, put the lid on and cook on High for 4 hours. Add the spinach, toss, put the lid on, cook on High for 30 minutes more, divide into bowls and serve.

Nutrition: calories 160, fat 1, fiber 4, carbs 18, protein 4

Chicken Meatballs

***Preparation time:** 10 minutes | **Cooking time:** 7 hours | **Servings:** 2*

Ingredients:
- A pinch of red pepper flakes, crushed
- ½ pound chicken breast, skinless, boneless, ground
- 1 egg, whisked
- ½ cup salsa Verde
- 1 teaspoon oregano, dried
- ½ teaspoon chili powder
- ½ teaspoon rosemary, dried
- 1 tablespoon parsley, chopped
- A pinch of salt and black pepper

Directions:

In a bowl, mix the chicken with the egg and the other ingredients except the salsa, stir well and shape medium meatballs out of this mix. Put the meatballs in the slow cooker, add the salsa Verde, toss gently, put the lid on and cook on Low for 7 hours. Arrange the meatballs on a platter and serve.

Nutrition: calories 201, fat 4, fiber 5, carbs 8, protein 2

Cinnamon Pecans Snack

***Preparation time:** 10 minutes | **Cooking time:** 3 hours | **Servings:** 2*

Ingredients:
- ½ tablespoon cinnamon powder
- ¼ cup water
- ½ tablespoon avocado oil
- ½ teaspoon chili powder
- 2 cups pecans

Directions:

In your slow cooker, mix the pecans with the cinnamon and the other ingredients, toss, put the lid on and cook on Low for 3 hours. Divide the pecans into bowls and serve as a snack.

Nutrition: calories 172, fat 3, fiber 5, carbs 8, protein 2

Seasoned Peanuts

***Preparation time:** 10 minutes | **Cooking time:** 8 hours | **Servings:** 2*

Ingredients:
- ½ pounds green peanuts
- 1 cup water
- A pinch of sea salt
- ½ tablespoon Cajun seasoning

Directions:

In your slow cooker, mix peanuts with water, salt and Cajun seasoning, stir, cover, cook on Low for 8 hours, drain, transfer to bowls and serve as a snack.

Nutrition: calories 100, fat 2, fiber 3, carbs 7, protein 3

Broccoli Dip

Preparation time: 10 minutes | Cooking time: 2 hours | Servings: 2

Ingredients:
- 1 green chili pepper, minced
- 2 tablespoons heavy cream
- 1 cup broccoli florets
- 1 tablespoon mayonnaise
- 2 tablespoons cream cheese, cubed
- A pinch of salt and black pepper
- 1 tablespoon chives, chopped

Directions:

In your slow cooker, mix the broccoli with the chili pepper, mayo and the other ingredients, toss, put the lid on and cook on Low for 2 hours. Blend using an immersion blender, divide into bowls and serve as a party dip.

Nutrition: calories 202, fat 3, fiber 3, carbs 7, protein 6

Walnuts Bowls

Preparation time: 10 minutes | Cooking time: 2 hours | Servings: 2

Ingredients:
- Cooking spray
- 1 cup walnuts, chopped
- 2 tablespoons balsamic vinegar
- 1 tablespoon smoked paprika
- ½ tablespoon lemon zest, grated
- ½ tablespoons olive oil
- 1 teaspoon rosemary, dried

Directions:

Grease your slow cooker with the cooking spray, add walnuts and the other ingredients inside, toss, put the lid on and cook on Low for 2 hours. Divide into bowls and serve them as a snack.

Nutrition: calories 100, fat 2, fiber 2, carbs 3, protein 2

Cauliflower Bites

Preparation time: 10 minutes | Cooking time: 4 hours | Servings: 2

Ingredients:
- 2 cups cauliflower florets
- 1 tablespoon Italian seasoning
- 1 tablespoon sweet paprika
- 2 tablespoons tomato sauce
- 1 teaspoon sweet paprika
- 1 tablespoon olive oil
- ¼ cup veggie stock

Directions:

In your slow cooker, mix the cauliflower florets with the Italian seasoning and the other ingredients, toss, put the lid on and cook on Low for 4 hours. Divide into bowls and serve as a snack.

Nutrition: calories 251, fat 4, fiber 6, carbs 7, protein 3

Beef Dip

Preparation time: 10 minutes | Cooking time: 4 hours | Servings: 2

Ingredients:
- 1 pound beef meat, ground
- 1 carrot, peeled and grated
- 2 spring onions, chopped
- 1 tablespoon sriracha sauce
- 3 tablespoons beef stock
- 1 teaspoon hot sauce
- 3 ounces heavy cream

Directions:

In your slow cooker, mix the beef meat with the stock, hot sauce and the other ingredients, whisk, put the lid on and cook on Low for 4 hours. Divide the mix into bowls and serve as a party dip.

Nutrition: calories 301, fat 3, fiber 6, carbs 11, protein 5

Zucchini Spread

Preparation time: 10 minutes | *Cooking time: 6 hours* | *Servings: 2*

Ingredients:
- 1 tablespoon walnuts, chopped
- 2 zucchinis, grated
- 1 cup heavy cream
- 1 teaspoon balsamic vinegar
- 1 tablespoon tahini paste
- 1 tablespoon chives, chopped

Directions:
In your slow cooker, combine the zucchinis with the cream, walnuts and the other ingredients, whisk, put the lid on and cook on Low for 6 hours. Blend using an immersion blender, divide into bowls and serve as a party spread.

Nutrition: calories 221, fat 6, fiber 5, carbs 9, protein 3

Beef Dip

Preparation time: 10 minutes | *Cooking time: 7 hours and 10 minutes* | *Servings: 2*

Ingredients:
- ½ pounds beef, minced
- 3 spring onions, minced
- 1 tablespoon olive oil
- 1 cup mild salsa
- 2 ounces white mushrooms, chopped
- ¼ cup pine nuts, toasted
- 2 garlic cloves, minced
- 1 tablespoon hives, chopped
- ½ teaspoon coriander, ground
- ½ teaspoon rosemary, dried
- A pinch of salt and black pepper

Directions:
Heat up a pan with the oil over medium heat, add the spring onions, mushrooms, garlic and the meat, stir, brown for 10 minutes and transfer to your slow cooker. Add the rest of the ingredients, toss, put the lid on and cook on Low for 7 hours. Divide the dip into bowls and serve.

Nutrition: calories 361, fat 6, fiber 6, carbs 12, protein 3

Eggplant Salsa

Preparation time: 10 minutes | *Cooking time: 4 hours* | *Servings: 2*

Ingredients:
- 1 cup cherry tomatoes, cubed
- 2 cups eggplant, cubed
- 1 tablespoon capers, drained
- 1 tablespoon black olives, pitted and sliced
- 1 tablespoon lemon juice
- 1 tablespoon olive oil
- ¼ cup mild salsa
- 2 teaspoons balsamic vinegar
- 1 tablespoon basil, chopped
- 1 tablespoon chives, chopped
- Salt and black pepper to the taste

Directions:
In your slow cooker, mix the eggplant with the cherry tomatoes, capers, olives and the other ingredients, toss, put the lid on and cook on High for 4 hours. Divide salsa into small bowls and serve.

Nutrition: calories 200, fat 6, fiber 5, carbs 9, protein 2

Carrots Spread

Preparation time: 10 minutes | Cooking time: 7 hours | Servings: 4

Ingredients:
- 2 cups carrots, peeled and grated
- ½ cup heavy cream
- 1 teaspoon turmeric powder
- 1 teaspoon sweet paprika
- 1 cup coconut milk
- 1 teaspoon garlic powder
- ¼ teaspoon mustard powder
- A pinch of salt and black pepper

Directions:
In your slow cooker, mix the carrots with the cream, turmeric and the other ingredients, whisk, put the lid on and cook on Low for 7 hours. Divide the mix into bowls and serve as a party spread.

Nutrition: calories 291, fat 7, fiber 4, carbs 14, protein 3

Cauliflower Dip

Preparation time: 10 minutes | Cooking time: 5 hours | Servings: 2

Ingredients:
- 1 cup cauliflower florets
- ½ cup heavy cream
- 1 tablespoon tahini paste
- ½ cup white mushrooms, chopped
- 2 garlic cloves, minced
- 2 tablespoons lemon juice
- 1 tablespoon basil, chopped
- 1 teaspoon rosemary, dried
- A pinch of salt and black pepper

Directions:
In your slow cooker, mix the cauliflower with the cream, tahini paste and the other ingredients, toss, put the lid on and cook on Low for 5 hours. Transfer to a blender, pulse well, divide into bowls and serve as a party dip.

Nutrition: calories 301, fat 7, fiber 6, carbs 10, protein 6

Lentils Hummus

Preparation time: 10 minutes | Cooking time: 4 hours | Servings: 2

Ingredients:
- 1 cup chicken stock
- 1 cup canned lentils, drained
- 2 tablespoons tahini paste
- ¼ teaspoon onion powder
- ¼ cup heavy cream
- A pinch of salt and black pepper
- ¼ teaspoon turmeric powder
- 1 teaspoon lemon juice

Directions:
In your slow cooker, mix the lentils with the stock, onion powder, salt and pepper, toss, put the lid on and cook on High for 4 hours. Drain the lentils, transfer to your blender, add the rest of the ingredients, pulse well, divide into bowls and serve.

Nutrition: calories 192, fat 7, fiber 7, carbs 12, protein 4

Spinach Dip

Preparation time: 10 minutes | Cooking time: 1 hour | Servings: 2

Ingredients:
- 1 cup coconut cream
- 10 ounces spinach, torn
- 2 spring onions, chopped
- 1 teaspoon rosemary, dried
- ½ teaspoon garam masala
- 1 garlic clove, minced
- A pinch of salt and black pepper

Directions:
In your slow cooker, mix the spinach with the cream, spring onions and the other ingredients, toss, put the lid on and cook on High for 1 hour. Blend using an immersion blender, divide into bowls and serve as a party dip.

Nutrition: calories 241, fat 5, fiber 7, carbs 12, protein 5

Peppers Salsa

Preparation time: 10 minutes | Cooking time: 5 hours and 5 minutes | Servings: 2

Ingredients:
- 1 yellow onion, chopped
- 2 spring onions, chopped
- 2 teaspoons olive oil
- 1 teaspoon turmeric powder
- 1 red bell pepper, roughly cubed
- 1 green bell pepper, roughly cubed
- 1 orange bell pepper, roughly cubed
- 1 cup cherry tomatoes, halved
- 1 tablespoon chili powder
- 3 garlic cloves, minced
- ½ cup mild salsa
- 1 teaspoon oregano, dried
- A pinch of salt and black pepper

Directions:
Heat up a pan with the oil over medium-high heat, add the spring onions, onion and garlic, sauté for 5 minutes and transfer to the slow cooker. Add the rest of the ingredients, toss, put the lid on and cook on Low for 5 hours. Divide the mix into bowls and serve as a snack.

Nutrition: calories 221, fat 5, fiber 4, carbs 9, protein 3

Artichoke Dip

Preparation time: 10 minutes | Cooking time: 4 hours | Servings: 2

Ingredients:
- 1 cup canned artichoke hearts, drained and chopped
- 1 cup baby spinach
- 1 cup heavy cream
- 2 spring onions, chopped
- ½ teaspoon sweet paprika
- ½ teaspoon turmeric powder
- 2 garlic cloves, minced
- 1/3 cup mayonnaise
- 1 tablespoon lemon juice
- A pinch of salt and black pepper

Directions:
In your slow cooker, mix the artichoke hearts with the spinach, cream and the other ingredients, toss, put the lid on and cook on Low for 4 hours. Divide into bowls and serve as a party dip.

Nutrition: calories 305, fat 14, fiber 4, carbs 9, protein 13

Mushroom Salsa

Preparation time: 10 minutes | Cooking time: 5 hours | Servings: 4

Ingredients:
- 2 cups white mushrooms, sliced
- 1 cup cherry tomatoes halved
- 1 cup spring onions, chopped
- ½ teaspoon chili powder
- ½ teaspoon rosemary, dried
- ½ teaspoon oregano, dried
- ½ cup black olives, pitted and sliced
- 3 garlic cloves, minced
- 1 cup mild salsa
- Salt and black pepper to the taste

Directions:
In your slow cooker, mix the mushrooms with the cherry tomatoes and the other ingredients, toss, put the lid on and cook on Low for 5 hours. Divide into bowls and serve as a snack.

Nutrition: calories 205, fat 4, fiber 7, carbs 9, protein 3

Slow Cooker Poultry Recipes for 2

Garlic Chicken and Green Beans

Preparation time: 10 minutes | Cooking time: 6 hours and 10 minutes. | Servings: 2

Ingredients:

- 1 pound chicken thighs, boneless, skinless and cubed
- 1 teaspoon sweet paprika
- ½ teaspoon garam masala
- 1 cup green beans, trimmed and halved
- 1 red onion, chopped
- 2 tablespoons olive oil
- 4 garlic cloves, minced
- 1 cup chicken stock
- 1 tablespoon chives, chopped
- A pinch of salt and black pepper

Directions:

Heat up a pan with the oil over medium-high heat, add the chicken, onion and garlic, cook for 10 minutes and transfer to the slow cooker. Add the rest of the ingredients, toss, put the lid on and cook on Low for 6 hours. Divide everything into bowls and serve.

Nutrition: calories 263, fat 12, fiber 3, carbs 6, protein 14

Oregano Turkey and Tomatoes

Preparation time: 10 minutes | Cooking time: 7 hours | Servings: 4

Ingredients:

- 1 pound turkey breast, skinless, boneless and sliced
- 1 tablespoon oregano, chopped
- 1 cup chicken stock
- 1 cup cherry tomatoes, halved
- 1 teaspoon turmeric powder
- 2 tablespoons olive oil
- 1 cup scallions, chopped
- 1 teaspoon chili powder
- A pinch of salt and black pepper
- ½ cup tomato sauce

Directions:

In your slow cooker, mix the turkey with the oregano, stock and the other ingredients, toss, put the lid on and cook on Low for 7 hours. Divide the mix between plates and serve.

Nutrition: calories 162, fat 8, fiber 2, carbs 5, protein 9

Mustard Chicken Mix

Preparation time: 10 minutes | Cooking time: 6 hours | Servings: 4

Ingredients:

- 1 tablespoon olive oil
- 1 pound chicken breast, skinless, boneless and roughly cubed
- 2 tablespoons mustard
- ¾ cup chicken stock
- 1 teaspoon sweet paprika
- 1 teaspoon rosemary, dried
- 1 tablespoon lemon juice
- A pinch of salt and black pepper
- 1 tablespoon chives, chopped

Directions:

In your slow cooker, mix the chicken with the oil, mustard and the other ingredients, toss, put the lid on and cook on Low for 6 hours. Divide the mix into bowls and serve.

Nutrition: calories 200, fat 9, fiber 2, carbs 5, protein 10

Lemon Turkey and Spinach

Preparation time: 10 minutes | Cooking time: 7 hours | Servings: 4

Ingredients:

- 1 pound turkey breasts, skinless, boneless and roughly cubed
- 1 cup baby spinach
- Juice of ½ lemon
- 2 spring onions, chopped
- ½ teaspoon chili powder
- 1 cup chicken stock
- 1 tablespoon oregano, chopped
- A pinch of salt and black pepper
- 1 teaspoon garam masala

Directions:

In your slow cooker, mix the turkey with the lemon juice, spring onions and the other ingredients except the baby spinach, toss, put the lid on and cook on Low for 6 hours and 30 minutes. Add the spinach, cook everything on Low for 30 minutes more, divide between plates and serve.

Nutrition: calories 200, fat 7, fiber 2, carbs 6, protein 11

Paprika Chicken and Artichokes

Preparation time: 10 minutes | Cooking time: 7 hours and 10 minutes | Servings: 2

Ingredients:

- 1 pound chicken breast, skinless, boneless and cut into strips
- 1 cup canned artichoke hearts, drained and halved
- 3 scallions, chopped
- 2 garlic cloves, minced
- 1 tablespoon olive oil
- 1 tablespoon sweet paprika
- 1 cup chicken stock
- ½ cup parsley, chopped

Directions:

Heat up a pan with the oil over medium-high heat, add the scallions, garlic and the chicken, brown for 10 minutes and transfer to the slow cooker. Add the rest of the ingredients, toss, put the lid on and cook on Low for 7 hours. Divide everything between plates and serve.

Nutrition: calories 210, fat 8, fiber 2, carbs 6, protein 11

Chives Chicken Wings

Preparation time: 10 minutes | Cooking time: 6 hours | Servings: 2

Ingredients:

- 1 cup chicken stock
- 1 pound chicken wings
- ½ cup chives, chopped
- ½ teaspoon chili powder
- ½ teaspoon coriander, ground
- ½ teaspoon cumin, ground
- 1 teaspoon oregano, dried
- A pinch of salt and black pepper

Directions:

In your slow cooker, mix the chicken with the stock, chives and the other ingredients, toss, put the lid on and cook on Low for 6 hours Divide the mix between plates and serve with a side salad.

Nutrition: calories 220, fat 8, fiber 2, carbs 5, protein 11

Lime Chicken Mix

Preparation time: 10 minutes | Cooking time: 7 hours | Servings: 2

Ingredients:

- 1 pound chicken thighs, boneless and skinless
- 1 tablespoon olive oil
- Juice of 1 lime
- Zest of 1 lime, grated
- ½ cup tomato sauce
- 2 spring onions, chopped
- Salt and black pepper to the taste
- 1 tablespoon oregano, chopped

Directions:

In your slow cooker, mix the chicken with the oil, lime juice and the other ingredients, toss, put the lid on and cook on Low for 7 hours Divide the mix between plates and serve.

Nutrition: calories 192, fat 12, fiber 3, carbs 5, protein 12

Chicken and Olives

Preparation time: 10 minutes | Cooking time: 5 hours | Servings: 2

Ingredients:

- 1 pound chicken breasts, skinless, boneless and sliced
- 1 cup black olives, pitted and halved
- ½ cup chicken stock
- ½ cup tomato sauce
- 1 tablespoon lime juice
- 1 tablespoon lime zest, grated
- 1 teaspoon chili powder
- 2 spring onions, chopped
- 1 tablespoon chives, chopped

Directions:

In your slow cooker, mix the chicken with the olives, stock and the other ingredients except the chives, toss, put the lid on and cook on High for 5 hours. Divide the mix into bowls, sprinkle the chives on top and serve.

Nutrition: calories 200, fat 7, fiber 1, carbs 5, protein 12

Turkey, Tomato and Fennel Mix

Preparation time: 10 minutes | Cooking time: 7 hours and 10 minutes | Servings: 2

Ingredients:

- 1 pound turkey breast, skinless, boneless and cut into strips
- 1 fennel bulb, sliced
- 1 cup cherry tomatoes, halved
- ¼ cup chicken stock
- ½ cup tomato sauce
- ½ teaspoon hot paprika
- ½ teaspoon cumin, ground
- ½ teaspoon fennel seeds, crushed
- 1 tablespoon olive oil
- 1 red onion, chopped
- A pinch of salt and black pepper
- 1 tablespoon cilantro, chopped

Directions:

Heat up a pan with the oil over medium-high heat, add the meat, onion and fennel seeds, stir, brown for 10 minutes and transfer to the slow cooker. Add the rest of the ingredients, toss, put the lid on, cook on Low for 7 hours, divide between plates and serve.

Nutrition: calories 231, fat 7, fiber 2, carbs 6, protein 12

Chicken with Tomatoes and Eggplant Mix

Preparation time: 10 minutes | Cooking time: 5 hours and 10 minutes. | Servings: 2

Ingredients:

- 1 pound chicken breast, skinless, boneless and cubed
- 2 small eggplants, cubed
- 1 red onion, sliced
- 1 tablespoon olive oil
- ½ teaspoon cumin, ground
- ½ teaspoon sweet paprika
- ½ teaspoon red pepper flakes, crushed
- ½ cup canned tomatoes, crushed
- 1 cup chicken stock
- 1 teaspoon coriander, ground
- A pinch of salt and black pepper
- 1 tablespoon oregano, chopped

Directions:

Heat up a pan with the oil over medium-high heat, add the chicken, onion and pepper flakes, stir, brown for 10 minutes and transfer to your slow cooker. Add the rest of the ingredients, toss, put the lid on and cook on High for 5 hours. Divide everything between plates and serve.

Nutrition: calories 252, fat 12, fiber 4, carbs 7, protein 13

Chicken and Onions Mix

Preparation time: 10 minutes | Cooking time: 7 hours | Servings: 2

Ingredients:

- 1 pound chicken breasts, skinless, boneless and cubed
- 2 red onions, sliced
- ½ cup chicken stock
- ½ cup tomato pasata
- 2 teaspoons olive oil
- A pinch of salt and black pepper
- 1 teaspoon black peppercorns, crushed
- 2 garlic cloves, minced
- 1 tablespoon chives, chopped

Directions:

Grease the slow cooker with the oil and mix the chicken with the onions, stock and the other ingredients inside. Put the lid on, cook on Low for 7 hours, divide between plates and serve.

Nutrition: calories 221, fat 14, fiber 3, carbs 7, protein 14

Pesto Chicken Mix

Preparation time: 10 minutes | Cooking time: 6 hours and 10 minutes | Servings: 2

Ingredients:

- 1 pound chicken breast, skinless, boneless and cut into strips
- 1 tablespoon basil pesto
- 1 tablespoon olive oil
- 4 scallions, chopped
- ½ cup kalamata olives, pitted and halved
- 1 cup chicken stock
- 1 tablespoon cilantro, chopped
- A pinch of salt and black pepper

Directions:

Heat up a pan with the oil over medium-high heat, add the scallions and the meat, brown for 10 minutes, transfer to the slow cooker and mix with the remaining ingredients. Toss, put the lid on, cook on Low for 6 hours, divide the mix between plates and serve.

Nutrition: calories 263, fat 14, fiber 1, carbs 8, protein 12

Ginger Turkey Mix

Preparation time: 10 minutes | Cooking time: 6 hours | Servings: 2

Ingredients:

1. 1 pound turkey breast, skinless, boneless and roughly cubed
2. 1 tablespoon ginger, grated
3. 2 teaspoons olive oil
4. 1 cup tomato passata
5. ½ cup chicken stock
6. A pinch of salt and black pepper
7. 1 teaspoon chili powder
8. 2 garlic cloves, minced
9. 1 tablespoon cilantro, chopped

Directions:

Grease the slow cooker with the oil and mix the turkey with the ginger and the other ingredients inside. Put the lid on, cook on High for 6 hours, divide between plates and serve.

Nutrition: calories 263, fat 12, fiber 3, carbs 6, protein 14

Turkey and Plums Mix

Preparation time: 10 minutes | Cooking time: 7 hours | Servings: 2

Ingredients:

- 1 pound turkey breast, skinless, boneless and sliced
- 1 cup plums, pitted and halved
- ½ cup chicken stock
- ½ teaspoon chili powder
- ½ teaspoon turmeric powder
- ½ teaspoon cumin, ground
- 1 tablespoon rosemary, chopped
- A pinch of salt and black pepper

Directions:

In your slow cooker, mix the turkey with the plums, stock and the other ingredients, toss, put the lid on and cook on Low for 7 hours. Divide the mix between plates and serve right away.

Nutrition: calories 253, fat 13, fiber 2, carbs 7, protein 16

Creamy Turkey Mix

Preparation time: 10 minutes | Cooking time: 7 hours | Servings: 2

Ingredients:

- 1 pound turkey breast, skinless, boneless and cubed
- 1 teaspoon turmeric powder
- ½ teaspoon garam masala
- ½ cup heavy cream
- 1 red onion, chopped
- ½ cup chicken stock
- 4 garlic cloves, minced
- ¼ cup chives, chopped
- A pinch of salt and black pepper
- 1 tablespoon chives, chopped

Directions:

In your slow cooker, mix the turkey with turmeric, garam masala and the other ingredients except the cream, toss, put the lid on and cook on Low for 6 hours. Add the cream, toss, put the lid on again, cook on Low for 1 more hour, divide everything between plates and serve.

Nutrition: calories 234, fat 14, fiber 4, carbs 7, protein 15

Chicken and Apples Mix

Preparation time: 10 minutes | Cooking time: 7 hours | Servings: 2

Ingredients:

- 1 pound chicken breast, skinless, boneless and sliced
- 1 cup apples, cored and cubed
- 1 teaspoon olive oil
- 1 red onion, sliced
- 1 tablespoon oregano, chopped
- ½ teaspoon turmeric powder
- ½ teaspoon chili powder
- 1 cup chicken stock
- A pinch of salt and black pepper
- 1 tablespoon chives, chopped

Directions:

Grease the slow cooker with the oil, and mix the chicken with the apples, onion and the other ingredients inside. Toss, put the lid on, cook on Low for 7 hours, divide the mix between plates and serve.

Nutrition: calories 263, fat 13, fiber 2, carbs 7, protein 15

Chicken and Endives

Preparation time: 5 minutes | Cooking time: 7 hours | Servings: 2

Ingredients:

- 1 pound chicken breasts, skinless, boneless and sliced
- 4 scallions, chopped
- 2 endives, shredded
- ½ cup tomatoes, cubed
- 1 cup chicken stock
- 1 tablespoon oregano, chopped
- A pinch of salt and black pepper

Directions:

In your slow cooker, combine the chicken slices with the scallions and the other ingredients except the endives and the oregano, toss, put the lid on and cook on Low for 6 hours. Add the remaining ingredients, cook on Low for 1 more hour, divide everything between plates and serve.

Nutrition: calories 200, fat 13, fiber 2, carbs 5, protein 16

Basil Chicken Wings

Preparation time: 5 minutes | Cooking time: 5 hours | Servings: 2

Ingredients:

- 1 pound chicken wings, halved
- 1 tablespoon olive oil
- 1 tablespoon honey
- 1 cup chicken stock
- A pinch of salt and black pepper
- 1 tablespoon basil, chopped
- ½ teaspoon cumin, ground

Directions:

In your slow cooker, mix the chicken wings with the oil, honey and the other ingredients, toss, put the lid on and cook on High for 5 hours. Divide the mix between plates and serve with a side salad.

Nutrition: calories 200, fat 12, fiber 2, carbs 6, protein 15

Chicken and Broccoli

Preparation time: 10 minutes | Cooking time: 5 hours | Servings: 2

Ingredients:
- 1 pound chicken breast, skinless, boneless and sliced
- 1 cup broccoli florets
- ½ cup tomato sauce
- ½ cup chicken stock
- 1 tablespoon avocado oil
- 1 yellow onion, sliced
- 3 garlic cloves, minced
- A pinch of salt and black pepper
- 1 tablespoon cilantro, chopped

Directions:
In your slow cooker, mix the chicken with the broccoli, tomato sauce and the other ingredients, toss, put the lid on and cook on High for 5 hours. Divide the mix between plates and serve hot.

Nutrition: calories 253, fat 14, fiber 2, carbs 7, protein 16

Rosemary Chicken

Preparation time: 10 minutes | Cooking time: 7 hours | Servings: 2

Ingredients:
- 1 pound chicken thighs, boneless, skinless and sliced
- 1 tablespoon avocado oil
- 1 teaspoon cumin, ground
- 1 tablespoon rosemary, chopped
- 1 cup chicken stock
- A pinch of salt and black pepper
- 1 tablespoon chives, chopped

Directions:
In your slow cooker, mix the chicken with the oil, cumin and the other ingredients, toss, put the lid on and cook on Low for 7 hours. Divide the mix between plates and serve.

Nutrition: calories 273, fat 13, fiber 3, carbs 7, protein 17

Chicken Curry

Preparation time: 10 minutes | Cooking time: 7 hours | Servings: 2

Ingredients:
- 1 pound chicken breast, skinless, boneless and cubed
- 1 tablespoon yellow curry paste
- 1 yellow onion, chopped
- 1 tablespoon olive oil
- 1 teaspoon basil, dried
- 1 teaspoon black peppercorns, crushed
- 1 cup chicken stock
- ¼ cup coconut cream
- 1 tablespoon lime juice
- 1 tablespoon cilantro, chopped

Directions:
In your slow cooker, mix the chicken with the curry paste, onion and the other ingredients, toss, put the lid on and cook on Low for 7 hours. Divide everything into bowls and serve hot.

Nutrition: calories 276, fat 15, fiber 3, carbs 7, protein 16

Balsamic Turkey

Preparation time: 10 minutes | Cooking time: 5 hours | Servings: 2

Ingredients:
- 1 pound turkey breast, skinless, boneless and cubed
- 1 tablespoon lemon juice
- 4 scallions, chopped
- 1 tablespoon balsamic vinegar
- 2 tablespoons avocado oil
- A pinch of salt and black pepper
- 1 tablespoon chives, chopped
- ½ cup chicken stock

Directions:
In your slow cooker, mix the turkey with the lemon juice, scallions and the other ingredients, toss, put the lid on and cook on High for 5 hours. Divide the mix between plates and serve right away.

Nutrition: calories 252, fat 15, fiber 2, carbs 6, protein 15

Turkey and Scallions Mix

Preparation time: 10 minutes | Cooking time: 7 hours | Servings: 2

Ingredients:

- 1 pound turkey breasts, skinless, boneless and cubed
- 1 tablespoon avocado oil
- ½ cup tomato sauce
- ½ cup chicken stock
- ½ teaspoon sweet paprika
- 4 scallions, chopped
- 1 tablespoons lemon zest, grated
- 1 tablespoon lemon juice
- A pinch of salt and black pepper
- 1 tablespoon chives, chopped

Directions:

In your slow cooker, mix the turkey with the oil, tomato sauce and the other ingredients, toss, put the lid on and cook on Low for 7 hours. Divide everything between plates and serve.

Nutrition: calories 234, fat 12, fiber 3, carbs 5, protein 7

Parsley Chicken Mix

Preparation time: 10 minutes | Cooking time: 5 hours | Servings: 2

Ingredients:

- 1 pound chicken breast, skinless, boneless and sliced
- ½ cup parsley, chopped
- 2 tablespoons olive oil
- 1 tablespoon pine nuts
- 1 tablespoon lemon juice
- ½ cup chicken stock
- ¼ cup black olives, pitted and halved
- 1 teaspoon hot paprika
- A pinch of salt and black pepper

Directions:

In a blender, mix the parsley with the oil, pine nuts and lemon juice and pulse well. In your slow cooker, mix the chicken with the parsley mix and the remaining ingredients, toss, put the lid on and cook on High for 5 hours. Divide everything between plates and serve.

Nutrition: calories 263, fat 14, fiber 3, carbs 7, protein 16

Turkey Chili

Preparation time: 10 minutes | Cooking time: 5 hours | Servings: 2

Ingredients:

- 1 pound turkey breast, skinless, boneless and cubed
- 1 red chili, minced
- 1 teaspoon chili powder
- 1 red onion, chopped
- 1 tablespoon avocado oil
- ½ cup tomato passata
- ½ cup chicken stock
- A pinch of salt and black pepper
- 1 tablespoon cilantro, chopped

Directions:

In your slow cooker, mix the turkey with the chili, chili powder and the other ingredients, toss, put the lid on and cook on High for 5 hours. Divide the mix into bowls and serve.

Nutrition: calories 263, fat 12, fiber 2, carbs 7, protein 18

Masala Turkey

Preparation time: 10 minutes | Cooking time: 5 hours | Servings: 2

Ingredients:
- 1 pound turkey breasts, skinless, boneless and cubed
- A pinch of salt and black pepper
- 2 scallions, chopped
- 1 teaspoon garam masala
- 1 cup coconut cream
- 1 cup chicken stock
- 1 tablespoon basil, chopped
- 1 tablespoon lime juice

Directions:

In your slow cooker, mix the turkey with the scallions, garam masala and the other ingredients, toss, put the lid on and cook on High for 5 hours. Divide the mix into bowls and serve.

Nutrition: calories 201, fat 7, fiber 3, carbs 6, protein 8

Chicken and Beans

Preparation time: 10 minutes | Cooking time: 7 hours | Servings: 2

Ingredients:
- 1 cup canned black beans, drained and rinsed
- ½ cup canned kidney beans, drained and rinsed
- 1 pound chicken breast, skinless, boneless and cubed
- 1 red onion, chopped
- 2 garlic cloves, minced
- 1 tablespoon olive oil
- ½ teaspoon sweet paprika
- 1 tablespoon chili powder
- 1 cup tomato sauce
- A pinch of salt and black pepper
- 1 tablespoon parsley, chopped

Directions:

In your slow cooker, mix the chicken with the beans, onion and the other ingredients, toss, put the lid on and cook on Low for 7 hours. Divide the mix into bowls and serve hot.

Nutrition: calories 263, fat 12, fiber 3, carbs 7, protein 15

Turkey and Corn

Preparation time: 10 minutes | Cooking time: 7 hours | Servings: 2

Ingredients:
- 1 red onion
- 1 cup corn
- 1 pound turkey breasts, skinless, boneless and cubed
- 1 cup heavy cream
- 2 tablespoons olive oil
- 1 tablespoon cumin, ground
- ½ cup chicken stock
- ½ teaspoon rosemary, dried
- A pinch of salt and black pepper
- 1 tablespoon cilantro, chopped

Directions:

In your slow cooker, mix the turkey with the corn, onion and the other ingredients, toss, put the lid on and cook on Low for 7 hours. Divide everything into bowls and serve.

Nutrition: calories 214, fat 14, fiber 2, carbs 6, protein 15

Coriander Turkey Mix

Preparation time: 10 minutes | Cooking time: 6 hours | Servings: 2

Ingredients:
- 1 pound turkey breasts, skinless, boneless and cubed
- 1 tablespoon olive oil
- 3 scallions, chopped
- 1 cup chicken stock
- 1 teaspoon sweet paprika
- 1 tablespoon coriander, chopped

Directions:
In your slow cooker, mix the turkey with the oil, scallions and the other ingredients, toss, put the lid on and cook Low for 6 hours. Divide the mix into bowls and serve.

Nutrition: calories 231, fat 12, fiber 4, carbs 7, protein 15

Turkey with Olives and Corn

Preparation time: 10 minutes | Cooking time: 4 hours | Servings: 2

Ingredients:
- 1 pound turkey breast, skinless, boneless and cubed
- 1 tablespoon olive oil
- ½ cup kalamata olives, pitted and halved
- 1 cup corn
- 1 red onion, sliced
- 1 cup tomato passata
- 1 tablespoon parsley, chopped

Directions:
In your slow cooker, mix the turkey with the olives, corn and the other ingredients, toss, put the lid on and cook on High for 4 hours. Divide everything between plates and serve.

Nutrition: calories 263, fat 12, fiber 5, carbs 7, protein 16

Dill Turkey and Peas

Preparation time: 10 minutes | Cooking time: 5 hours | Servings: 2

Ingredients:
- 1 pound turkey breast, skinless, boneless and sliced
- 1 cup green peas
- ½ cup tomato sauce
- ½ cup scallions, chopped
- A pinch of salt and black pepper
- 1 cup chicken stock
- 1 teaspoon garam masala
- 1 tablespoon dill, chopped

Directions:
In your slow cooker, mix the turkey with the peas, tomato sauce and the other ingredients, toss, put the lid on and cook on High for 5 hours Divide the mix into bowls and serve right away.

Nutrition: calories 242, fat 14, fiber 3, carbs 7, protein 14

Turkey with Rice

Preparation time: 10 minutes | Cooking time: 7 hours | Servings: 2

Ingredients:
- 1 pound turkey breasts, skinless, boneless and cubed
- 1 cup wild rice
- 2 cups chicken stock
- 1 tablespoon cilantro, chopped
- 1 tablespoon oregano, chopped
- 2 tablespoons green onions, chopped
- ½ teaspoon coriander, ground
- ½ teaspoon rosemary, dried
- ½ teaspoon turmeric powder
- A pinch of salt and black pepper

Directions:
In your slow cooker, mix the turkey with the rice, stock and the other ingredients, toss, put the lid on and cook on Low for 7 hours. Divide everything between plates and serve.

Nutrition: calories 232, fat 12, fiber 2, carbs 6, protein 15

Italian Turkey

Preparation time: 10 minutes | Cooking time: 6 hours | Servings: 2

Ingredients:
- 1 pound turkey breasts, skinless, boneless and roughly cubed
- 1 tablespoon olive oil
- ½ cup black olives, pitted and halved
- ½ cup pearl onions, peeled
- 1 cup chicken stock
- 1 tablespoon Italian seasoning
- A pinch of salt and black pepper

Directions:
In your slow cooker, mix the turkey with the olives, onions and the other ingredients, toss, put the lid on and coo on Low for 6 hours. Divide the mix between plates and serve.

Nutrition: calories 263, fat 14, fiber 4, carbs 6, protein 18

Duck and Mushrooms

Preparation time: 10 minutes | Cooking time: 6 hours | Servings: 2

Ingredients:
- 1 pound duck leg, skinless, boneless and sliced
- 1 cup chicken stock
- 1 cup white mushrooms, sliced
- ½ teaspoon rosemary, dried
- ½ teaspoon cumin, ground
- ½ cup heavy cream
- 1 tablespoon olive oil
- ¼ cup chives, chopped

Directions:
In your slow cooker, mix the duck with the stock, mushrooms and the other ingredients, toss, put the lid on and cook on Low for 6 hours. Divide everything between plates and serve.

Nutrition: calories 262, fat 16, fiber 2, carbs 8, protein 16

Turkey and Tomato Sauce

Preparation time: 10 minutes | Cooking time: 7 hours | Servings: 2

Ingredients:
- 1 cup tomato sauce
- ½ cup chicken stock
- ½ tablespoon rosemary, chopped
- 1 pound turkey breast, skinless, boneless and roughly cubed
- 1 teaspoon rosemary, dried
- 1 tablespoon cilantro, chopped
- A pinch of salt and black pepper

Directions:
In your slow cooker, mix the turkey with the sauce, stock and the other ingredients, toss, put the lid on and cook on Low for 7 hours. Divide everything between plates and serve.

Nutrition: calories 283, fat 16, fiber 2, carbs 6, protein 17

Tomato Chicken and Chickpeas

Preparation time: 10 minutes | Cooking time: 7 hours | Servings: 2

Ingredients:
- 1 tablespoon olive oil
- 1 red onion, chopped
- 1 cup canned chickpeas, drained
- 1 pound chicken breast, skinless, boneless and cubed
- ½ cup tomato sauce
- ½ cup cherry tomatoes, halved
- ½ teaspoon rosemary, dried
- ½ teaspoon turmeric powder
- 1 cup chicken stock
- A pinch of salt and black pepper
- 1 tablespoon chives, chopped

Directions:
Grease the slow cooker with the oil and mix the chicken with the onion, chickpeas and the other ingredients inside the pot. Put the lid on, cook on Low for 7 hours, divide between plates and serve.

Nutrition: calories 291, fat 17, fiber 3, carbs 7, protein 16

Turkey with Leeks and Radishes

Preparation time: 10 minutes | Cooking time: 6 hours | Servings: 2

Ingredients:

- 1 pound turkey breast, skinless, boneless and cubed
- 1 leek, sliced
- 1 cup radishes, sliced
- 1 red onion, chopped
- 1 tablespoon olive oil
- A pinch of salt and black pepper
- 1 cup chicken stock
- ½ teaspoon sweet paprika
- ½ teaspoon coriander, ground
- 1 tablespoon cilantro, chopped

Directions:

In your slow cooker, combine the turkey with the leek, radishes, onion and the other ingredients, toss, put the lid on and cook on High for 6 hours. Divide everything between plates and serve.

Nutrition: calories 226, fat 9, fiber 1, carbs 6, protein 12

Coconut Turkey

Preparation time: 10 minutes | Cooking time: 5 hours | Servings: 2

Ingredients:

- 1 yellow onion, chopped
- 1 tablespoon olive oil
- 1 cup coconut cream
- ½ teaspoon curry powder
- 1 pound turkey breast, skinless, boneless and cubed
- 1 teaspoon turmeric powder
- ½ cup chicken stock
- 1 tablespoon parsley, chopped
- A pinch of salt and black pepper

Directions:

In your slow cooker, mix the turkey with the onion, oil and the other ingredients except the cream and the parsley, stir, put the lid on and cook on High for 4 hours and 30 minutes. Add the remaining ingredients, toss, put the lid on again, cook on High for 30 minutes more, divide the mix between plates and serve.

Nutrition: calories 283, fat 11, fiber 2, carbs 8, protein 15

Hot Chicken and Zucchinis

Preparation time: 10 minutes | Cooking time: 6 hours | Servings: 2

Ingredients:

- 1 pound chicken breasts, skinless, boneless and cubed
- 1 zucchini, cubed
- 2 garlic cloves, minced
- 1 red chili, minced
- ½ teaspoon hot paprika
- 1 red onion, chopped
- 2 tablespoons olive oil
- A pinch of salt and black pepper
- 1 cup chicken stock
- 1 tablespoon chives, chopped

Directions:

In your slow cooker, mix the chicken with the zucchini, garlic, chili pepper and the other ingredients, toss, put the lid on and cook on Low for 6 hours. Divide everything between plates and serve.

Nutrition: calories 221, fat 12, fiber 2, carbs 5, protein 17

Turkey with Radishes

Preparation time: 10 minutes | Cooking time: 7 hours | Servings: 2

Ingredients:

- 1 tablespoon olive oil
- 2 scallions, minced
- 1 pound turkey breast, skinless, boneless and cubed
- 2 garlic cloves, minced
- 1 cup radishes, sliced
- ½ cup tomato passata
- ½ cup chicken stock
- 1 teaspoon sweet paprika
- A pinch of salt and black pepper
- ½ teaspoon coriander, ground
- 1 tablespoon parsley, chopped

Directions:

In your slow cooker, mix the turkey with the oil, scallions and the other ingredients, toss, put the lid on and cook on Low for 7 hours. Divide the mix between plates and serve.

Nutrition: calories 227, fat 12, fiber 3, carbs 7, protein 18

Chives Duck

Preparation time: 10 minutes | Cooking time: 20 minutes | Servings: 4

Ingredients:

- 1 pound duck breasts, boneless, skinless and sliced
- 1 tablespoon olive oil
- 1 red bell pepper, cut into strips
- 1 yellow onion, chopped
- 1 cup chicken stock
- ½ cup heavy cream
- A pinch of salt and black pepper
- 1 tablespoon chives, chopped

Directions:

Set the instant pot on Sauté mode, add the oil, heat it up, add the onion and the bell pepper and sauté for 5 minutes. Add the duck and the rest of the ingredients except the chives, put the lid on and cook on High for 15 minutes. Release the pressure naturally for 10 minutes, divide everything between plates, sprinkle the chives on top and serve.

Nutrition: calories 293, fat 15, fiber 4, carbs 6, protein 14

Cilantro Chicken and Eggplant Mix

Preparation time: 10 minutes | Cooking time: 7 hours | Servings: 2

Ingredients:

- 1 pound chicken breasts, skinless, boneless and sliced
- 2 eggplants, roughly cubed
- ½ cup chicken stock
- ½ cup tomato sauce
- 3 scallions, chopped
- A pinch of salt and black pepper
- 1 teaspoon chili powder
- 1 tablespoon cilantro, chopped

Directions:

In your slow cooker, mix the chicken with the eggplant, stock and the other ingredients, toss, put the lid on, cook on Low for 7 hours, divide the mix between plates and serve.

Nutrition: calories 223, fat 9, fiber 2, carbs 4, protein 11

Chicken with Brussels Sprouts

Preparation time: 10 minutes | Cooking time: 7 hours | Servings: 2

Ingredients:
- 1 pound chicken breasts, skinless, boneless and roughly cubed
- 1 tablespoon olive oil
- 1 cup Brussels sprouts, halved
- ½ teaspoon garam masala
- 1 cup chicken stock
- 1 tablespoon olive oil
- 1 red onion, sliced
- 1 tablespoon cilantro, chopped

Directions:
In your slow cooker, mix the chicken with the sprouts, oil and the other ingredients, toss, put the lid on and cook on Low for 7 hours. Divide the mix between plates and serve right away.

Nutrition: calories 210, fat 11, fiber 2, carbs 7, protein 14

Chicken and Mango Mix

Preparation time: 10 minutes | Cooking time: 5 hours | Servings: 2

Ingredients:
- 1 pound chicken breast, skinless, boneless and sliced
- 1 cup mango, peeled and cubed
- 4 scallions, chopped
- 1 tablespoon avocado oil
- ½ teaspoon chili powder
- ½ teaspoon rosemary, dried
- 1 cup chicken stock
- 1 tablespoon sweet paprika
- A pinch of salt and black pepper
- 1 tablespoon chives, chopped

Directions:
In your slow cooker, mix the chicken with the mango, scallions, chili powder and the other ingredients, toss, put the lid on and cook on Low for 5 hours. Divide the mix between plates and serve.

Nutrition: calories 263, fat 8, fiber 2, carbs 7, protein 12

Turkey and Avocado

Preparation time: 10 minutes | Cooking time: 6 hours | Servings: 2

Ingredients:
- 1 pound turkey breasts, skinless, boneless and cubed
- 1 cup avocado, peeled, pitted and cubed
- 1 cup tomatoes, cubed
- 1 tablespoon chives, chopped
- ½ teaspoon chili powder
- 4 garlic cloves, minced
- ¼ cup chicken stock

Directions:
In slow cooker, mix the turkey with the tomatoes, chives and the other ingredients except the avocado, toss, put the lid on and cook on Low for 5 hours and 30 minutes. Add the avocado, toss, cook on Low for 30 minutes more, divide everything between plates and serve.

Nutrition: calories 220, fat 8, fiber 2, carbs 7, protein 15

Chicken and Peppers

Preparation time: 10 minutes | Cooking time: 6 hours | Servings: 2

Ingredients:

- 1 pound chicken breasts, skinless, boneless and cubed
- ¼ cup tomato sauce
- 2 red bell peppers, cut into strips
- 1 teaspoon olive oil
- ½ teaspoon rosemary, dried
- ½ teaspoon coriander, ground
- 1 teaspoon Italian seasoning
- A pinch of cayenne pepper
- 1 cup chicken stock

Directions:

In your slow cooker, mix the chicken with the peppers, tomato sauce and the other ingredients, toss, put the lid on and cook on Low for 6 hours. divide everything between plates and serve.

Nutrition: calories 282, fat 12, fiber 2, carbs 6, protein 18

Chicken and Cabbage Mix

Preparation time: 5 minutes | Cooking time: 7 hours | Servings: 2

Ingredients:

- 1 pound chicken breasts, skinless, boneless and halved
- 2 cups red cabbage, shredded
- 1 cup chicken stock
- ½ teaspoon rosemary, dried
- ½ teaspoon sweet paprika
- 2 teaspoons cumin, ground
- A pinch of salt and black pepper
- ¼ cup cilantro, chopped

Directions:

In slow cooker, mix the chicken with the cabbage, stock and the other ingredients, toss, put the lid on and cook on Low for 7 hours. Divide everything between plates and serve.

Nutrition: calories 285, fat 16, fiber 4, carbs 8, protein 18

Lime Turkey and Chard

Preparation time: 10 minutes | Cooking time: 6 hours | Servings: 2

Ingredients:

- 1 pound turkey breasts, skinless, boneless and cubed
- 2 teaspoons olive oil
- 1 cup red chard, torn
- ½ teaspoon sweet paprika
- 1 cup chicken stock
- A pinch of salt and black pepper
- 2 tablespoons lime juice
- 1 tablespoon lime zest, grated
- 1 tablespoon tomato paste

Directions:

In your slow cooker, mix the turkey with the oil, paprika and the other ingredients, toss, put the lid on and cook on Low for 6 hours. Divide everything into bowls and serve.

Nutrition: calories 292, fat 17, fiber 2, carbs 7, protein 16

BBQ Turkey mix

Preparation time: 10 minutes | Cooking time: 6 hours | Servings: 2

Ingredients:
- 1 pound turkey breast, skinless, boneless and sliced
- 1 teaspoon sweet paprika
- ½ teaspoon red pepper flakes, crushed
- ½ teaspoon turmeric powder
- 1 cup bbq sauce
- A pinch of salt and black pepper
- ¼ cup cilantro, chopped
- 1 cup chicken stock

Directions:

In slow cooker, mix the turkey with the paprika, pepper flakes and the other ingredients, toss, put the lid on and cook on Low for 6 hours. Divide everything between plates and serve.

Nutrition: calories 224, fat 11, fiber 2, carbs 9, protein 11

Chicken and Asparagus

Preparation time: 10 minutes | Cooking time: 5 hours | Servings: 2

Ingredients:
- 1 pound chicken breast, skinless, boneless and cubed
- 1 cup asparagus, sliced
- 1 tablespoon olive oil
- 2 scallions, chopped
- A pinch of salt and black pepper
- 1 teaspoon garam masala
- 1 cup chicken stock
- 1 cup tomatoes, cubed
- 1 tablespoon parsley, chopped

Directions:

In your slow cooker, mix the chicken with the asparagus, oil and the other ingredients except the asparagus, toss, put the lid on and cook on High for 4 hours. Add the asparagus, toss, cook on High for 1 more hour, divide everything between plates and serve.

Nutrition: calories 229, fat 9, fiber 4, carbs 7, protein 16

Lemon Turkey and Potatoes

Preparation time: 10 minutes | Cooking time: 7 hours | Servings: 2

Ingredients:
- 1 pound turkey breast, skinless, boneless and cubed
- 2 teaspoons olive oil
- 1 tablespoon lemon juice
- 2 gold potatoes, peeled and cubed
- 1 red onion, chopped
- ½ cup tomato sauce
- ¼ cup chicken stock
- 1 tablespoon chives, chopped
- A pinch of salt and black pepper

Directions:

In your slow cooker, mix the turkey with the oil, lemon juice, potatoes and the other ingredients, toss, put the lid on and cook on Low for 7 hours. Divide everything between plates and serve.

Nutrition: calories 263, fat 12, fiber 3, carbs 6, protein 14

Turkey and Okra

Preparation time: 10 minutes | Cooking time: 5 hours | Servings: 2

Ingredients:

- 1 pound turkey breasts, skinless, boneless and cubed
- 1 cup okra, halved
- 1 tablespoon lime zest, grated
- ½ cup chicken stock
- 1 tablespoon lime juice
- 1 teaspoon olive oil
- ½ teaspoon sweet paprika
- ½ teaspoon coriander, ground
- ½ teaspoon oregano, dried
- 1 teaspoon chili powder
- A pinch of salt and black pepper
- 1 tablespoon cilantro, chopped

Directions:

In your slow cooker, mix the turkey with the okra, lime zest, juice and the other ingredients, toss, put the lid on and cook on High for 5 hours. Divide everything between plates and serve.

Nutrition: calories 162, fat 8, fiber 2, carbs 5, protein 9

Mustard Duck Mix

Preparation time: 10 minutes | Cooking time: 5 hours | Servings: 2

Ingredients:

- 2 teaspoons olive oil
- 1 red onion, sliced
- 1 pound duck leg, skinless, boneless and cut into strips
- 1 tablespoon mustard
- 1 tablespoon lemon juice
- ¾ cup chicken stock
- 1 teaspoon sweet paprika
- A pinch of salt and black pepper
- 1 tablespoon coriander, chopped

Directions:

In your slow cooker, mix the duck with the oil, onion, mustard and the other ingredients, toss, put the lid on and cook on High for 5 hours. Divide the mix between plates and serve with a side salad.

Nutrition: calories 200, fat 9, fiber 2, carbs 5, protein 10

Orange Chicken Mix

Preparation time: 10 minutes | Cooking time: 6 hours | Servings: 2

Ingredients:

- 1 pound chicken breast, skinless, boneless and cubed
- 1 cup oranges, peeled and cut into segments
- 2 teaspoons olive oil
- 1 teaspoon turmeric powder
- 1 teaspoon balsamic vinegar
- 4 scallions, minced
- 1 cup orange juice
- 1 tablespoon mint, chopped
- A pinch of salt and black pepper

Directions:

In your slow cooker, mix the chicken with the oranges, scallions and the other ingredients, toss, put the lid on and cook on Low for 6 hours. Divide the mix between plates and serve.

Nutrition: calories 200, fat 7, fiber 2, carbs 6, protein 11

Turkey and Carrots

Preparation time: 10 minutes | Cooking time: 7 hours | Servings: 2

Ingredients:
- 1 pound turkey breasts, skinless, boneless and cubed
- 1 cup carrots, peeled and sliced
- 2 tablespoons avocado oil
- 1 tablespoon balsamic vinegar
- 2 scallions, chopped
- 1 teaspoon turmeric powder
- 1 cup chicken stock
- ½ cup chives, chopped

Directions:

In your slow cooker, mix the turkey with the carrots, oil, vinegar and the other ingredients, toss, put the lid on and cook on Low for 7 hours. Divide the mix between plates and serve right away.

Nutrition: calories 210, fat 8, fiber 2, carbs 6, protein 11

Rosemary Chicken Thighs

Preparation time: 10 minutes | Cooking time: 7 hours | Servings: 2

Ingredients:
- 1 pound chicken thighs, boneless
- 1 teaspoon rosemary, dried
- ½ teaspoon sweet paprika
- ½ teaspoon garam masala
- 1 tablespoon olive oil
- ½ cup chicken stock
- A pinch of salt and black pepper
- 1 tablespoon cilantro, chopped

Directions:

In your slow cooker, mix the chicken with the rosemary, paprika and the other ingredients, toss, put the lid on and cook on Low for 7 hours. Divide the chicken between plates and serve with a side salad.

Nutrition: calories 220, fat 8, fiber 2, carbs 5, protein 11

Turkey and Kidney Beans

Preparation time: 10 minutes | Cooking time: 6 hours | Servings: 2

Ingredients:
- 1 pound turkey breasts, skinless, boneless and cut into strips
- 2 cups canned red kidney beans, drained and rinsed
- ¼ cup chicken stock
- 1 cup tomato passata
- 1 tablespoon avocado oil
- Salt and black pepper to the taste
- ½ teaspoon chili powder
- 1 tablespoon tarragon, chopped

Directions:

In your slow cooker, mix the turkey with the beans, stock and the other ingredients, toss, put the lid on and cook on Low for 6 hours. Divide the mix between plates and serve.

Nutrition: calories 192, fat 12, fiber 3, carbs 5, protein 12

Coriander and Turmeric Chicken

Preparation time: 10 minutes | Cooking time: 6 hours | Servings: 2

Ingredients:

- 1 pound chicken breasts, skinless, boneless and cubed
- 1 tablespoon coriander, chopped
- ½ teaspoon turmeric powder
- 2 scallions, minced
- 1 tablespoon olive oil
- 1 tablespoon lime zest, grated
- 1 cup lime juice
- 1 tablespoon chives, chopped
- ¼ cup tomato sauce

Directions:

In your slow cooker, mix the chicken with the coriander, turmeric, scallions and the other ingredients, toss, put the lid on and cook on Low for 6 hours. Divide the mix between plates and serve right away.

Nutrition: calories 200, fat 7, fiber 1, carbs 5, protein 12

Garlic Turkey

Preparation time: 10 minutes | Cooking time: 6 hours | Servings: 2

Ingredients:

- 1 pound turkey breast, skinless, boneless and cubed
- 1 tablespoon avocado oil
- ½ cup chicken stock
- 2 tablespoons tomato paste
- 2 tablespoons garlic, minced
- ½ teaspoon chili powder
- ½ teaspoon oregano, dried
- A pinch of salt and black pepper
- 1 tablespoon parsley, chopped

Directions:

In your slow cooker, mix the turkey with the oil, stock, tomato paste and the other ingredients, toss, put the lid on and cook on Low for 6 hours. Divide the mix between plates and serve with a side salad.

Nutrition: calories 231, fat 7, fiber 2, carbs 6, protein 12

Cumin Chicken Mix

Preparation time: 10 minutes | Cooking time: 6 hours | Servings: 2

Ingredients:

- 1 pound chicken breast, skinless, boneless and cubed
- 2 teaspoons olive oil
- ½ cup tomato sauce
- ¼ cup chicken stock
- ½ teaspoon garam masala
- ½ teaspoon chili powder
- ½ teaspoon cumin, ground
- 1 yellow onion, chopped
- ½ teaspoon sweet paprika
- A pinch of salt and black pepper
- 1 tablespoon chives, chopped

Directions:

In your slow cooker, mix the chicken with the oil, tomato sauce, stock and the other ingredients, toss, put the lid on and cook on Low for 6 hours. Divide everything between plates and serve right away.

Nutrition: calories 252, fat 12, fiber 4, carbs 7, protein 13

Slow Cooker Meat Recipes for 2
Pork Chops and Mango Mix
Preparation time: 10 minutes | *Cooking time:* 6 hours | *Servings:* 2

Ingredients:
- 1 pound pork chops
- 1 teaspoon sweet paprika
- ½ teaspoon chili powder
- 1 cup mango, peeled, and cubed
- 2 tablespoons ketchup
- 1 tablespoon balsamic vinegar
- ¼ cup beef stock
- 1 tablespoon cilantro, chopped

Directions:
In your slow cooker, mix the pork chops with the paprika, chili powder, ketchup and the other ingredients, toss, put the lid on and cook on Low for 6 hours. Divide everything between plates and serve.

Nutrition: calories 345, fat 5, fiber 7, carbs 17, protein 14

Beef and Zucchinis Mix
Preparation time: 10 minutes | *Cooking time:* 8 hours | *Servings:* 2

Ingredients:
- 1 pound beef stew meat, cut into strips
- 1 tablespoon olive oil
- ¼ cup beef stock
- ½ teaspoon sweet paprika
- ½ teaspoon chili powder
- 2 small zucchinis, cubed
- 1 tablespoon balsamic vinegar
- 1 tablespoon chives, chopped

Directions:
In your slow cooker, mix the beef with the oil, stock and the other ingredients, toss, put the lid on and cook on Low for 8 hours. Divide the mix between plates and serve.

Nutrition: calories 400, fat 12, fiber 8, carbs 18, protein 20

Pork and Olives Mix
Preparation time: 10 minutes | *Cooking time:* 8 hours | *Servings:* 2

Ingredients:
- 1 pound pork roast, sliced
- ½ cup tomato passata
- 1 red onion, sliced
- 1 cup kalamata olives, pitted and halved
- Juice of ½ lime
- ¼ cup beef stock
- Salt and black pepper to the taste
- 1 tablespoon chives, hopped

Directions:
In your slow cooker, mix the pork slices with the passata, onion, olives and the other ingredients, toss, put the lid on and cook on Low for 8 hours. Divide the mix between plates and serve.

Nutrition: calories 360, fat 4, fiber 3, carbs 17, protein 27

Pork and Soy Sauce Mix
Preparation time: 10 minutes | *Cooking time:* 8 hours | *Servings:* 2

Ingredients:
- 1 pound pork loin roast, boneless and roughly cubed
- 1 tablespoon soy sauce
- 3 tablespoons honey
- ½ tablespoons oregano, dried
- 1 tablespoon garlic, minced
- 1 tablespoons olive oil
- Salt and black pepper to the taste
- ½ cup beef stock
- ½ teaspoon sweet paprika

Directions:
In your slow cooker, mix the pork loin with the honey, soy sauce and the other ingredients, toss, put the lid on and cook on Low for 8 hours. Divide everything between plates and serve.

Nutrition: calories 374, fat 6, fiber 8, carbs 29, protein 6

Beef and Sauce

Preparation time: 10 minutes | Cooking time: 8 hours | Servings: 2

Ingredients:
- 1 pound beef stew meat, cubed
- 1 teaspoon garam masala
- ½ teaspoon turmeric powder
- Salt and black pepper to the taste
- 1 cup beef stock
- 1 teaspoon garlic, minced
- ½ cup sour cream
- 2 ounces cream cheese, soft
- 1 tablespoon chives, chopped

Directions:
In your slow cooker, mix the beef with the turmeric, garam masala and the other ingredients, toss, put the lid on and cook on Low for 8 hours. Divide everything into bowls and serve.

Nutrition: calories 372, fat 6, fiber 9, carbs 18, protein 22

Pork and Beans Mix

Preparation time: 10 minutes | Cooking time: 8 hours | Servings: 2

Ingredients:
- 1 red bell pepper, chopped
- 1 pound pork stew meat, cubed
- 1 tablespoon olive oil
- 1 cup canned black beans, drained and rinsed
- ½ cup tomato sauce
- 1 yellow onion, chopped
- 1 teaspoon Italian seasoning
- Salt and black pepper to the taste
- 1 tablespoon oregano, chopped

Directions:
In your slow cooker, mix the pork with the bell pepper, oil and the other ingredients, toss, put the lid on and cook on Low for 8 hours. Divide the mix between plates and serve.

Nutrition: calories 385, fat 12, fiber 5, carbs 18, protein 40

Beef with Spinach

Preparation time: 10 minutes | Cooking time: 7 hours | Servings: 2

Ingredients:
- 1 red onion, sliced
- 1 pound beef stew meat, cubed
- 1 cup tomato passata
- 1 cup baby spinach
- 1 teaspoon olive oil
- Salt and black pepper to the taste
- ½ cup bee stock
- 1 tablespoon basil, chopped

Directions:
In your slow cooker, mix the beef with the onion, passata and the other ingredients except the spinach, toss, put the lid on and cook on Low for 6 hours and 30 minutes. Add the spinach, toss, put the lid on, cook on Low for 30 minutes more, divide into bowls and serve.

Nutrition: calories 400, fat 15, fiber 4, carbs 25, protein 14

Pork and Chilies Mix

Preparation time: 10 minutes | Cooking time: 7 hours | Servings: 2

Ingredients:
- 1 pound pork stew meat, cubed
- 1 tablespoon olive oil
- ½ green bell pepper, chopped
- 1 red onion, sliced
- ½ red bell pepper, chopped
- 1 garlic clove, minced
- 2 ounces canned green chilies, chopped
- ½ cup tomato passata
- Salt and black pepper to the taste
- 1 tablespoon chili powder
- 1 tablespoon cilantro, chopped

Directions:
In your slow cooker, mix the pork with the oil, bell pepper and the other ingredients, toss, put the lid on and cook on Low for 7 hours. Divide into bowls and serve right away.

Nutrition: calories 400, fat 14, fiber 5, carbs 29, protein 22

Mustard Ribs

Preparation time: 10 minutes | Cooking time: 8 hours | Servings: 2

Ingredients:
- 2 beef short ribs, cut into individual ribs
- Salt and black pepper to the taste
- ½ cup ketchup
- 1 tablespoon balsamic vinegar
- 1 tablespoon mustard
- 1 tablespoon chives, chopped

Directions:
In your slow cooker, combine the ribs with the ketchup, salt, pepper and the other ingredients, toss, put the lid on and cook on Low for 8 hours. Divide between plates and serve with a side salad.
Nutrition: calories 284, fat 7, 4, carbs 18, protein 20

Beef and Corn Mix

Preparation time: 10 minutes | Cooking time: 8 hours | Servings: 2

Ingredients:
- 2 teaspoons olive oil
- 3 scallions, chopped
- 1 pound beef stew meat, cubed
- 1 cup corn
- ½ cup heavy cream
- ½ cup beef stock
- 2 garlic cloves, minced
- Salt and black pepper to the taste
- 1 tablespoon soy sauce
- 1 tablespoon parsley, chopped

Directions:
In your slow cooker, combine the beef with the corn, oil, scallions and the other ingredients except the cream, toss, put the lid on and cook on Low for 7 hours. Add the cream, toss, cook on Low for 1 more hour, divide into bowls and serve.
Nutrition: calories 400, fat 10, fiber 4, carbs 15, protein 20

Cider Beef Mix

Preparation time: 10 minutes | Cooking time: 8 hours | Servings: 2

Ingredients:
- 1 pound beef stew meat, cubed
- 1 tablespoon olive oil
- Salt and black pepper to the taste
- 3 garlic cloves, minced
- ½ yellow onion, chopped
- ½ cup beef stock
- 1 tablespoon apple cider vinegar
- 1 tablespoon lime zest, grated

Directions:
In your slow cooker, mix the beef with the oil, salt, pepper, garlic and the other ingredients, toss, put the lid on, and cook on Low for 8 hours. Divide everything between plates and serve.
Nutrition: calories 453, fat 10, fiber 12, carbs 20, protein 36

Tarragon Pork Chops

Preparation time: 10 minutes | Cooking time: 6 hours | Servings: 2

Ingredients:
- ½ pound pork chops
- ¼ tablespoons olive oil
- 2 garlic clove, minced
- ¼ teaspoon chili powder
- ½ cup beef stock
- ½ teaspoon coriander, ground
- Salt and black pepper to the taste
- ¼ teaspoon mustard powder
- 1 tablespoon tarragon, chopped

Directions:
Grease your slow cooker with the oil and mix the pork chops with the garlic, stock and the other ingredients inside. Toss, put the lid on, cook on Low for 6 hours, divide between plates and serve with a side salad.
Nutrition: calories 453, fat 16, fiber 8, carbs 7, protein 27

Honey Pork Chops

Preparation time: 10 minutes | Cooking time: 5 hours | Servings: 2

Ingredients:
- 2 teaspoons avocado oil
- 1 pound pork chops, bone in
- 2 tablespoons mayonnaise
- 1 tablespoon ketchup
- ½ tablespoon honey
- ¼ cup beef stock
- ½ tablespoon lime juice

Directions:
In your slow cooker, mix the pork chops with the oil, honey and the other ingredients, toss well, put the lid on, and cook on High for 5 hours. Divide pork chops between plates and serve.

Nutrition: calories 300, fat 8, fiber 10, carbs 16, protein 16

Turmeric Lamb

Preparation time: 10 minutes | Cooking time: 5 hours | Servings: 2

Ingredients:
- 1 pound lamb chops
- 2 teaspoons avocado oil
- 1 teaspoon turmeric powder
- ½ teaspoon sweet paprika
- 1 cup beef stock
- 1 red onion, sliced
- Salt and black pepper to the taste
- 1 tablespoon chives, chopped

Directions:
In your slow cooker, mix the lamb chops with the oil, turmeric and the other ingredients, toss, put the lid on and cook on High for 5 hours. Divide everything between plates and serve.

Nutrition: calories 254, fat 12, fiber 2, carbs 6, protein 16

Chili Lamb

Preparation time: 10 minutes | Cooking time: 4 hours | Servings: 2

Ingredients:
- 1 pound lamb chops
- 2 teaspoons avocado oil
- 2 scallions, chopped
- 1 green chili pepper, minced
- ½ teaspoon turmeric powder
- 1 teaspoon chili powder
- ½ cup veggie stock
- 2 garlic cloves, minced
- A pinch of salt and black pepper

Directions:
In your slow cooker, mix the lamb chops with the oil, scallions and the other ingredients, toss, put the lid on and cook on High for 4 hours. Divide everything between plates and serve.

Nutrition: calories 243, fat 15, fiber 3, carbs 6, protein 20

Beef and Red Onions Mix

Preparation time: 10 minutes | Cooking time: 7 hours | Servings: 2

Ingredients:
- 1 pound beef stew meat, cubed
- 2 teaspoons olive oil
- 2 red onions, sliced
- 1 cup heavy cream
- ¼ cup beef stock
- 1 teaspoon chili powder
- ½ teaspoon rosemary, dried
- 1 tablespoon parsley, chopped
- A pinch of salt and black pepper

Directions:
In your slow cooker, mix the beef with the onions, oil and the other ingredients, toss, put the lid on and cook on low for 7 hours. Divide everything between plates and serve.

Nutrition: calories 263, fat 14, fiber 3, carbs 6, protein 16

Pork and Okra

Preparation time: 10 minutes | Cooking time: 6 hours | Servings: 2

Ingredients:
- 1 pound pork stew meat, cubed
- 1 cup okra, sliced
- 2 teaspoons olive oil
- 1 red onion, chopped
- ¼ cup beef stock
- ½ teaspoon chili powder
- ½ teaspoon turmeric powder
- 1 cup tomato passata
- A pinch of salt and black pepper

Directions:
In your slow cooker, combine the pork with the okra, oil and the other ingredients, toss, put the lid on and cook on High for 6 hours. Divide the mix between plates and serve.

Nutrition: calories 264, fat 14, fiber 4, carbs 7, protein 15

Chives Lamb

Preparation time: 10 minutes | Cooking time: 4 hours | Servings: 2

Ingredients:
- 1 pound lamb chops
- ½ cup chives, chopped
- ½ cup tomato passata
- 2 scallions, chopped
- 2 teaspoons olive oil
- 2 garlic cloves, minced
- ½ teaspoon sweet paprika
- 1 teaspoon cumin, ground
- A pinch of salt and black pepper

Directions:
In your slow cooer, mix the lamb chops with the chives, passata and the other ingredients, toss, put the lid on and cook on High for 4 hours, Divide the mix between plates and serve.

Nutrition: calories 263, fat 12, fiber 4, carbs 6, protein 16

Oregano Beef

Preparation time: 10 minutes | Cooking time: 4 hours | Servings: 2

Ingredients:
- 1 pound beef stew meat, cubed
- 1 tablespoon olive oil
- 1 tablespoon balsamic vinegar
- ½ tablespoon lemon juice
- 1 tablespoon oregano, chopped
- ½ cup tomato sauce
- 1 red onion, chopped
- A pinch of salt and black pepper
- ½ teaspoon chili powder

Directions:
In your slow cooker, mix the beef with the oil, vinegar, lemon juice and the other ingredients, toss, put the lid on and cook on High for 4 hours. Divide the mix between plates and serve right away.

Nutrition: calories 263, fat 14, fiber 4, carbs 6, protein 18

Pork and Green Beans

Preparation time: 10 minutes | Cooking time: 6 hours | Servings: 2

Ingredients:
- 1 pound pork stew meat, cubed
- 1 tablespoon balsamic vinegar
- 1 cup green beans, trimmed and halved
- 1 tablespoon lime juice
- 1 tablespoon avocado oil
- ½ teaspoon rosemary, dried
- A pinch of salt and black pepper
- 1 cup beef stock
- 1 tablespoon chives, chopped

Directions:
In your slow cooker, mix the pork stew meat with the green beans, vinegar and the other ingredients, toss, put the lid on and cook on Low for 6 hours. Divide the mix between plates and serve.

Nutrition: calories 264, fat 14, fiber 4, carbs 6, protein 17

Mint Lamb Chops

Preparation time: 10 minutes | Cooking time: 4 hours | Servings: 2

Ingredients:
- 2 tablespoons olive oil
- 1 pound lamb chops
- 1 tablespoon mint, chopped
- ½ teaspoon garam masala
- ½ cup coconut cream
- 1 red onion, chopped
- 2 tablespoons garlic, minced
- ½ cup beef stock
- A pinch of salt and black pepper

Directions:
In your slow cooker, mix the lamb chops with the oil, mint and the other ingredients, toss, put the lid on and cook on High for 4 hours. Divide the mix between plates and serve warm.

Nutrition: calories 263, fat 14, fiber 3, carbs 7, protein 20

Beef and Artichokes

Preparation time: 10 minutes | Cooking time: 7 hours | Servings: 2

Ingredients:
- 1 tablespoon avocado oil
- 1 pound beef stew meat, cubed
- 2 scallions, chopped
- 1 cup canned artichoke hearts, drained and quartered
- ½ teaspoon chili powder
- A pinch of salt and black pepper
- 1 cup tomato passata
- A pinch of salt and black pepper
- ¼ tablespoon dill, chopped

Directions:
In your slow cooker, combine the beef with the artichokes and the other ingredients, toss, put the lid on and cook on Low for 7 hours. Divide the mix between plates and serve.

Nutrition: calories 263, fat 14, fiber 5, carbs 7, protein 15

Lamb and Potatoes

Preparation time: 10 minutes | Cooking time: 4 hours | Servings: 2

Ingredients:
- 1 pound lamb stew meat, roughly cubed
- 2 sweet potatoes, peeled and cubed
- ½ cup beef stock
- ½ cup tomato sauce
- ½ teaspoon sweet paprika
- ½ teaspoon coriander, ground
- 1 tablespoon avocado oil
- 1 tablespoon balsamic vinegar
- 1 tablespoon cilantro, chopped
- A pinch of salt and black pepper

Directions:
In your slow cooker, mix the lamb with the potatoes, stock, sauce and the other ingredients, toss, put the lid on and cook on High for 4 hours Divide everything between plates and serve.

Nutrition: calories 253, fat 14, fiber 3, carbs 7, protein 17

Lamb and Tomatoes Mix

Preparation time: 10 minutes | Cooking time: 4 hours | Servings: 2

Ingredients:
- 1 teaspoon olive oil
- 1 pound lamb stew meat, cubed
- 1 cup cherry tomatoes, halved
- 1 tablespoon basil, chopped
- ½ teaspoon rosemary, dried
- 1 tablespoon oregano, chopped
- 1 cup beef stock
- ½ teaspoon sweet paprika
- A pinch of salt and black pepper
- 1 tablespoon parsley, chopped

Directions:
Grease the slow cooker with the oil and mix the lamb with the tomatoes, basil and the other ingredients inside. Toss, put the lid on, cook on High for 4 hours, divide the mix between plates and serve.

Nutrition: calories 276, fat 14, fiber 3, carbs 7, protein 20

Pork and Eggplant Mix

Preparation time: 10 minutes | Cooking time: 7 hours | Servings: 2

Ingredients:
- 1 pound pork stew meat, cubed
- 1 eggplant, cubed
- 2 scallions, chopped
- 2 garlic cloves, minced
- ½ cup beef stock
- ¼ cup tomato sauce
- 1 teaspoon sweet paprika
- 1 tablespoon chives, chopped

Directions:
In your slow cooker, mix the pork stew meat with the scallions, eggplant and the other ingredients, toss, put the lid on and cook on Low for 7 hours. Divide the mix between plates and serve right away.

Nutrition: calories 287, fat 16, fiber 4, carbs 6, protein 20

Lemon Lamb

Preparation time: 10 minutes | Cooking time: 7 hours | Servings: 2

Ingredients:
- 1 pound lamb stew meat, cubed
- 1 red onion, sliced
- ½ cup tomato sauce
- 1 tablespoon balsamic vinegar
- 1 tablespoon lemon juice
- 1 tablespoon lemon zest, grated
- 1 teaspoon olive oil
- 3 garlic cloves, chopped
- A pinch of salt and black pepper
- 1 tablespoon chives, chopped

Directions:
In your slow cooker, mix the lamb with the onion, tomato sauce and the other ingredients, toss, put the lid on and cook on Low for 7 hours. Divide the mix between plates and serve right away.

Nutrition: calories 264, fat 8, fiber 3, carbs 6, protein 17

Rosemary Lamb with Olives

Preparation time: 10 minutes | Cooking time: 4 hours | Servings: 2

Ingredients:
- 1 pound lamb chops
- 1 tablespoon olive oil
- 3 garlic cloves, minced
- 1 tablespoon rosemary, chopped
- 1 cup kalamata olives, pitted and halved
- 3 scallions, chopped
- 1 teaspoon turmeric powder
- 1 cup beef stock
- A pinch of salt and black pepper

Directions:
In your slow cooker, mix the lamb chops with the oil, rosemary and the other ingredients, toss, put the lid on and cook on High for 4 hours. Divide the mix between plates and serve.

Nutrition: calories 275, fat 13, fiber 4, carbs 7, protein 20

Nutmeg Lamb and Squash

Preparation time: 10 minutes | Cooking time: 6 hours | Servings: 2

Ingredients:
- 1 pound lamb stew meat, roughly cubed
- 1 cup butternut squash, peeled and cubed
- ½ teaspoon nutmeg, ground
- ½ teaspoon chili powder
- ½ teaspoon coriander, ground
- 2 teaspoons olive oil
- 1 cup beef stock
- A pinch of salt and black pepper
- 1 tablespoon cilantro, chopped

Directions:
In your slow cooker, mix the lamb with the squash, nutmeg and the other ingredients, toss, put the lid on and cook on Low for 6 hours. Divide the mix between plates and serve.

Nutrition: calories 263, fat 12, fiber 4, carbs 7, protein 12

Lamb and Fennel Mix

Preparation time: 10 minutes | Cooking time: 4 hours | Servings: 2

Ingredients:
- 1 pound lamb stew meat, roughly cubed
- 1 fennel bulb, sliced
- 1 tablespoon lemon juice
- 1 teaspoon avocado oil
- ½ teaspoon coriander, ground
- 1 cup tomato passata
- A pinch of salt and black pepper
- 1 tablespoon cilantro, chopped

Directions:
In your slow cooker, combine the lamb with the fennel, lemon juice and the other ingredients, toss, put the lid on and cook on High for 4 hours. Divide the mix between plates and serve.

Nutrition: calories 263, fat 12, fiber 3, carbs 7, protein 10

Creamy Lamb

Preparation time: 10 minutes | Cooking time: 6 hours | Servings: 2

Ingredients:
- 2 pounds lamb shoulder, cubed
- 1 cup heavy cream
- 1/3 cup beef stock
- 2 teaspoons avocado oil
- 1 teaspoon turmeric powder
- 1 red onion, sliced
- A pinch of salt and black pepper
- 1 tablespoon cilantro, chopped

Directions:
In your slow cooker, mix the lamb with the stock, oil and the other ingredients except the cream, toss, put the lid on and cook on Low for 5 hours. Add the cream, toss, cook on Low for 1 more hour, divide the mix into bowls and serve.

Nutrition: calories 233, fat 7, fiber 2, carbs 6, protein 12

Beef and Capers Sauce

Preparation time: 10 minutes | Cooking time: 7 hours | Servings: 2

Ingredients:
- 1 pound beef stew meat, cubed
- 1 tablespoon capers, drained
- 1 cup heavy cream
- ½ cup beef stock
- ½ tablespoon mustard
- 3 scallions, chopped
- 2 teaspoons avocado oil
- 1 teaspoon cumin, ground
- A pinch of salt and black pepper
- 1 tablespoon parsley, chopped

Directions:
In your slow cooker, mix the beef with capers, stock and the other ingredients except the cream, toss, put the lid on and cook on Low for 6 hours. Add the cream, toss, cook on Low for 1 more hour, divide the mix between plates and serve.

Nutrition: calories 235, fat 12, fiber 5, carbs 7, protein 10

Masala Beef and Sauce

Preparation time: 10 minutes | Cooking time: 7 hours | Servings: 2

Ingredients:
- 1 pound beef stew meat, cubed
- 1 teaspoon garam masala
- 1 tablespoon olive oil
- 1 tablespoon lime zest, grated
- 1 tablespoon lime juice
- ½ teaspoon sweet paprika
- ½ teaspoon coriander, ground
- 1 cup beef stock
- A pinch of salt and black pepper

Directions:
In your slow cooker, mix the beef with the garam masala, oil and the other ingredients, toss, put the lid on and cook on Low for 7 hours. Divide the mix between plates and serve.

Nutrition: calories 211, fat 9, fiber 2, carbs 6, protein 12

Lamb and Cabbage

Preparation time: 10 minutes | Cooking time: 5 hours | Servings: 2

Ingredients:
- 2 pounds lamb stew meat, cubed
- 1 cup red cabbage, shredded
- 1 cup beef stock
- 1 teaspoon avocado oil
- 1 teaspoon sweet paprika
- 2 tablespoons tomato paste
- A pinch of salt and black pepper
- 1 tablespoon cilantro, chopped

Directions:
In your slow cooker, mix the lamb with the cabbage, stock and the other ingredients, toss, put the lid on and cook on High for 5 hours. Divide everything between plates and serve.

Nutrition: calories 254, fat 12, fiber 3, carbs 6, protein 16

Pork and Lentils

Preparation time: 10 minutes | Cooking time: 7 hours | Servings: 2

Ingredients:
- 1 pound pork stew meat, cubed
- 1 cup canned lentils, drained and rinsed
- 1 tablespoon olive oil
- 1 yellow onion, chopped
- ¼ cup tomato sauce
- ¼ cup beef stock
- A pinch of salt and black pepper
- 1 tablespoon cilantro, chopped

Directions:
In your slow cooker, mix the pork with the lentils, oil, onion and the other ingredients, toss, put the lid on and cook on Low for 7 hours. Divide the mix between plates and serve.

Nutrition: calories 232, fat 10, fiber 5, carbs 7, protein 11

Balsamic Lamb Mix

Preparation time: 10 minutes | Cooking time: 7 hours | Servings: 2

Ingredients:
- 1 pound lamb stew meat, cubed
- 2 teaspoons avocado oil
- 1 tablespoon balsamic vinegar
- ½ teaspoon coriander, ground
- A pinch of salt and black pepper
- 1 cup beef stock

Directions:
In your slow cooker, mix the lamb with the oil, vinegar and the other ingredients, toss, put the lid on and cook on Low for 7 hours. Divide the mix between plates and serve with a side salad.

Nutrition: calories 243, fat 11, fiber 4, carbs 6, protein 10

Beef and Endives

Preparation time: 10 minutes | Cooking time: 7 hours | Servings: 2

Ingredients:
- 1 pound beef stew meat, cubed
- 2 teaspoons avocado oil
- 2 endives, shredded
- ½ cup beef stock
- ½ teaspoon sweet paprika
- ¼ cup tomato passata
- 3 garlic cloves, minced
- A pinch of salt and black pepper
- 1 tablespoon chives, chopped

Directions:
In your slow cooker, mix the meat with the oil, endives and the other ingredients, toss, put the lid on and cook on Low for 7 hours. Divide the mix between plates and serve.

Nutrition: calories 232, fat 12, fiber 4, carbs 6, protein 9

Lamb and Lime Zucchinis

Preparation time: 10 minutes | Cooking time: 4 hours | Servings: 2

Ingredients:
- 1 pound lamb stew meat, roughly cubed
- 2 small zucchinis, cubed
- Juice of 1 lime
- ½ teaspoon rosemary, dried
- 2 tablespoons avocado oil
- 1 red onion, chopped
- ½ cup beef stock
- 1 tablespoon garlic, minced
- A pinch of salt and black pepper
- 1 tablespoon cilantro, chopped

Directions:
In your slow cooker, mix the lamb with the zucchinis, lime juice and the other ingredients, toss, put the lid on and cook on High for 4 hours. Divide the mix between plates and serve.

Nutrition: calories 274, fat 9, fiber 5, carbs 6, protein 12

Beef and Peas

Preparation time: 10 minutes | Cooking time: 5 hours | Servings: 2

Ingredients:
- 1 pound beef stew meat, cubed
- 1 tablespoon olive oil
- ½ teaspoon coriander, ground
- ½ teaspoon sweet paprika
- ½ cup beef stock
- ½ cup tomato sauce
- 1 cup fresh peas
- 1 tablespoon lime juice
- A pinch of salt and black pepper
- 1 tablespoon dill, chopped

Directions:
In your slow cooker, mix the beef with the oil, coriander, peas and the other ingredients, toss, put the lid on and cook on High for 5 hours. Divide everything between plates and serve.

Nutrition: calories 232, fat 9, fiber 3, carbs 6, protein 10

Maple Beef

Preparation time: 10 minutes | Cooking time: 7 hours | Servings: 2

Ingredients:
- 1 pound beef roast, sliced
- 1 tablespoon maple syrup
- 2 tablespoons balsamic vinegar
- 2 teaspoons olive oil
- ½ teaspoon Italian seasoning
- A pinch of salt and black pepper
- 1 tablespoon coriander, chopped
- ½ cup beef stock

Directions:
In your slow cooker, mix the roast with the maple syrup, vinegar and the other ingredients, toss, put the lid on and cook on Low for 7 hours. Divide the mix between plates and serve.

Nutrition: calories 200, fat 11, fiber 3, carbs 6, protein 15

Rosemary Beef

Preparation time: 10 minutes | Cooking time: 7 hours | Servings: 2

Ingredients:
- 1 pound beef roast, sliced
- 1 tablespoon rosemary, chopped
- Juice of ½ lemon
- 1 tablespoon olive oil
- ½ cup tomato sauce
- A pinch of salt and black pepper

Directions:
In your slow cooker, mix the roast with the rosemary, lemon juice and the other ingredients, toss, put the lid on and cook on Low for 7 hours. Divide everything between plates and serve.

Nutrition: calories 210, fat 5, fiber 3, carbs 8, protein 12

Parsley and Chili Lamb

Preparation time: 10 minutes | Cooking time: 4 hours | Servings: 2

Ingredients:
- 1 pound lamb meat, roughly cubed
- 1 tablespoon avocado oil
- 2 red chilies, chopped
- ½ teaspoon chili powder
- 1 tablespoon parsley, chopped
- ½ cup tomato sauce
- ½ teaspoon oregano, dried
- Juice of 1 lime
- Salt and black pepper to the taste

Directions:
In your slow cooker, mix the lamb with the oil, chilies and the other ingredients, toss, put the lid on and cook on High for 4 hours. Divide the mix between plates and serve right away.

Nutrition: calories 248, fat 11, fiber 3, carbs 6, protein 15

Cumin Pork Chops

Preparation time: 10 minutes | Cooking time: 5 hours | Servings: 2

Ingredients:
- 1 pound pork chops
- 2 tablespoons olive oil
- 2 tablespoons balsamic vinegar
- ½ teaspoon cumin, ground
- ½ cup beef stock
- A pinch of salt and black pepper
- 1 tablespoon chives, chopped

Directions:
In your slow cooker, mix the pork chops with the oil, vinegar and the other ingredients, toss, put the lid on and cook on High for 5 hours. Divide everything between plates and serve.

Nutrition: calories 233, fat 9, fiber 3, carbs 7, protein 14

Paprika Lamb

Preparation time: 10 minutes | Cooking time: 4 hours | Servings: 2

Ingredients:
- 1 pound lamb chops
- 1 tablespoon sweet paprika
- ½ cup beef stock
- 2 tablespoons avocado oil
- 2 scallions, chopped
- A pinch of salt and black pepper

Directions:
In your slow cooker, mix the lamb chops with the paprika, stock and the other ingredients, toss, put the lid on and cook on High for 4 hours. Divide the mix between plates and serve with a side salad.

Nutrition: calories 227, fat 14, fiber 4, carbs 6, protein 16

Beef with Peas and Corn

Preparation time: 10 minutes | Cooking time: 7 hours | Servings: 2

Ingredients:
- 1 pound beef stew meat, cubed
- ½ cup corn
- ½ cup fresh peas
- 2 scallions, chopped
- 1 tablespoon lime juice
- 1 cup beef stock
- 2 tablespoons tomato paste
- ½ cup chives, chopped

Directions:
In your slow cooker, mix the beef with the corn, peas and the other ingredients, toss, put the lid on and cook on Low for 7 hours. Divide the mix between plates and serve right away.

Nutrition: calories 236, fat 12, fiber 2, carbs 7, protein 15

Lime Pork Chops

Preparation time: 10 minutes | Cooking time: 7 hours | Servings: 2

Ingredients:
- 1 pound pork chops
- 1 tablespoon lime zest, grated
- Juice of 1 lime
- ½ teaspoon turmeric powder
- 1 cup beef stock
- 2 tablespoons olive oil
- A pinch of salt and black pepper

Directions:
In your slow cooker, mix the pork chops with the lime juice, zest and the other ingredients, toss, put the lid on and cook on Low for 7 hours. Divide the mix between plates and serve.

Nutrition: calories 273, fat 12, fiber 4, carbs 7, protein 17

Lamb with Capers

Preparation time: 10 minutes | Cooking time: 4 hours | Servings: 2

Ingredients:
- 1 pound lamb chops
- 1 tablespoon capers
- ½ cup beef stock
- ¼ cup tomato passata
- ½ teaspoon sweet paprika
- ½ teaspoon chili powder
- 2 tablespoons olive oil
- 3 scallions, chopped
- A pinch of salt and black pepper

Directions:
In your slow cooker, mix the lamb chops with the capers, stock and the other ingredients, toss, put the lid on and cook on High for 4 hours. Divide the mix between plates and serve.

Nutrition: calories 244, fat 12, fiber 2, carbs 5, protein 16

Lamb and Zucchini Mix

Preparation time: 10 minutes | Cooking time: 4 hours | Servings: 2

Ingredients:
- 1 pound lamb stew meat, ground
- 2 zucchinis, cubed
- 2 teaspoons olive oil
- 1 carrot, peeled and sliced
- ½ cup beef stock
- 2 tablespoons tomato paste
- ½ teaspoon cumin, ground
- 1 tablespoon chives, chopped
- A pinch of salt and black pepper

Directions:
In your slow cooker, mix the lamb with the zucchinis, oil, carrot and the other ingredients, toss, put the lid on and cook on High for 4 hours. Divide the mix into bowls and serve hot.

Nutrition: calories 254, fat 14, fiber 3, carbs 6, protein 17

Beef and Peppers

Preparation time: 10 minutes | Cooking time: 4 hours | Servings: 2

Ingredients:
- 1 pound lamb stew meat, cubed
- 1 red bell pepper, cut into strips
- 1 green bell pepper, cut into strips
- 1 orange bell pepper, cut into strips
- 2 teaspoons olive oil
- A pinch of salt and black pepper
- 1 cup beef stock
- 1 tablespoon chives, chopped
- ½ teaspoon sweet paprika

Directions:
In your slow cooker, mix the lamb with the peppers and the other ingredients, toss, put the lid on and cook on High for 4 hours. Divide the mix between plate sand serve.

Nutrition: calories 263, fat 14, fiber 3, carbs 6, protein 20

Cayenne Lamb Mix

Preparation time: 10 minutes | Cooking time: 4 hours | Servings: 2

Ingredients:
- 1 pound lamb stew meat, cubed
- ½ cup tomato sauce
- ½ teaspoon cayenne pepper
- 1 red onion, sliced
- 2 teaspoons olive oil
- ½ teaspoon sweet paprika
- A pinch of salt and black pepper
- 1 tablespoon cilantro, chopped

Directions:
In your slow cooker, mix the lamb with the tomato sauce, cayenne and the other ingredients, toss, put the lid on and cook on High for 4 hours.. Divide the mix between plates and serve.

Nutrition: calories 283, fat 13, fiber 4, carbs 6, protein 16

Cinnamon Lamb

Preparation time: 10 minutes | Cooking time: 6 hours | Servings: 2

Ingredients:
- 1 pound lamb chops
- 1 teaspoon cinnamon powder
- 1 red onion, chopped
- 1 tablespoon avocado oil
- 1 tablespoon oregano, chopped
- ½ cup beef stock
- 1 tablespoon chives, chopped

Directions:
In your slow cooker, mix the lamb chops with the cinnamon and the other ingredients, toss, put the lid on and cook on Low for 6 hours. Divide the chops between plates and serve with a side salad.

Nutrition: calories 253, fat 14, fiber 2, carbs 6, protein 18

Lamb and Kale

Preparation time: 10 minutes | Cooking time: 4 hours | Servings: 2

Ingredients:
- 1 pound lamb shoulder, cubed
- 1 cup baby kale
- 1 tablespoon olive oil
- 1 yellow onion, chopped
- ½ teaspoon coriander, ground
- ½ teaspoon cumin, ground
- ½ teaspoon sweet paprika
- A pinch of salt and black pepper
- ¼ cup beef stock
- 1 tablespoon chives, chopped

Directions:
In your slow cooker, mix the lamb with the kale, oil, onion and the other ingredients, toss, put the lid on and cook on High for 4 hours. Divide everything between plates and serve.

Nutrition: calories 264, fat 14, fiber 3, carbs 6, protein 17

Beef and Sprouts

Preparation time: 10 minutes | Cooking time: 7 hours | Servings: 2

Ingredients:
- 1 teaspoon olive oil
- 1 pound beef stew meat, roughly cubed
- 1 cup Brussels sprouts, trimmed and halved
- 1 red onion, chopped
- 1 cup tomato passata
- A pinch of salt and black pepper
- 1 tablespoon chives, chopped

Directions:
In your slow cooker, mix the beef with the sprouts, oil and the other ingredients, toss, put the lid on and cook on Low for 7 hours. Divide the mix between plates and serve.

Nutrition: calories 273, fat 13, fiber 2, carbs 6, protein 15

Pork Chops and Spinach

Preparation time: 10 minutes | Cooking time: 4 hours | Servings: 2

Ingredients:
- 1 pound pork chops
- 1 cup baby spinach
- ½ cup beef stock
- ¼ cup tomato passata
- ½ teaspoon sweet paprika
- ½ teaspoon coriander, ground
- 4 scallions, chopped
- 2 teaspoons olive oil
- A pinch of salt and black pepper
- 1 tablespoon chives, chopped

Directions:
In your slow cooker, mix the pork chops with the stock, passata and the other ingredients except the spinach, toss, put the lid on and cook on High for 3 hours and 30 minutes. Add the spinach, cook on High for 30 minutes more, divide the mix between plates and serve.

Nutrition: calories 274, fat 14, fiber 2, carbs 6, protein 16

Green Curry Lamb

Preparation time: 10 minutes | Cooking time: 6 hours | Servings: 2

Ingredients:
- 1 pound lamb stew meat, cubed
- 2 garlic cloves, minced
- 1 tablespoon green curry paste
- A pinch of salt and black pepper
- 1 cup beef stock
- ½ teaspoon rosemary, dried
- 1 tablespoon cilantro, chopped

Directions:
In your slow cooker, mix the lamb with the garlic, curry paste and the other ingredients, toss, put the lid on and cook on Low for 6 hours. Divide the mix between plates and serve.

Nutrition: calories 264, fat 14, fiber 2, carbs 8, protein 12

Oregano Lamb

Preparation time: 10 minutes | Cooking time: 6 hours | Servings: 2

Ingredients:
- 1 pound lamb stew meat, roughly cubed
- 1 teaspoon hot paprika
- 1 tablespoon oregano, chopped
- ½ teaspoon turmeric powder
- 4 scallions, chopped
- A pinch of salt and black pepper
- 1 cup beef stock

Directions:
In your slow cooker, mix the lamb with the paprika, oregano and the other ingredients, toss, put the lid on and cook on Low for 6 hours. Divide the mix between plates and serve with a side salad.

Nutrition: calories 200, fat 9, fiber 2, carbs 6, protein 12

Pesto Lamb Chops

Preparation time: 10 minutes | Cooking time: 6 hours | Servings: 2

Ingredients:
- 1 pound lamb chops
- 2 tablespoons basil pesto
- 1 tablespoon sweet paprika
- 2 tablespoons olive oil
- A pinch of salt and black pepper
- ½ cup beef stock

Directions:
In your slow cooker, mix the lamb chops with the pesto, paprika and the other ingredients, toss, put the lid on and cook on Low for 6 hours. Divide the mix between plates and serve.

Nutrition: calories 234, fat 11, fiber 3, carbs 7, protein 15

Beef with Green Beans and Cilantro

Preparation time: 10 minutes | Cooking time: 7 hours | Servings: 2

Ingredients:
- 1 pound beef stew meat, cubed
- 1 cup green beans, trimmed and halved
- 1 red onion, sliced
- ½ teaspoon chili powder
- ½ teaspoon rosemary, chopped
- 2 teaspoons olive oil
- 1 cup beef stock
- 1 tablespoon cilantro, chopped

Directions:
In your slow cooker, mix the beef with the green beans, onion and the other ingredients, toss, put the lid on and cook on Low for 7 hours. Divide the mix between plates and serve right away.

Nutrition: calories 273, fat 14, fiber 2, carbs 6, protein 15

Balsamic Lamb Chops

Preparation time: 10 minutes | Cooking time: 6 hours | Servings: 2

Ingredients:
- 1 pound lamb chops
- 2 tablespoons balsamic vinegar
- 1 tablespoon chives, chopped
- 1 tablespoon olive oil
- 4 garlic cloves, minced
- ½ cup beef stock
- A pinch of salt and black pepper

Directions:
In your slow cooker, mix the lamb chops with the vinegar and the other ingredients, toss, put the lid on and cook on Low for 6 hours. Divide everything between plates and serve.

Nutrition: calories 292, fat 12, fiber 3, carbs 7, protein 16

Creamy Beef

Preparation time: 10 minutes | Cooking time: 6 hours | Servings: 2

Ingredients:

- 1 pound beef stew meat, cubed
- 1 cup heavy cream
- 1 red onion, sliced
- ½ teaspoon turmeric powder
- 2 tablespoons olive oil
- 3 scallions, chopped
- 1 tablespoon chives, chopped
- A pinch of salt and black pepper

Directions:

In your slow cooker, mix the beef with the cream, onion and the other ingredients, toss, put the lid on and cook on Low for 6 hours. Divide everything between plates and serve.

Nutrition: calories 277, fat 14, fiber 3, carbs 7, protein 17

Walnut and Coconut Beef

Preparation time: 10 minutes | Cooking time: 7 hours | Servings: 2

Ingredients:

- 1 pound beef stew meat, cubed
- 2 tablespoons walnuts, chopped
- ½ cup coconut cream
- 2 scallions, chopped
- 1 cup beef stock
- ½ teaspoon Italian seasoning
- A pinch of salt and black pepper
- 1 tablespoon rosemary, chopped

Directions:

In your slow cooker, mix the beef with the walnuts, scallions and the other ingredients except the cream, toss, put the lid on and cook on Low for 6 hours. Add the cream, toss, cook on Low for 1 more hour, divide everything between plates and serve.

Nutrition: calories 274, fat 12, fiber 4, carbs 7, protein 16

Slow Cooker Fish and Seafood Recipes for 2

Lime Shrimp

Preparation time: 10 minutes | Cooking time: 1 hour | Servings: 2

Ingredients:
- 1 pound shrimp, peeled and deveined
- Juice of 1 lime
- 2 scallions, chopped
- ½ teaspoon turmeric powder
- ¼ cup chickens stock
- A pinch of salt and black pepper
- 1 tablespoon chives, chopped

Directions:
In your slow cooker, mix the shrimp with the lime juice, scallions and the other ingredients, toss, put the lid on and cook on High for 1 hour. Divide the mix into bowls and serve.

Nutrition: calories 198, fat 7, fiber 2, carbs 6, protein 7

Chili Salmon

Preparation time: 10 minutes | Cooking time: 3 hours | Servings: 2

Ingredients:
- 1 tablespoon avocado oil
- 1 pound salmon fillets, boneless
- 1 red chili pepper, minced
- ½ teaspoon chili powder
- 2 scallions, chopped
- ½ cup chicken stock
- A pinch of salt and black pepper

Directions:
In your slow cooker, mix the salmon with the chili pepper, the oil and the other ingredients, rub gently, put the lid on and cook on High for 3 hours. Divide the salmon between plates and serve with a side salad.

Nutrition: calories 221, fat 8, fiber 3, carbs 6, protein 7

Rosemary Shrimp

Preparation time: 10 minutes | Cooking time: 1 hour | Servings: 2

Ingredients:
- 1 pound shrimp, peeled and deveined
- 1 tablespoon avocado oil
- 1 tablespoon rosemary, chopped
- ½ teaspoon sweet paprika
- ½ teaspoon cumin, ground
- 3 garlic cloves, crushed
- 1 cup chicken stock
- A pinch of salt and black pepper

Directions:
In your slow cooker, mix the shrimp with the oil, rosemary and the other ingredients, toss, put the lid on and cook on High for 1 hour. Divide the mix into bowls and serve.

Nutrition: calories 235, fat 8, fiber 4, carbs 7, protein 9

Paprika Cod

Preparation time: 10 minutes | Cooking time: 3 hours | Servings: 2

Ingredients:
- 1 tablespoon olive oil
- 1 pound cod fillets, boneless
- 1 teaspoon sweet paprika
- ¼ cup chicken stock
- ¼ cup white wine
- 2 scallions, chopped
- ½ teaspoon rosemary, dried
- A pinch of salt and black pepper

Directions:
In your slow cooker, mix the cod with the paprika, oil and the other ingredients, toss gently, put the lid on and cook on High for 3 hours. Divide everything between plates and serve.

Nutrition: calories 211, fat 8, fiber 4, carbs 8, protein 8

Spicy Tuna

Preparation time: 10 minutes | Cooking time: 2 hours | Servings: 2

Ingredients:

- 1 pound tuna fillets, boneless and cubed
- ½ teaspoon red pepper flakes, crushed
- ¼ teaspoon cayenne pepper
- ½ cup chicken stock
- ½ teaspoon chili powder
- 1 tablespoon olive oil
- A pinch of salt and black pepper
- 1 tablespoon chives, chopped

Directions:

In your slow cooker, mix the tuna with the pepper flakes, cayenne and the other ingredients, toss, put the lid on and cook on High for 2 hours. Divide the tuna mix between plates and serve.

Nutrition: calories 193, fat 7, fiber 3, carbs 6, protein 6

Ginger Tuna

Preparation time: 5 minutes | Cooking time: 2 hours | Servings: 2

Ingredients:

- 1 pound tuna fillets, boneless and roughly cubed
- 1 tablespoon ginger, grated
- 1 red onion, chopped
- 2 teaspoons olive oil
- Juice of 1 lime
- ¼ cup chicken stock
- 1 tablespoon chives, chopped
- A pinch of salt and black pepper

Directions:

In your slow cooker, mix the tuna with the ginger, onion and the other ingredients, toss, put the lid on and cook on High for 2 hours. Divide the mix into bowls and serve.

Nutrition: calories 200, fat 11, fiber 4, carbs 5, protein 12

Chives Shrimp

Preparation time: 10 minutes | Cooking time: 1 hour | Servings: 2

Ingredients:

- 1 pound shrimp, peeled and deveined
- 1 tablespoon chives, chopped
- ½ teaspoon basil, dried
- 1 teaspoon turmeric powder
- 1 tablespoon olive oil
- ½ cup chicken stock

Directions:

In your slow cooker, mix the shrimp with the basil, chives and the other ingredients, toss, put the lid on and cook on High for 1 hour. Divide the shrimp between plates and serve with a side salad.

Nutrition: calories 200, fat 12, fiber 3, carbs 7, protein 9

Coriander Salmon Mix

Preparation time: 5 minutes | Cooking time: 3 hours | Servings: 2

Ingredients:

- 1 pound salmon fillets, boneless and roughly cubed
- 1 tablespoon coriander, chopped
- ½ teaspoon chili powder
- ¼ cup chicken stock
- 3 scallions, chopped
- Juice of 1 lime
- 2 teaspoons avocado oil
- A pinch of salt and black pepper

Directions:

In your slow cooker, mix the salmon with the coriander, chili powder and the other ingredients, toss gently, put the lid on and cook on High for 3 hours. Divide the mix between plates and serve.

Nutrition: calories 232, fat 10, fiber 4, carbs 6, protein 9

Tuna and Green Beans

Preparation time: 10 minutes | *Cooking time:* 3 hours | *Servings:* 2

Ingredients:
- 1 pound tuna fillets, boneless
- 1 cup green beans, trimmed and halved
- ½ cup chicken stock
- ½ teaspoon sweet paprika
- ½ teaspoon garam masala
- 3 scallions, minced
- ½ teaspoon ginger, ground
- 1 tablespoon olive oil
- 1 tablespoon chives, chopped
- Salt and black pepper to the taste

Directions:
In your slow cooker, mix the tuna with the green beans, stock and the other ingredients, toss gently, put the lid on and cook on High for 3 hours. Divide the mix between plates and serve.

Nutrition: calories 182, fat 7, fiber 3, carbs 6, protein 9

Cod and Corn

Preparation time: 5 minutes | *Cooking time:* 2 hours | *Servings:* 2

Ingredients:
- 1 pound cod fillets, boneless
- 1 tablespoon avocado oil
- ½ teaspoon chili powder
- ½ teaspoon coriander, ground
- 1 cup corn
- ½ tablespoon lime juice
- 1 tablespoon chives, chopped
- ¼ cup chicken stock
- A pinch of salt and black pepper

Directions:
In your slow cooker, mix the cod with the oil, corn and the other ingredients, toss, put the lid on and cook on High for 2 hours. Divide the mix between plates and serve.

Nutrition: calories 210, fat 8, fiber 3, carbs 6, protein 14

Turmeric Salmon

Preparation time: 5 minutes | *Cooking time:* 2 hours | *Servings:* 2

Ingredients:
- 1 pound salmon fillets, boneless
- 1 red onion, chopped
- ½ teaspoon turmeric powder
- ½ teaspoon oregano, dried
- ½ cup chicken stock
- 1 teaspoon olive oil
- Salt and black pepper to the taste
- 1 tablespoon chives, chopped

Directions:
In your slow cooker, mix the salmon with the turmeric, onion and the other ingredients, toss gently, put the lid on and cook on High for 2 hours. Divide the mix between plates and serve.

Nutrition: calories 200, fat 12, fiber 3, carbs 6, protein 11

Sea Bass and Chickpeas

Preparation time: 5 minutes | *Cooking time:* 3 hours | *Servings:* 2

Ingredients:
- 1 pound sea bass fillets, boneless
- ½ cup chicken stock
- ½ cup canned chickpeas, drained and rinsed
- 2 tablespoons tomato paste
- ½ teaspoon rosemary, dried
- ½ teaspoon oregano, dried
- 2 scallions, minced
- 1 tablespoon olive oil
- Salt and black pepper to the taste

Directions:
In your slow cooker, mix the sea bass with the chickpeas, stock and the other ingredients, toss, put the lid on and cook on High for 3 hours. Divide everything between plates and serve.

Nutrition: calories 132, fat 9, fiber 2, carbs 5, protein 11

Creamy Shrimp

Preparation time: 10 minutes | Cooking time: 1 hour | Servings: 2

Ingredients:
- 1 pound shrimp, peeled and deveined
- 2 scallions, chopped
- ¼ cup chicken stock
- 2 tablespoons avocado oil
- ½ cup heavy cream
- 1 teaspoon garam masala
- 1 tablespoon ginger, grated
- A pinch of salt and black pepper
- 1 tablespoon parsley, chopped

Directions:
In your slow cooker, mix the shrimp with the scallions, stock and the other ingredients, toss, put the lid on and cook on High for 1 hour. Divide the mix into bowls and serve.

Nutrition: calories 200, fat 12, fiber 2, carbs 6, protein 11

Parsley Cod

Preparation time: 5 minutes | Cooking time: 2 hours | Servings: 2

Ingredients:
- 1 pound cod fillets, boneless
- 3 scallions, chopped
- 2 teaspoons olive oil
- Juice of 1 lime
- 1 teaspoon coriander, ground
- Salt and black pepper to the taste
- 1 tablespoon parsley, chopped

Directions:
In your slow cooker, mix the cod with the scallions, the oil and the other ingredients, rub gently, put the lid on and cook on High for 1 hour. Divide everything between plates and serve.

Nutrition: calories 200, fat 12, fiber 2, carbs 6, protein 9

Pesto Cod and Tomatoes

Preparation time: 10 minutes | Cooking time: 3 hours | Servings: 2

Ingredients:
- 1 pound cod, boneless and roughly cubed
- 2 tablespoons basil pesto
- 1 tablespoon olive oil
- 1 cup cherry tomatoes, halved
- 1 tablespoon chives, chopped
- ½ cup veggie stock
- A pinch of salt and black pepper

Directions:
In your slow cooker, mix the cod with the pesto, oil and the other ingredients, toss, put the lid on and cook on High for 3 hours. Divide the mix between plates and serve.

Nutrition: calories 211, fat 13, fiber 2, carbs 7, protein 11

Orange Cod

Preparation time: 5 minutes | Cooking time: 3 hours | Servings: 2

Ingredients:
- 1 pound cod fillets, boneless
- Juice of 1 orange
- 1 tablespoon avocado oil
- 2 scallions, chopped
- ½ teaspoon turmeric powder
- ½ teaspoon sweet paprika
- A pinch of salt and black pepper

Directions:
In your slow cooker, mix the cod with the orange juice, oil and the other ingredients, toss, put the lid on and cook on High 3 hours. Divide the mix between plates and serve.

Nutrition: calories 200, fat 12, fiber 4, carbs 6, protein 8

Garlic Sea Bass

Preparation time: 5 minutes | Cooking time: 4 hours | Servings: 2

Ingredients:
- 1 pound sea bass fillets, boneless
- 2 teaspoons avocado oil
- 3 garlic cloves, minced
- 1 green chili pepper, minced
- ½ teaspoon rosemary, dried
- ½ cup chicken stock
- A pinch of salt and black pepper
- 1 tablespoon cilantro, chopped

Directions:
In your slow cooker, mix the sea bass with the oil, garlic and the other ingredients, toss gently, put the lid on and cook on Low for 4 hours. Divide the mix between plates and serve.
Nutrition: calories 232, fat 7, fiber 3, carbs 7, protein 9

Tuna and Brussels Sprouts

Preparation time: 5 minutes | Cooking time: 3 hours | Servings: 2

Ingredients:
- 1 pound tuna fillets, boneless
- ½ cup chicken stock
- 1 teaspoon sweet paprika
- ½ teaspoon chili powder
- 1 cup Brussels sprouts, trimmed and halved
- 1 red onion, chopped
- ½ teaspoon garlic powder
- A pinch of salt and black pepper
- 1 tablespoon cilantro, chopped

Directions:
In your slow cooker, mix the tuna with the stock, sprouts and the other ingredients, put the lid on and cook on High for 3 hours. Divide the mix between plates and serve.
Nutrition: calories 232, fat 9, fiber 2, carbs 6, protein 8

Shrimp with Spinach

Preparation time: 10 minutes | Cooking time: 1 hour | Servings: 2

Ingredients:
- 1 pound shrimp, peeled and deveined
- 1 cup baby spinach
- ¼ cup tomato passata
- ½ cup chicken stock
- 3 scallions, chopped
- 1 tablespoon olive oil
- ½ teaspoon sweet paprika
- A pinch of salt and black pepper
- 1 tablespoon chives, chopped

Directions:
In your slow cooker, mix the shrimp with the spinach, tomato passata and the other ingredients, toss, put the lid on and cook on High for 1 hour. Divide the mix between plates and serve.
Nutrition: calories 200, fat 13, fiber 3, carbs 6, protein 11

Shrimp and Avocado

Preparation time: 5 minutes | Cooking time: 1 hour | Servings: 2

Ingredients:
- 1 pound shrimp, peeled and deveined
- 1 cup avocado, peeled, pitted and cubed
- ½ cup chicken stock
- ½ teaspoon sweet paprika
- Juice of 1 lime
- 1 tablespoon olive oil
- 2 tablespoons chili pepper, minced
- A pinch of salt and black pepper
- 1 tablespoon chives, chopped

Directions:
In your slow cooker, mix the shrimp with the avocado, stock and the other ingredients, toss, put the lid on and cook on High for 1 hour. Divide the mix into bowls and serve.
Nutrition: calories 200, fat 12, fiber 2, carbs 6, protein 9

Chives Mackerel

Preparation time: 10 minutes | Cooking time: 4 hours | Servings: 2

Ingredients:
- 1 pound mackerel fillets, boneless
- ½ teaspoon cumin, ground
- ½ teaspoon coriander, ground
- 2 garlic cloves, minced
- 1 tablespoon avocado oil
- 1 tablespoon lime juice
- ½ cup chicken stock
- A pinch of salt and black pepper
- 2 tablespoons chives, chopped

Directions:
In your slow cooker, mix the mackerel with the cumin, coriander and the other ingredients, put the lid on and cook on Low for 4 hours. Divide the mix between plates and serve with a side salad.

Nutrition: calories 200, fat 12, fiber 2, carbs 5, protein 6

Dill Cod

Preparation time: 10 minutes | Cooking time: 3 hours | Servings: 2

Ingredients:
- 1 tablespoon olive oil
- 1 pound cod fillets, boneless and cubed
- 1 tablespoon dill, chopped
- ½ teaspoon sweet paprika
- ½ teaspoon cumin, ground
- 2 garlic cloves, minced
- 1 teaspoon lemon juice
- 1 cup tomato passata
- A pinch of salt and black pepper

Directions:
In your slow cooker, mix the cod with the oil, dill and the other ingredients, toss, put the lid on and cook on Low for 3 hours. Divide the mix between plates and serve.

Nutrition: calories 192, fat 9, fiber 2, carbs 8, protein 7

Shrimp and Mango Mix

Preparation time: 10 minutes | Cooking time: 1 hour | Servings: 2

Ingredients:
- 1 pound shrimp, peeled and deveined
- ½ cup mango, peeled and cubed
- ½ cup cherry tomatoes, halved
- ½ cup shallots, chopped
- 1 tablespoon lime juice
- ½ teaspoon rosemary, dried
- 1 tablespoon olive oil
- ½ teaspoon chili powder
- ½ cup chicken stock
- A pinch of salt and black pepper
- 1 tablespoon chives, chopped

Directions:
In your slow cooker, mix the shrimp with the mango, tomatoes and the other ingredients, toss, put the lid on and cook on High for 1 hour. Divide the mix into bowls and serve.

Nutrition: calories 210, fat 9, fiber 2, carbs 6, protein 7

Balsamic Tuna

Preparation time: 5 minutes | *Cooking time:* 3 hours | *Servings:* 2

Ingredients:
- 1 pound tuna fillets, boneless and roughly cubed
- 1 tablespoon balsamic vinegar
- 3 garlic cloves, minced
- 1 tablespoon avocado oil
- ¼ cup chicken stock
- 1 tablespoon hives, chopped
- A pinch of salt and black pepper

Directions:
In your slow cooker, mix the tuna with the garlic, vinegar and the other ingredients, toss, put the lid on and cook on Low for 3 hours. Divide the mix into bowls and serve.

Nutrition: calories 200, fat 10, fiber 2, carbs 5, protein 9

Lime Trout Mix

Preparation time: 10 minutes | *Cooking time:* 2 hours | *Servings:* 2

Ingredients:
- 1 pound trout fillets, boneless
- 1 tablespoon olive oil
- ½ cup chicken stock
- 2 tablespoons lime zest, grated
- 2 tablespoons lemon juice
- 1 teaspoon garam masala
- A pinch of salt and black pepper

Directions:
In your slow cooker, mix the trout with the olive oil, lime juice and the other ingredients, toss, put the lid on and cook on High for 2 hours. Divide everything between plates and serve.

Nutrition: calories 200, fat 13, fiber 3, carbs 6, protein 11

Creamy Tuna and Scallions

Preparation time: 10 minutes | *Cooking time:* 2 hours | *Servings:* 2

Ingredients:
- 1 pound tuna fillets, boneless and cubed
- 4 scallions, chopped
- ½ cup heavy cream
- ½ cup chicken stock
- 1 tablespoon olive oil
- 1 teaspoon turmeric powder
- A pinch of salt and black pepper
- 1 tablespoon chives, chopped

Directions:
In your slow cooker, mix the tuna with the scallions, cream and the other ingredients, toss, put the lid on and cook on High for 2 hours. Divide the mix into bowls and serve.

Nutrition: calories 198, fat 7, fiber 2, carbs 6, protein 7

Cod and Mustard Sauce

Preparation time: 10 minutes | *Cooking time:* 3 hours | *Servings:* 2

Ingredients:
- 1 tablespoon olive oil
- 1 pound cod fillets, boneless
- 2 tablespoons mustard
- ½ cup heavy cream
- ¼ cup chicken stock
- 2 garlic cloves, minced
- A pinch of salt and black pepper
- 1 tablespoon chives, chopped

Directions:
In your slow cooker, mix the cod with the oil, mustard and the other ingredients, toss gently, put the lid on and cook on Low for 3 hours. Divide the mix between plates and serve.

Nutrition: calories 221, fat 8, fiber 3, carbs 6, protein 7

Shrimp and Pineapple Bowls

***Preparation time:** 5 minutes | **Cooking time:** 1 hour | **Servings:** 2*

Ingredients:
- 1 pound shrimp, peeled and deveined
- 1 cup pineapple, peeled and cubed
- 1 teaspoon sweet paprika
- 1 tablespoon avocado oil
- 3 scallions, chopped
- ½ cup chicken stock
- A pinch of salt and black pepper

Directions:

In your slow cooker, mix the shrimp with the pineapple, paprika and the other ingredients, toss, put the lid on and cook on High for 1 hour. Divide the mix into bowls and serve.

Nutrition: calories 235, fat 8, fiber 4, carbs 7, protein 9

Lime Crab

***Preparation time:** 10 minutes | **Cooking time:** 2 hours | **Servings:** 2*

Ingredients:
- 1 tablespoon avocado oil
- 1 pound crab meat
- ¼ cup shallots, chopped
- 1 tablespoon lime juice
- ½ cup fish stock
- 1 teaspoon sweet paprika
- 1 tablespoon chives, chopped
- A pinch of salt and black pepper

Directions:

In your slow cooker, mix the crab with the oil, shallots and the other ingredients, toss, put the lid on and cook on High for 2 hours. Divide everything into bowls and serve.

Nutrition: calories 211, fat 8, fiber 4, carbs 8, protein 8

Hot Salmon and Carrots

***Preparation time:** 10 minutes | **Cooking time:** 3 hours | **Servings:** 2*

Ingredients:
- 1 pound salmon fillets, boneless
- 1 cup baby carrots, peeled
- ½ teaspoon hot paprika
- ½ teaspoon chili powder
- ¼ cup chicken stock
- 2 scallions, chopped
- 1 tablespoon smoked paprika
- A pinch of salt and black pepper
- 2 tablespoons chives, chopped

Directions:

In your slow cooker, mix the salmon with the carrots, paprika and the other ingredients, toss, put the lid on and cook on Low for 3 hours. Divide the mix between plates and serve.

Nutrition: calories 193, fat 7, fiber 3, carbs 6, protein 6

Shrimp and Eggplant

***Preparation time:** 5 minutes | **Cooking time:** 1 hour | **Servings:** 2*

Ingredients:
- 1 pound shrimp, peeled and deveined
- 2 teaspoons avocado oil
- 1 eggplant, cubed
- 2 tomatoes, cubed
- Juice of 1 lime
- ½ cup chicken stock
- 4 garlic cloves, minced
- 1 tablespoon coriander, chopped
- 1 tablespoon chives, chopped
- A pinch of salt and black pepper

Directions:

In your slow cooker, mix the shrimp with the oil, eggplant, tomatoes and the other ingredients, toss, put the lid on and cook on High for 1 hour. Divide the mix into bowls and serve.

Nutrition: calories 200, fat 11, fiber 4, carbs 5, protein 12

Sea Bass and Squash

Preparation time: 10 minutes | Cooking time: 3 hours | Servings: 2

Ingredients:
- 1 pound sea bass, boneless and cubed
- 1 cup butternut squash, peeled and cubed
- 1 teaspoon olive oil
- ½ teaspoon turmeric powder
- ½ teaspoon Italian seasoning
- 1 cup chicken stock
- 1 tablespoon cilantro, chopped

Directions:
In your slow cooker, mix the sea bass with the squash, oil, turmeric and the other ingredients, toss, the lid on and cook on Low for 3 hours. Divide everything between plates and serve.

Nutrition: calories 200, fat 12, fiber 3, carbs 7, protein 9

Coconut Mackerel

Preparation time: 5 minutes | Cooking time: 3 hours | Servings: 2

Ingredients:
- 1 pound mackerel fillets, boneless, skinless and cubed
- 1 tablespoon avocado oil
- 1 cup coconut cream
- ½ teaspoon cumin, ground
- 2 scallions, chopped
- A pinch of salt and black pepper
- ½ teaspoon garam masala
- 1 tablespoon cilantro, chopped

Directions:
In your slow cooker, mix the mackerel with the oil, cream and the other ingredients, toss, put the lid on and cook on Low for 3 hours. Divide the mix into bowls and serve.

Nutrition: calories 232, fat 10, fiber 4, carbs 6, protein 9

Salmon and Peas

Preparation time: 10 minutes | Cooking time: 2 hours | Servings: 2

Ingredients:
- 1 pound salmon fillets, boneless and cubed
- 1 tablespoon olive oil
- 1 cup sugar snap peas
- 1 tablespoon lemon juice
- ½ cup tomato passata
- 1 tablespoon chives, chopped
- Salt and black pepper to the taste

Directions:
In your slow cooker, mix the salmon with the peas, oil and the other ingredients, toss, put the lid on and cook on High for 2 hour. Divide the mix between plates and serve.

Nutrition: calories 182, fat 7, fiber 3, carbs 6, protein 9

Chili Shrimp and Zucchinis

Preparation time: 10 minutes | Cooking time: 1 hour | Servings: 4

Ingredients:
- 1 pound shrimp, peeled and deveined
- 1 zucchini, cubed
- 2 scallions, minced
- 1 cup tomato passata
- 2 green chilies, chopped
- A pinch of salt and black pepper
- 1 tablespoon chives, chopped

Directions:
In your slow cooker, mix the shrimp with the zucchini and the other ingredients, toss, put the lid on and cook on High for 1 hour. Divide the shrimp mix into bowls and serve.

Nutrition: calories 210, fat 8, fiber 3, carbs 6, protein 14

Italian Shrimp

Preparation time: 5 minutes | Cooking time: 1 hour | Servings: 2

Ingredients:

- 1 pound shrimp, peeled and deveined
- 1 tablespoon avocado oil
- ½ teaspoon sweet paprika
- 1 teaspoon Italian seasoning
- Salt and black pepper to the taste
- Juice of 1 lime
- ¼ cup chicken stock
- 1 tablespoon chives, chopped

Directions:

In your slow cooker, mix the shrimp with the oil, seasoning and the other ingredients, toss, put the lid on and cook on High for 1 hour. Divide the mix into bowls and serve.

Nutrition: calories 200, fat 12, fiber 3, carbs 6, protein 11

Basil Cod and Olives

Preparation time: 5 minutes | Cooking time: 3 hours | Servings: 2

Ingredients:

- 1 pound cod fillets, boneless
- 1 cup black olives, pitted and halved
- ½ tablespoon tomato paste
- 1 tablespoon basil, chopped
- ¼ cup chicken stock
- 1 red onion, sliced
- 1 tablespoon lime juice
- 1 tablespoon chives, chopped
- Salt and black pepper to the taste

Directions:

In your slow cooker, mix the cod with the olives, basil and the other ingredients, toss, put the lid on and cook on Low for 3 hours. Divide everything between plates and serve.

Nutrition: calories 132, fat 9, fiber 2, carbs 5, protein 11

Tuna and Fennel

Preparation time: 10 minutes | Cooking time: 2 hours | Servings: 2

Ingredients:

- 1 pound tuna fillets, boneless and cubed
- 1 fennel bulb, sliced
- ½ cup chicken stock
- ½ teaspoon sweet paprika
- ½ teaspoon chili powder
- 1 red onion, chopped
- A pinch of salt and black pepper
- 2 tablespoons cilantro, chopped

Directions:

In your slow cooker, mix the tuna with the fennel, stock and the other ingredients, toss, put the lid on and cook on High for 2 hour. Divide the mix between plates and serve.

Nutrition: calories 200, fat 12, fiber 2, carbs 6, protein 11

Shrimp and Mushrooms

Preparation time: 10 minutes | Cooking time: 1 hour | Servings: 2

Ingredients:

- 1 pound shrimp, peeled and deveined
- 1 cup white mushrooms, halved
- 1 tablespoon avocado oil
- ½ tablespoon tomato paste
- 4 scallions, minced
- ½ cup chicken stock
- Juice of 1 lime
- Salt and black pepper to the taste
- 1 tablespoon chives, minced

Directions:

In your slow cooker, mix the shrimp with the mushrooms, oil and the other ingredients, toss, put the lid on and cook on High for 1 hour. Divide the mix into bowls and serve.

Nutrition: calories 200, fat 12, fiber 2, carbs 6, protein 9

Salmon and Berries

Preparation time: 10 minutes | Cooking time: 3 hours | Servings: 2

Ingredients:

- 1 pound salmon fillets, boneless and roughly cubed
- ½ cup blackberries
- Juice of 1 lime
- 1 tablespoon avocado oil
- 2 scallions, chopped
- ½ teaspoon Italian seasoning
- ½ cup fish stock
- A pinch of salt and black pepper

Directions:

In your slow cooker, mix the salmon with the berries, lime juice and the other ingredients, toss, put the lid on and cook on Low for 3 hours. Divide the mix between plates and serve.

Nutrition: calories 211, fat 13, fiber 2, carbs 7, protein 11

Cod and Artichokes

Preparation time: 5 minutes | Cooking time: 3 hours | Servings: 2

Ingredients:

- 1 pound cod fillets, boneless and roughly cubed
- 1 cup canned artichoke hearts, drained and quartered
- 2 scallions, chopped
- 1 tablespoon olive oil
- ½ cup chicken stock
- 1 tablespoon lime juice
- 1 tablespoon cilantro, chopped
- A pinch of salt and black pepper

Directions:

In your slow cooker, mix the cod with the artichokes, scallions and the other ingredients, toss, put the lid on and cook on Low for 3 hours. Divide the mix between plates and serve.

Nutrition: calories 200, fat 12, fiber 4, carbs 6, protein 8

Salmon, Tomatoes and Green Beans

Preparation time: 5 minutes | Cooking time: 2 hours | Servings: 2

Ingredients:

- 1 pound salmon fillets, boneless and cubed
- 1 cup cherry tomatoes, halved
- 1 cup green beans, trimmed and halved
- 1 cup tomato passata
- ½ cup chicken stock
- A pinch of salt and black pepper
- 1 tablespoon parsley, chopped

Directions:

In your slow cooker, mix the salmon with the tomatoes, green beans and the other ingredients, toss, put the lid on and cook on High for 2 hours. Divide the mix into bowls and serve.

Nutrition: calories 232, fat 7, fiber 3, carbs 7, protein 9

Shrimp and Rice Mix

Preparation time: 5 minutes | Cooking time: 1 hour and 30 minutes | Servings: 2

Ingredients:

- 1 pound shrimp, peeled and deveined
- 1 cup chicken stock
- ½ cup wild rice
- ½ cup carrots, peeled and cubed
- 1 green bell pepper, cubed
- ½ teaspoon turmeric powder
- ½ teaspoon coriander, ground
- 1 tablespoon olive oil
- 1 red onion, chopped
- A pinch of salt and black pepper
- 1 tablespoon cilantro, chopped

Directions:

In your slow cooker, mix the stock with the rice, carrots and the other ingredients except the shrimp, toss, put the lid on and cook on High for 1 hour. Add the shrimp, toss, put the lid back on and cook on High for 30 minutes. Divide the mix between plates and serve.

Nutrition: calories 232, fat 9, fiber 2, carbs 6, protein 8

Shrimp and Red Chard

Preparation time: 5 minutes | Cooking time: 1 hour | Servings: 2

Ingredients:

- 1 pound shrimp, peeled and deveined
- Juice of 1 lime
- 1 cup red chard, torn
- ½ cup tomato sauce
- 2 garlic cloves, minced
- 1 red onion, sliced
- 1 tablespoon olive oil
- ½ teaspoon sweet paprika
- A pinch of salt and black pepper
- 1 tablespoon parsley, chopped

Directions:

In your slow cooker, mix the shrimp with the lime juice, chard and the other ingredients, toss, put the lid on and cook on High for 1 hour. Divide the mix into bowls and serve.

Nutrition: calories 200, fat 13, fiber 3, carbs 6, protein 11

Chives Mussels

Preparation time: 5 minutes | Cooking time: 1 hour | Servings: 2

Ingredients:

- 1 pound mussels, debearded
- ½ teaspoon coriander, ground
- ½ teaspoon rosemary, dried
- 1 tablespoon lime zest, grated
- Juice of 1 lime
- 1 cup tomato passata
- ¼ cup chicken stock
- A pinch of salt and black pepper
- 1 tablespoon chives, chopped

Directions:

In your slow cooker, mix the mussels with the coriander, rosemary and the other ingredients, toss, put the lid on and cook on High for 1 hour. Divide the mix into bowls and serve.

Nutrition: calories 200, fat 12, fiber 2, carbs 6, protein 9

Calamari and Sauce

Preparation time: 10 minutes | Cooking time: 2 hours | Servings: 2

Ingredients:
- 1 pound calamari rings
- 2 scallions, chopped
- 2 garlic cloves, minced
- ½ cup heavy cream
- ½ cup chicken stock
- 1 tablespoon lime juice
- ½ cup black olives, pitted and halved
- A pinch of salt and black pepper
- 2 tablespoons chives, chopped

Directions:

In your slow cooker, mix the calamari with the scallions, garlic and the other ingredients except the cream, toss, put the lid on and cook on High for 1 hour. Add the cream, toss, cook on High for 1 more hour, divide into bowls and serve.

Nutrition: calories 200, fat 12, fiber 2, carbs 5, protein 6

Salmon Salad

Preparation time: 5 minutes | Cooking time: 3 hours | Servings: 2

Ingredients:
- 1 pound salmon fillets, boneless and cubed
- ¼ cup chicken stock
- 1 zucchini, cut with a spiralizer
- 1 carrot, sliced
- 1 eggplant, cubed
- ½ cup cherry tomatoes, halved
- 1 red onion, sliced
- ½ teaspoon turmeric powder
- ½ teaspoon chili powder
- ½ tablespoon rosemary, chopped
- A pinch of salt and black pepper
- 1 tablespoon chives, chopped

Directions:

In your slow cooker, mix the salmon with the zucchini, stock, carrot and the other ingredients,, toss , put the lid on and cook on High for 3 hours. Divide the mix into bowls and serve.

Nutrition: calories 210, fat 9, fiber 2, carbs 6, protein 7

Walnut Tuna Mix

Preparation time: 10 minutes | Cooking time: 3 hours | Servings: 2

Ingredients:
- 1 pound tuna fillets, boneless
- ½ tablespoon walnuts, chopped
- ½ cup chicken stock
- ½ teaspoon chili powder
- ½ teaspoon sweet paprika
- 1 red onion, sliced
- 2 tablespoons parsley, chopped
- A pinch of salt and black pepper

Directions:

In your slow cooker, mix the tuna with the walnuts, stock and the other ingredients, toss, put the lid on and cook on High for 3 hours. Divide everything between plates and serve.

Nutrition: calories 200, fat 10, fiber 2, carbs 5, protein 9

Almond Shrimp and Cabbage

Preparation time: 5 minutes | Cooking time: 1 hour | Servings: 2

Ingredients:

- 1 pound shrimp, peeled and deveined
- 1 cup red cabbage, shredded
- 1 tablespoon almonds, chopped
- 1 cup cherry tomatoes, halved
- 1 tablespoon balsamic vinegar
- 2 tablespoons olive oil
- ½ cup tomato passata
- A pinch of salt and black pepper

Directions:

In your slow cooker, mix the shrimp with the cabbage, almonds and the other ingredients, toss, put the lid on and cook on High for 1 hour. Divide everything into bowls and serve.

Nutrition: calories 200, fat 13, fiber 3, carbs 6, protein 11

Indian Shrimp

Preparation time: 5 minutes | Cooking time: 1 hours | Servings: 2

Ingredients:

- 4 scallions, chopped
- 1 tablespoon olive oil
- 1 pound shrimp, peeled and deveined
- ½ teaspoon garam masala
- ½ teaspoon coriander, ground
- ½ teaspoon turmeric powder
- 1 tablespoon lime juice
- ½ cup chicken stock
- ¼ cup lime leaves, torn

Directions:

In your slow cooker, mix the shrimp with the oil, scallions, masala and the other ingredients, toss, put the lid on and cook on High for 1 hour. Divide the mix into bowls and serve.

Nutrition: calories 211, fat 12, fiber 3, carbs 6, protein 7

Shrimp, Tomatoes and Kale

Preparation time: 5 minutes | Cooking time: 1 hour | Servings: 2

Ingredients:

- 1 pound shrimp, peeled and deveined
- ½ cup cherry tomatoes, halved
- 1 cup baby kale
- ½ cup chicken stock
- 1 tablespoon olive oil
- Salt and black pepper to the taste
- Juice of 1 lime
- ½ teaspoon sweet paprika
- 1 tablespoon cilantro, chopped

Directions:

In your slow cooker, mix the shrimp with the cherry tomatoes, kale and the other ingredients, toss, put the lid on and cook on High for 1 hour. Divide the mix into bowls and serve.

Nutrition: calories 200, fat 12, fiber 3, carbs 6, protein 11

Trout Bowls

Preparation time: 5 minutes | Cooking time: 3 hours | Servings: 2

Ingredients:

- 1 pound trout fillets, boneless, skinless and cubed
- 1 cup kalamata olives, pitted and chopped
- 1 cup baby spinach
- 2 garlic cloves, minced
- 1 tablespoon olive oil
- Juice of ½ lime
- Salt and black pepper to the taste
- 1 tablespoon parsley, chopped

Directions:

In your slow cooker, mix the trout with the olives, spinach and the other ingredients, toss, put the lid on and cook on Low for 3 hours. Divide everything into bowls and serve.

Nutrition: calories 132, fat 9, fiber 2, carbs 5, protein 11

Calamari Curry

Preparation time: 10 minutes | Cooking time: 3 hours | Servings: 2

Ingredients:

- 1 pound calamari rings
- ½ tablespoon yellow curry paste
- 1 cup coconut milk
- ½ teaspoon turmeric powder
- ½ cup chicken stock
- 2 garlic cloves, minced
- ½ tablespoon coriander, chopped
- A pinch of salt and black pepper
- 2 tablespoons lemon juice

Directions:

In your slow cooker, mix the rings with the curry paste, coconut milk and the other ingredients, toss, put the lid on and cook on High for 3 hours. Divide the curry into bowls and serve.

Nutrition: calories 200, fat 12, fiber 2, carbs 6, protein 11

Balsamic Trout

Preparation time: 10 minutes | Cooking time: 3 hours | Servings: 2

Ingredients:

- 1 pound trout fillets, boneless
- ½ cup chicken stock
- 2 garlic cloves, minced
- 2 tablespoons balsamic vinegar
- ½ teaspoon cumin, ground
- Salt and black pepper to the taste
- 1 tablespoon parsley, chopped
- 1 tablespoon olive oil

Directions:

In your slow cooker, mix the trout with the stock, garlic and the other ingredients, toss gently, put the lid on and cook on High for 3 hours. Divide the mix between plates and serve.

Nutrition: calories 200, fat 12, fiber 2, carbs 6, protein 9

Oregano Shrimp Bowls

Preparation time: 10 minutes | Cooking time: 1 hour | Servings: 2

Ingredients:

- 1 pound shrimp, peeled and deveined
- ½ cup cherry tomatoes, halved
- ½ cup baby spinach
- 1 tablespoon lime juice
- 1 tablespoon oregano, chopped
- ¼ cup fish stock
- ½ teaspoon sweet paprika
- 2 garlic cloves, chopped
- A pinch of salt and black pepper

Directions:

In your slow cooker, mix the shrimp with the cherry tomatoes, spinach and the other ingredients, toss, put the lid on and cook on High for 1 hour. Divide everything between plates and serve.

Nutrition: calories 211, fat 13, fiber 2, carbs 7, protein 11

Salmon and Strawberries Mix

Preparation time: 10 minutes | Cooking time: 2 hours | Servings: 2

Ingredients:

- 1 pound salmon fillets, boneless
- 1 cup strawberries, halved
- ½ cup orange juice
- Zest of 1 lemon, grated
- 4 scallions, chopped
- 1 teaspoon balsamic vinegar
- 1 tablespoon chives, chopped
- A pinch of salt and black pepper

Directions:

In your slow cooker, mix the salmon with the strawberries, orange juice and the other ingredients, toss, put the lid on and cook on High for 2 hours. Divide everything into bowls and serve.

Nutrition: calories 200, fat 12, fiber 4, carbs 6, protein 8

Shrimp, Salmon and Tomatoes Mix

Preparation time: 5 minutes | Cooking time: 1 hour and 30 minutes | Servings: 2

Ingredients:

- 1 pound shrimp, peeled and deveined
- ½ pound salmon fillets, boneless and cubed
- 1 cup cherry tomatoes, halved
- ½ cup chicken stock
- ½ teaspoon chili powder
- ½ teaspoon rosemary, dried
- A pinch of salt and black pepper
- 1 tablespoon parsley, chopped
- 2 tablespoons tomato sauce
- 2 garlic cloves, minced

Directions:

In your slow cooker, combine the shrimp with the salmon, tomatoes and the other ingredients, toss gently, put the lid on and cook on High for 1 hour and 30 minutes. Divide the mix into bowls and serve.

Nutrition: calories 232, fat 7, fiber 3, carbs 7, protein 9

Shrimp and Cauliflower Bowls

Preparation time: 5 minutes | Cooking time: 2 hours | Servings: 2

Ingredients:

- 1 pound shrimp, peeled and deveined
- ½ cup chicken stock
- 1 cup cauliflower florets
- ½ teaspoon turmeric powder
- ½ teaspoon coriander, ground
- ½ cup tomato passata
- A pinch of salt and black pepper
- 1 tablespoon cilantro, chopped

Directions:

In your slow cooker, mix the cauliflower with the stock, turmeric and the other ingredients except the shrimp, toss, put the lid on and cook on High for 1 hour. Add the shrimp, toss, cook on High for 1 more hour, divide into bowls and serve.

Nutrition: calories 232, fat 9, fiber 2, carbs 6, protein 8

Cod and Broccoli

***Preparation time:** 10 minutes | **Cooking time:** 3 hours | **Servings:** 2*

Ingredients:
- 1 pound cod fillets, boneless
- 1 cup broccoli florets
- ½ cup veggie stock
- 2 tablespoons tomato paste
- 2 garlic cloves, minced
- 1 red onion, minced
- ½ teaspoon rosemary, dried
- A pinch of salt and black pepper
- 1 tablespoon chives, chopped

Directions:

In your slow cooker, mix the cod with the broccoli, stock, tomato paste and the other ingredients, toss, put the lid on and cook on Low for 3 hours. Divide the mix between plates and serve.

Nutrition: calories 200, fat 13, fiber 3, carbs 6, protein 11

Cinnamon Trout

***Preparation time:** 5 minutes | **Cooking time:** 3 hours | **Servings:** 2*

Ingredients:
- 1 pound trout fillets, boneless
- 1 tablespoon cinnamon powder
- ¼ cup chicken stock
- 2 tablespoons chili pepper, minced
- A pinch of salt and black pepper
- A pinch of cayenne pepper
- 1 tablespoon chives, chopped

Directions:

In your slow cooker, mix the trout with the cinnamon, stock and the other ingredients, toss gently, put the lid on and cook on Low for 3 hours. Divide the mix between plates and serve with a side salad.

Nutrition: calories 200, fat 12, fiber 2, carbs 6, protein 9

Slow Cooker Dessert Recipes for 2

Cinnamon Apples
Preparation time: 10 minutes | Cooking time: 2 hours | Servings: 2

Ingredients:
- 2 tablespoons brown sugar
- 1 pound apples, cored and cut into wedges
- 1 tablespoon cinnamon powder
- 2 tablespoons walnuts, chopped
- A pinch of nutmeg, ground
- ½ tablespoon lemon juice
- ¼ cup water
- 2 apples, cored and tops cut off

Directions:
In your slow cooker, mix the apples with the sugar, cinnamon and the other ingredients, toss, put the lid on and cook on High for 2 hours. Divide the mix between plates and serve.

Nutrition: calories 189, fat 4, fiber 7, carbs 19, protein 2

Vanilla Pears
Preparation time: 10 minutes | Cooking time: 2 hours | Servings: 2

Ingredients:
- 2 tablespoons avocado oil
- 1 teaspoon vanilla extract
- 2 pears, cored and halved
- ½ tablespoon lime juice
- 1 tablespoon sugar

Directions:
In your slow cooker combine the pears with the sugar, oil and the other ingredients, toss, put the lid on and cook on High for 2 hours. Divide between plates and serve.

Nutrition: calories 200, fat 4, fiber 6, carbs 16, protein 3

Avocado Cake
Preparation time: 10 minutes | Cooking time: 2 hours | Servings: 2

Ingredients:
- ½ cup brown sugar
- 2 tablespoons coconut oil, melted
- 1 cup avocado, peeled and mashed
- ½ teaspoon vanilla extract
- 1 egg
- ½ teaspoon baking powder
- 1 cup almond flour
- ¼ cup almond milk
- Cooking spray

Directions:
In a bowl, mix the sugar with the oil, avocado and the other ingredients except the cooking spray and whisk well. Grease your slow cooker with cooking spray, add the cake batter, spread, put the lid on and cook on High for 2 hours. Leave the cake to cool down, slice and serve.

Nutrition: calories 300, fat 4, fiber 4, carbs 27, protein 4

Coconut Cream
Preparation time: 10 minutes | Cooking time: 1 hour | Servings: 2

Ingredients:
- 2 ounces coconut cream
- 1 cup coconut milk
- ½ teaspoon almond extract
- 2 tablespoons sugar

Directions:
In your slow cooker, mix the cream with the milk and the other ingredients, whisk, put the lid on, cook on High for 1 hour, divide into bowls and serve cold.

Nutrition: calories 242, fat 12, fiber 6, carbs 9, protein 4

Almond Rice Pudding

Preparation time: 10 minutes | Cooking time: 1 hour | Servings: 2

Ingredients:
- 2 tablespoons almonds, chopped
- 1 cup white rice
- 2 cups almond milk
- 1 tablespoon sugar
- 1 tablespoons maple syrup
- ¼ teaspoon cinnamon powder
- ¼ teaspoon ginger, grated

Directions:

In your slow cooker, mix the milk with the rice, sugar and the other ingredients, toss, put the lid on and cook on High for 1 hour. Divide the pudding into bowls and serve cold

Nutrition: calories 205, fat 2, fiber 7, carbs 11, protein 4

Cherry Bowls

Preparation time: 10 minutes | Cooking time: 1 hour | Servings: 2

Ingredients:
- 1 cup cherries, pitted
- 1 tablespoon sugar
- ½ cup red cherry juice
- 2 tablespoons maple syrup

Directions:

In your slow cooker, mix the cherries with the sugar and the other ingredients, toss gently, put the lid on, cook on High for 1 hour, divide into bowls and serve.

Nutrition: calories 200, fat 1, fiber 4, carbs 5, protein 2

Berry Cream

Preparation time: 10 minutes | Cooking time: 2 hours | Servings: 2

Ingredients:
- 2 tablespoons cashews, chopped
- 1 cup heavy cream
- ½ cup blueberries
- ½ cup maple syrup
- ½ tablespoon coconut oil, melted

Directions:

In your slow cooker, mix the cream with the berries and the other ingredients, whisk, put the lid on and cook on Low for 2 hours. Divide the mix into bowls and serve cold.

Nutrition: calories 200, fat 3, fiber 5, carbs 12, protein 3

Maple Pudding

Preparation time: 10 minutes | Cooking time: 1 hour | Servings: 2

Ingredients:
- ¼ cup cashew butter
- 1 tablespoon coconut oil, melted
- ½ cup white rice
- 1 cup almond milk
- 2 tablespoons lemon juice
- ½ teaspoon lemon zest, grated
- 1 tablespoon maple syrup

Directions:

In your slow cooker, mix the rice with the milk, coconut oil and the other ingredients, whisk, put the lid on and cook on High for 1 hour. Divide into bowls and serve.

Nutrition: calories 202, fat 4, fiber 5, carbs 14, protein 1

Chia and Orange Pudding

Preparation time: 10 minutes | Cooking time: 1 hour | Servings: 2

Ingredients:
- 1 tablespoon chia seeds
- ½ cup almond milk
- ½ cup oranges, peeled and cut into segments
- 1 tablespoon sugar
- ½ teaspoon cinnamon powder
- 1 tablespoon coconut oil, melted
- 2 tablespoons pecans, chopped

Directions:
In your slow cooker, mix the chia seeds with the almond milk, orange segments and the other ingredients, toss, put the lid on and cook on High for 1 hour. Divide the pudding into bowls and serve cold.

Nutrition: calories 252, fat 3, fiber 3, carbs 7, protein 3

Creamy Berries Mix

Preparation time: 10 minutes | Cooking time: 1 hour | Servings: 2

Ingredients:
- ½ teaspoon nutmeg, ground
- ½ teaspoon vanilla extract
- ½ cup blackberries
- ½ cup blueberries
- ¼ cup whipping cream
- 1 tablespoon sugar
- 2 tablespoons walnuts, chopped

Directions:
In your slow cooker, combine the berries with the cream and the other ingredients, toss gently, put the lid on, cook on High for 1 hour, divide into bowls, and serve.

Nutrition: calories 260, fat 3, fiber 2, carbs 14, protein 3

Apple Compote

Preparation time: 10 minutes | Cooking time: 1 hour | Servings: 2

Ingredients:
- 1 pound apples, cored and cut into wedges
- ½ cup water
- 1 tablespoon sugar
- 1 teaspoon vanilla extract
- ½ teaspoon almond extract

Directions:
In your slow cooker, mix the apples with the water and the other ingredients, toss, put the lid on and cook on High for 1 hour. Divide into bowls and serve cold.

Nutrition: calories 203, fat 0, fiber 1, carbs 5, protein 4

Plums Stew

Preparation time: 10 minutes | Cooking time: 1 hour | Servings: 2

Ingredients:
- 1 pound plums, pitted and halved
- ½ teaspoon nutmeg, ground
- 1 cup water
- 1 and ½ tablespoons sugar
- 1 tablespoon vanilla extract

Directions:
In your slow cooker, mix the plums with the water and the other ingredients, toss gently, put the lid on and cook on High for 1 hour. Divide the mix into bowls and serve.

Nutrition: calories 200, fat 2, fiber 1, carbs 5, protein 4

Cinnamon Peach Mix

Preparation time: 10 minutes | Cooking time: 2 hours | Servings: 2

Ingredients:
- 2 cups peaches, peeled and halved
- 3 tablespoons sugar
- ½ teaspoon cinnamon powder
- ½ cup heavy cream
- 1 teaspoon vanilla extract

Directions:
In your slow cooker, mix the peaches with the sugar and the other ingredients, toss, put the lid on and cook on High for 2 hours. Divide the mix into bowls and serve.

Nutrition: calories 212, fat 4, fiber 4, carbs 7, protein 3

Strawberry Cake

Preparation time: 10 minutes | Cooking time: 1 hour | Servings: 2

Ingredients:
- ¼ cup coconut flour
- ¼ teaspoon baking soda
- 1 tablespoon sugar
- ¼ cup strawberries, chopped
- ½ cup coconut milk
- 1 teaspoon butter, melted
- ½ teaspoon lemon zest, grated
- ¼ teaspoon vanilla extract
- Cooking spray

Directions:
In a bowl, mix the coconut flour with the baking soda, sugar and the other ingredients except the cooking spray and stir well. Grease your slow cooker with the cooking spray, line it with parchment paper, pour the cake batter inside, put the lid on and cook on High for 1 hour. Leave the cake to cool down, slice and serve.

Nutrition: calories 200, fat 4, fiber 4, carbs 10, protein 4

Ginger Pears Mix

Preparation time: 10 minutes | Cooking time: 2 hours | Servings: 2

Ingredients:
- 2 pears, peeled and cored
- 1 cup apple juice
- ½ tablespoon brown sugar
- 1 tablespoon ginger, grated

Directions:
In your slow cooker, mix the pears with the apple juice and the other ingredients, toss, put the lid on and cook on Low for 2 hour. Divide the mix into bowls and serve warm.

Nutrition: calories 250, fat 1, fiber 2, carbs 12, protein 4

Raisin Cookies

Preparation time: 10 minutes | Cooking time: 2 hours and 30 minutes | Servings: 2

Ingredients:
- 1 tablespoon coconut oil, melted
- 2 eggs, whisked
- ¼ cup brown sugar
- ½ cup raisins
- ¼ cup almond milk
- ¼ teaspoon vanilla extract
- ¼ teaspoon baking powder
- 1 cup almond flour

Directions:
In a bowl, mix the eggs with the raisins, almond milk and the other ingredients and whisk well. Line your slow cooker with parchment paper, spread the cookie mix on the bottom of the pot, put the lid on, cook on Low for 2 hours and 30 minutes, leave aside to cool down, cut with a cookie cutter and serve.

Nutrition: calories 220, fat 2, fiber 1, carbs 6, protein 6

Blueberries Jam

Preparation time: 10 minutes | Cooking time: 4 hours | Servings: 2

Ingredients:
- 2 cups blueberries
- ½ cup water
- ¼ pound sugar
- Zest of 1 lime

Directions:
In your slow cooker, combine the berries with the water and the other ingredients, toss, put the lid on and cook on High for 4 hours. Divide into small jars and serve cold.

Nutrition: calories 250, fat 3, fiber 2, carbs 6, protein 1

Orange Bowls

Preparation time: 10 minutes | Cooking time: 3 hours | Servings: 2

Ingredients:
- ½ pound oranges, peeled and cut into segments
- 1 cup heavy cream
- ½ tablespoon almonds, chopped
- 1 tablespoon chia seeds
- 1 tablespoon sugar

Directions:
In your slow cooker, mix the oranges with the cream and the other ingredients, toss, put the lid on and cook on Low for 3 hours. Divide into bowls and serve.

Nutrition: calories 170, fat 0, fiber 2, carbs 7, protein 4

Quinoa Pudding

Preparation time: 10 minutes | Cooking time: 2 hours | Servings: 2

Ingredients:
- 1 cup quinoa
- 2 cups almond milk
- ½ cup sugar
- ½ tablespoon walnuts, chopped
- ½ tablespoon almonds, chopped

Directions:
In your slow cooker, mix the quinoa with the milk and the other ingredients, toss, put the lid on and cook on High for 2 hours. Divide the pudding into cups and serve.

Nutrition: calories 213, fat 4, fiber 6, carbs 10, protein 4

Chia and Avocado Pudding

Preparation time: 10 minutes | Cooking time: 3 hours | Servings: 2

Ingredients:
- ½ cup almond flour
- 1 tablespoon lime juice
- 2 tablespoons chia seeds
- 1 cup avocado, peeled, pitted and cubed
- 1 teaspoons baking powder
- ¼ teaspoon nutmeg, ground
- ¼ cup almond milk
- 2 tablespoons brown sugar
- 1 egg, whisked
- 2 tablespoons coconut oil, melted
- Cooking spray

Directions:
Grease your slow cooker with the cooking spray and mix the chia seeds with the flour, avocado and the other ingredients inside. Put the lid on, cook on High for 3 hours, leave the pudding to cool down, divide into bowls and serve

Nutrition: calories 220, fat 4, fiber 4, carbs 9, protein 6

Almond and Cherries Pudding

Preparation time: 10 minutes | Cooking time: 3 hours | Servings: 2

Ingredients:
- ½ cup almonds, chopped
- ½ cup cherries, pitted and halved
- ½ cup heavy cream
- ½ cup almond milk
- 1 tablespoon butter, soft
- 1 egg
- 2 tablespoons sugar
- ½ cup almond flour
- ½ teaspoon baking powder
- Cooking spray

Directions:
Grease the slow cooker with the cooking spray and mix the almonds with the cherries, cream and the other ingredients inside. Put the lid on, cook on High for 3 hours, divide into bowls and serve.

Nutrition: calories 200, fat 4, fiber 2, carbs 8, protein 6

Vanilla Peach Cream

Preparation time: 10 minutes | Cooking time: 3 hours | Servings: 2

Ingredients:
- ¼ teaspoon cinnamon powder
- 1 cup peaches, pitted and chopped
- ¼ cup heavy cream
- Cooking spray
- 1 tablespoon maple syrup
- ½ teaspoons vanilla extract
- 2 tablespoons sugar

Directions:
In a blender, mix the peaches with the cinnamon and the other ingredients except the cooking spray and pulse well. Grease the slow cooker with the cooking spray, pour the cream mix inside, put the lid on and cook on Low for 3 hours. Divide the cream into bowls and serve cold.

Nutrition: calories 200, fat 3, fiber 4, carbs 10, protein 9

Cinnamon Plums

Preparation time: 10 minutes | Cooking time: 2 hours | Servings: 2

Ingredients:
- ½ pound plums, pitted and halved
- 2 tablespoons sugar
- 1 teaspoon cinnamon, ground
- ½ cup orange juice

Directions:
In your slow cooker, mix the plums with the cinnamon and the other ingredients, toss, put the lid on and cook on Low for 2 hours. Divide into bowls and serve as a dessert.

Nutrition: calories 180, fat 2, fiber 1, carbs 8, protein 8

Cardamom Apples

Preparation time: 10 minutes | Cooking time: 2 hours | Servings: 2

Ingredients:
- 1 pound apples, cored and cut into wedges
- ½ cup almond milk
- ¼ teaspoon cardamom, ground
- 2 tablespoons brown sugar

Directions:
In your slow cooker, mix the apples with the cardamom and the other ingredients, toss, put the lid on and cook on High for 2 hours. Divide the mix into bowls and serve cold.

Nutrition: calories 280, fat 2, fiber 1, carbs 10, protein 6

Cherry and Rhubarb Mix

Preparation time: 10 minutes | Cooking time: 2 hours | Servings: 2

Ingredients:
- 2 cups rhubarb, sliced
- ½ cup cherries, pitted
- 1 tablespoon butter, melted
- ¼ cup coconut cream
- ½ cup sugar

Directions:
In your slow cooker, mix the rhubarb with the cherries and the other ingredients, toss, put the lid on and cook on High for 2 hours. Divide the mix into bowls and serve cold.

Nutrition: calories 200, fat 2, fiber 3, carbs 6, protein 1

Peaches and Wine Sauce

Preparation time: 10 minutes | Cooking time: 2 hours | Servings: 2

Ingredients:
- 3 tablespoons brown sugar
- 1 pound peaches, pitted and cut into wedges
- ½ cup red wine
- ½ teaspoon vanilla extract
- 1 teaspoon lemon zest, grated

Directions:
In your slow cooker, mix the peaches with the sugar and the other ingredients, toss, put the lid on and cook on High for 2 hours. Divide into bowls and serve.

Nutrition: calories 200, fat 4, fiber 6, carbs 9, protein 4

Apricot and Peaches Cream

Preparation time: 10 minutes | Cooking time: 2 hours | Servings: 2

Ingredients:
- 1 cup apricots, pitted and chopped
- 1 cup peaches, pitted and chopped
- 1 cup heavy cream
- 3 tablespoons brown sugar
- 1 teaspoon vanilla extract

Directions:
In a blender, mix the apricots with the peaches and the other ingredients, and pulse well. Put the cream in the slow cooker, put the lid on, cook on High for 2 hours, divide into bowls and serve.

Nutrition: calories 200, fat 4, fiber 5, carbs 10, protein 4

Vanilla Grapes Mix

Preparation time: 10 minutes | Cooking time: 2 hours | Servings: 2

Ingredients:
- 1 cup grapes, halved
- ½ teaspoon vanilla extract
- 1 cup oranges, peeled and cut into segments
- ¼ cup water
- 1 and ½ tablespoons sugar
- 1 teaspoon lemon juice

Directions:
In your slow cooker, mix the grapes with the oranges, water and the other ingredients, toss, put the lid on and cook on Low for 2 hours. Divide into bowls and serve.

Nutrition: calories 100, fat 3, fiber 6, carbs 8, protein 3

Pomegranate and Mango Bowls

Preparation time: 10 minutes | *Cooking time:* 3 hours | *Servings:* 2

Ingredients:
- 2 cups pomegranate seeds
- 1 cup mango, peeled and cubed
- ½ cup heavy cream
- 1 tablespoon lemon juice
- ½ teaspoon vanilla extract
- 2 tablespoons white sugar

Directions:
In your slow cooker, combine the mango with the pomegranate seeds and the other ingredients, toss, put the lid on and cook on Low for 3 hours. Divide into bowls and serve cold.

Nutrition: calories 162, fat 4, fiber 5, carbs 20, protein 6

Mandarin Cream

Preparation time: 10 minutes | *Cooking time:* 2 hours | *Servings:* 2

Ingredients:
- 1 tablespoon ginger, grated
- 3 tablespoons sugar
- 3 mandarins, peeled and chopped
- 2 tablespoons agave nectar
- ½ cup coconut cream

Directions:
In your slow cooker, mix the ginger with the sugar, mandarins and the other ingredients, whisk, put the lid on and cook on High for 2 hours. Blend the cream using an immersion blender, divide into bowls and serve cold.

Nutrition: calories 100, fat 4, fiber 5, carbs 6, protein 7

Cranberries Cream

Preparation time: 10 minutes | *Cooking time:* 1 hour | *Servings:* 2

Ingredients:
- 3 cups cranberries
- ½ cup water
- ½ cup coconut cream
- ½ teaspoon vanilla extract
- ½ teaspoon almond extract
- ½ cup sugar

Directions:
In your slow cooker, mix the cranberries with the water, cream and the other ingredients, whisk, put the lid on and cook on High for 1 hour. Transfer to a blender, pulse well, divide into bowls and serve cold.

Nutrition: calories 100, fat 3, fiber 6, carbs 7, protein 3

Buttery Pineapple

Preparation time: 10 minutes | *Cooking time:* 2 hours | *Servings:* 2

Ingredients:
- 2 cups pineapple, peeled and roughly cubed
- 1 and ½ tablespoons butter
- ½ cup heavy cream
- 2 tablespoons brown sugar
- ½ teaspoon cinnamon powder
- ½ teaspoon ginger, grated

Directions:
In your slow cooker, mix the pineapple with the butter, cream and the other ingredients, toss, put the lid on and cook on High for 2 hours. Divide into bowls and serve cold.

Nutrition: calories 152, fat 3, fiber 1, carbs 17, protein 3

Strawberry and Orange Mix

Preparation time: 10 minutes | Cooking time: 1 hour | Servings: 2

Ingredients:
- 2 tablespoons sugar
- 1 cup orange segments
- 1 cup strawberries, halved
- A pinch of ginger powder
- ½ teaspoon vanilla extract
- ½ cup orange juice
- 1 tablespoon chia seeds

Directions:
In your slow cooker, mix the oranges with the berries, ginger powder and the other ingredients, toss, put the lid on and cook on High for 1 hour. Divide into bowls and serve cold.

Nutrition: calories 100, fat 2, fiber 2, carbs 10, protein 2

Maple Plums and Mango

Preparation time: 10 minutes | Cooking time: 1 hour | Servings: 2

Ingredients:
- 2 teaspoons orange zest
- 1 tablespoon orange juice
- 1 cup plums, pitted and halved
- 1 cup mango, peeled and cubed
- 1 tablespoon maple syrup
- 3 tablespoons sugar

Directions:
In your slow cooker, mix the plums with the mango and the other ingredients, toss, put the lid on and cook on High for 1 hour. Divide into bowls and serve cold

Nutrition: calories 123, fat 1, fiber 2, carbs 20, protein 3

Cantaloupe Cream

Preparation time: 5 minutes | Cooking time: 1 hour | Servings: 2

Ingredients:
- 2 cups cantaloupe, peeled and cubed
- 2 tablespoons sugar
- 1 cup coconut cream
- 1 tablespoon butter
- 1 tablespoon lemon zest, grated
- Juice of ½ lemon

Directions:
In your slow cooker, mix the cantaloupe with the sugar, cream and the other ingredients, toss, put the lid on and cook on High for 1 hour. Blend using an immersion blender, divide into bowls and serve cold.

Nutrition: calories 100, fat 2, fiber 3, carbs 6, protein 1

Yogurt Cheesecake

Preparation time: 1 hour | Cooking time: 3 hours | Servings: 2

Ingredients:
For the crust:
- 1 tablespoon coconut oil, melted
- ½ cup graham cookies, crumbled

For the filling:
- 3 ounces cream cheese, soft
- 1 cup Greek yogurt
- ½ tablespoon cornstarch
- 3 tablespoons sugar
- 1 egg, whisked
- 1 teaspoon almond extract
- Cooking spray

Directions:
In a bowl mix the cookie crumbs with butter and stir well. Grease your slow cooker with the cooking spray, line it with parchment paper and press the crumbs on the bottom. In a bowl, mix the cream cheese with the yogurt and the other ingredients, whisk well and spread over the crust. Put the lid on, cook on Low for 3 hours, cool down and keep in the fridge for 1 hour before serving.

Nutrition: calories 276, fat 12, fiber 3, carbs 20, protein 4

Chocolate Mango Mix

Preparation time: 10 minutes | Cooking time: 1 hour | Servings: 2

Ingredients:
- 1 cup crème fraiche
- ¼ cup dark chocolate, cut into chunks
- 1 cup mango, peeled and chopped
- 2 tablespoons sugar
- ½ teaspoon almond extract

Directions:
In your slow cooker, mix the crème fraiche with the chocolate and the other ingredients, toss, put the lid on and cook on Low for 1 hour. Blend using an immersion blender, divide into bowls and serve.

Nutrition: calories 200, fat 12, fiber 4, carbs 7, protein 3

Lemon Jam

Preparation time: 10 minutes | Cooking time: 3 hours | Servings: 2

Ingredients:
- ½ cup lemon juice
- 1 orange, peeled and cut into segments
- 1 lemon, peeled and cut into segments
- ½ cup water
- 2 tablespoons lemon zest, grated
- ¼ cup sugar
- A pinch of cinnamon powder
- ½ tablespoon cornstarch

Directions:
In your slow cooker, mix the lemon juice with the sugar, water and the other ingredients, whisk, put the lid on and cook on Low for 3 hours. Divide into small jars and serve cold.

Nutrition: calories 70, fat 1, fiber 3, carbs 13, protein 1

Lemon Peach Mix

Preparation time: 10 minutes | Cooking time: 3 hours | Servings: 2

Ingredients:
- 1 cup peaches, peeled and halved
- 2 tablespoons sugar
- ½ tablespoon lemon juice
- ½ cup heavy cream
- 1 tablespoon lemon zest, grated

Directions:
In your slow cooker, mix the peaches with the sugar and the other ingredients, toss gently, put the lid on and cook on Low for 3 hours. Divide into cups and serve cold.

Nutrition: calories 50, fat 0, fiber 2, carbs 10, protein 0

Rhubarb Stew

Preparation time: 10 minutes | Cooking time: 2 hours | Servings: 2

Ingredients:
- ½ pound rhubarb, roughly sliced
- 2 tablespoons sugar
- ½ teaspoon vanilla extract
- ½ teaspoon lemon extract
- 1 tablespoon lemon juice
- ¼ cup water

Directions:
In your slow cooker, mix the rhubarb with the sugar, vanilla and the other ingredients, toss, put the lid on and cook on Low for 2 hours. Divide the mix into bowls and serve cold.

Nutrition: calories 60, fat 1, fiber 0, carbs 10, protein 1

Strawberry and Blackberry Jam

Preparation time: 10 minutes | Cooking time: 3 hours | Servings: 2

Ingredients:
- ½ pound strawberries, halved
- 1 cup blackberries
- 1 tablespoon lemon zest, grated
- ½ teaspoon almond extract
- 2 tablespoons lemon juice
- 1 cup sugar

Directions:
In your slow cooker, combine the berries with the lemon zest and the other ingredients, toss, put the lid on and cook on Low for 3 hours. Stir the mix well, divide into bowls and serve cold.

Nutrition: calories 90, fat 1, fiber 2, carbs 20, protein 1

Pear Cream

Preparation time: 10 minutes | Cooking time: 3 hours | Servings: 2

Ingredients:
- ½ pound pears, peeled and chopped
- ½ cup heavy cream
- ½ cup honey
- 1 tablespoon lemon zest, grated
- Juice of ½ lemon

Directions:
In your slow cooker, mix the pears with the cream and the other ingredients, whisk, put the lid on and cook on Low for 3 hours. Blend using an immersion blender, divide into cups and serve cold.

Nutrition: calories 134, fat 1, fiber 3, carbs 20, protein 1

Rhubarb Jam

Preparation time: 10 minutes | Cooking time: 2 hours | Servings: 2

Ingredients:
- ½ pound rhubarb, sliced
- ½ tablespoon cornstarch
- ¼ cup sugar
- 1 tablespoon lemon juice
- 1 cup water

Directions:
In your slow cooker, mix the rhubarb with the sugar and the other ingredients, toss, put the lid on and cook on High for 2 hours. Whisk the jam, divide into bowls and serve cold.

Nutrition: calories 40, fat 0, fiber 1, carbs 10, protein 1

Apricot Marmalade

Preparation time: 10 minutes | Cooking time: 3 hours | Servings: 2

Ingredients:
- 1 cup apricots, chopped
- ½ cup water
- 1 teaspoon vanilla extract
- 2 tablespoons lemon juice
- 1 teaspoon fruit pectin
- 2 cups sugar

Directions:
In your slow cooker, mix the apricots with the water, vanilla and the other ingredients, whisk, put the lid on and cook on High for 3 hours. Stir the marmalade, divide into bowls and serve cold.

Nutrition: calories 100, fat 1, fiber 2, carbs 20, protein 1

Apple, Avocado and Mango Bowls

Preparation time: 10 minutes | Cooking time: 2 hours | Servings: 2

Ingredients:
- 1 cup avocado, peeled, pitted and cubed
- 1 cup mango, peeled and cubed
- 1 apple, cored and cubed
- 2 tablespoons brown sugar
- 1 cup heavy cream
- 1 tablespoon lemon juice

Directions:
In your slow cooker, combine the avocado with the mango and the other ingredients, toss gently, put the lid on and cook on Low for 2 hours. Divide the mix into bowls and serve.

Nutrition: calories 60, fat 1, fiber 2, carbs 20, protein 1

Tomato Jam

Preparation time: 10 minutes | Cooking time: 3 hours | Servings: 2

Ingredients:
- ½ pound tomatoes, chopped
- 1 green apple, grated
- 2 tablespoons red wine vinegar
- 4 tablespoons sugar

Directions:
In your slow cooker, mix the tomatoes with the apple and the other ingredients, whisk, put the lid on and cook on Low for 3 hours. Whisk the jam well, blend a bit using an immersion blender, divide into bowls and serve cold.

Nutrition: calories 70, fat 1, fiber 1, carbs 18, protein 1

Cinnamon and Chocolate Peaches

Preparation time: 10 minutes | Cooking time: 2 hours | Servings: 2

Ingredients:
- 4 peaches, stoned and halved
- 1 tablespoon cinnamon powder
- 1 tablespoon cocoa powder
- 2 tablespoons coconut oil, melted
- 2 tablespoons sugar
- 1 cup heavy cream

Directions:
In your slow cooker, mix the peaches with the cinnamon, cocoa and the other ingredients, toss, put the lid on and cook on Low for 2 hours. Divide the mix into bowls and serve cold.

Nutrition: calories 40, fat 1, fiber 1, carbs 5, protein 0

Coconut Jam

Preparation time: 10 minutes | Cooking time: 3 hours | Servings: 2

Ingredients:
- ½ cup coconut flesh, shredded
- 1 cup coconut cream
- ½ cup heavy cream
- 3 tablespoons sugar
- 1 tablespoon lemon juice

Directions:
In your slow cooker, mix the coconut cream with the lemon juice and the other ingredients, whisk, put the lid on and cook on Low for 3 hours. Whisk well, divide into bowls and serve cold.

Nutrition: calories 50, fat 1, fiber 1, carbs 10, protein 2

Bread and Berries Pudding

Preparation time: 10 minutes | Cooking time: 3 hours | Servings: 2

Ingredients:
- 2 cups white bread, cubed
- 1 cup blackberries
- 2 tablespoons butter, melted
- 2 tablespoons white sugar
- 1 cup almond milk
- ¼ cup heavy cream
- 2 eggs, whisked
- 1 tablespoon lemon zest, grated
- ¼ teaspoon vanilla extract

Directions:
In your slow cooker, mix the bread with the berries, butter and the other ingredients, toss gently, put the lid on and cook on Low for 3 hours. Divide pudding between dessert plates and serve.

Nutrition: calories 354, fat 12, fiber 4, carbs 29, protein 11

Tapioca and Chia Pudding

Preparation time: 10 minutes | Cooking time: 3 hours | Servings: 2

Ingredients:
- 1 cup almond milk
- ¼ cup tapioca pearls
- 2 tablespoons chia seeds
- 2 eggs, whisked
- ½ teaspoon vanilla extract
- 3 tablespoons sugar
- ½ tablespoon lemon zest, grated

Directions:
In your slow cooker, mix the tapioca pearls with the milk, eggs and the other ingredients, whisk, put the lid on and cook on Low for 3 hours. Divide the pudding into bowls and serve cold.

Nutrition: calories 180, fat 3, fiber 4, carbs 12, protein 4

Dates and Rice Pudding

Preparation time: 10 minutes | Cooking time: 3 hours | Servings: 2

Ingredients:
- 1 cup dates, chopped
- ½ cup white rice
- 1 cup almond milk
- 2 tablespoons brown sugar
- 1 teaspoon almond extract

Directions:
In your slow cooker, mix the rice with the milk and the other ingredients, whisk, put the lid on and cook on Low for 3 hours. Divide the pudding into bowls and serve.

Nutrition: calories 152, fat 5, fiber 2, carb 6, protein 3

Almonds, Walnuts and Mango Bowls

Preparation time: 10 minutes | Cooking time: 2 hours | Servings: 2

Ingredients:
- 1 cup walnuts, chopped
- 2 tablespoons almonds, chopped
- 1 cup mango, peeled and roughly cubed
- 1 cup heavy cream
- ½ teaspoon vanilla extract
- 1 teaspoon almond extract
- 1 tablespoon brown sugar

Directions:
In your slow cooker, mix the nuts with the mango, cream and the other ingredients, toss, put the lid on and cook on High for 2 hours. Divide the mix into bowls and serve.

Nutrition: calories 220, fat 4, fiber 2, carbs 4, protein 6

Berries Salad

Preparation time: 10 minutes | Cooking time: 1 hour | Servings: 2

Ingredients:
- 2 tablespoons brown sugar
- 1 tablespoon lime juice
- 1 tablespoon lime zest, grated
- 1 cup blueberries
- ½ cup cranberries
- 1 cup blackberries
- 1 cup strawberries
- ½ cup heavy cream

Directions:
In your slow cooker, mix the berries with the sugar and the other ingredients, toss, put the lid on and cook on High for 1 hour. Divide the mix into bowls and serve.

Nutrition: calories 262, fat 7, fiber 2, carbs 5, protein 8

Pears and Apples Bowls

Preparation time: 10 minutes | Cooking time: 2 hours | Servings: 2

Ingredients:
- 1 teaspoon vanilla extract
- 2 pears, cored and cut into wedges
- 2 apples, cored and cut into wedges
- 1 tablespoon walnuts, chopped
- 2 tablespoons brown sugar
- ½ cup coconut cream

Directions:
In your slow cooker, mix the pears with the apples, nuts and the other ingredients, toss, put the lid on and cook on Low for 2 hours. Divide the mix into bowls and serve cold.

Nutrition: calories 120, fat 2, fiber 2, carbs 4, protein 3

Creamy Rhubarb and Plums Bowls

Preparation time: 10 minutes | Cooking time: 2 hours | Servings: 2

Ingredients:
- 1 cup plums, pitted and halved
- 1 cup rhubarb, sliced
- 1 cup coconut cream
- ½ teaspoon vanilla extract
- ½ cup sugar
- ½ tablespoon lemon juice
- 1 teaspoon almond extract

Directions:
In your slow cooker, mix the plums with the rhubarb, cream and the other ingredients, toss, put the lid on and cook on High for 2 hours. Divide the mix into bowls and serve.

Nutrition: calories 162, fat 2, fiber 2, carbs 4, protein 5

Greek Cream Cheese Pudding

Preparation time: 5 minutes | Cooking time: 2 hours | Servings: 2

Ingredients:
- 1 cup cream cheese, soft
- ½ cup Greek yogurt
- 2 eggs, whisked
- ½ teaspoon baking soda
- 1 cup almonds, chopped
- 1 tablespoon sugar
- ½ teaspoon almond extract
- ½ teaspoon cinnamon powder

Directions:
In your slow cooker, mix the cream cheese with the yogurt, eggs and the other ingredients, whisk, put the lid on and cook on Low for 2 hours. Divide the pudding into bowls and serve.

Nutrition: calories 172, fat 2, fiber 3, carbs 4, protein 5

Greek Cream

Preparation time: 10 minutes | Cooking time: 1 hour | Servings: 2

Ingredients:
- 1 cup heavy cream
- 1 cup Greek yogurt
- 2 tablespoons brown sugar
- ½ teaspoon vanilla extract
- ½ teaspoon ginger powder

Directions:
In your slow cooker, mix the cream with the yogurt and the other ingredients, whisk, put the lid on and cook on High for 1 hour. Divide the cream into bowls and serve cold.

Nutrition: calories 200, fat 5, fiber 3, carbs 4, protein 5

Ginger Cream

Preparation time: 10 minutes | Cooking time: 1 hour | Serving: 2

Ingredients:
- 1 cup coconut cream
- 1 tablespoon ginger, grated
- 2 eggs, whisked
- 1 cup Greek yogurt
- 2 tablespoons brown sugar
- 1 tablespoon lemon juice

Directions:
In your slow cooker, mix the cream with the ginger, eggs and the other ingredients, whisk, put the lid on and cook on High for 1 hour. Cool the cream down and serve.

Nutrition: calories 200, fat 5, fiber 2, carbs 5, protein 6

Bread and Quinoa Pudding

Preparation time: 10 minutes | Cooking time: 3 hours | Servings: 2

Ingredients:
- 1 cup quinoa
- 1 cup bread, cubed
- 2 cups almond milk
- 2 tablespoons honey
- 1 teaspoon cinnamon powder
- 1 teaspoon nutmeg, ground

Directions:
In your slow cooker, mix the quinoa with the milk and the other ingredients, whisk, put the lid on and cook on Low for 3 hours. Divide the pudding into bowls and serve.

Nutrition: calories 172, fat 4, fiber 2, carbs 4, protein 5

Melon Pudding

Preparation time: 10 minutes | Cooking time: 2 hours | Servings: 2

Ingredients:
- 1 cup melon, peeled and cubed
- ½ cup white rice
- 1 cup coconut milk
- 2 tablespoons honey
- 1 teaspoon vanilla extract
- 1 teaspoon ginger powder
- ½ tablespoon lime zest, grated

Directions:
In your slow cooker, mix the rice with the melon, milk and the other ingredients, whisk, put the lid on and cook on High for 2 hours. Divide the pudding into bowls and serve cold.

Nutrition: calories 172, fat 2, fiber 2, carbs 4, protein 6

Conclusion

Cooking for you and your loved one can be such a challenge sometimes but from now on you have the best journal at hand. The recipes collection you discovered today is pretty impressive and it's full of great and delicious recipes for 2.
The best thing about this collection is that all the dishes are made using one single kitchen tool: the slow cooker. You get some of the best recipes for 2 made in one of the most popular and easy to use appliances.
Check out all our suggestions and discover some of the most textured and flavored slow cooker dishes for 2!

Get a copy of this amazing cookbook today and prepare real culinary feasts for you and your loved one in the comfort of your own kitchen. Enjoy the best and most delightful dishes for 2 and have fun cooking!

Recipe Index

ALLSPICE
Spinach Frittata, 18
Peas and Rice Bowls, 28
Cinnamon Pork Ribs, 43

ALMOND MILK
Cinnamon Berries Oatmeal, 12
Cinnamon French Toast, 13
Carrots Oatmeal, 13
Maple Banana Oatmeal, 14
Chia Oatmeal, 14
Ginger Raisins Oatmeal, 15
Apple and Chia Mix, 15
Pumpkin and Quinoa Mix, 15
Cocoa and Berries Quinoa, 15
Quinoa and Veggies Casserole, 16
Peach, Vanilla and Oats Mix, 18
Almond and Quinoa Bowls, 20
Cranberry Maple Oatmeal, 20
Cherries and Cocoa Oats, 23
Quinoa and Chia Pudding, 25
Avocado Cake, 137
Almond Rice Pudding, 138
Maple Pudding, 138
Chia and Orange Pudding, 139
Raisin Cookies, 140
Quinoa Pudding, 141
Chia and Avocado Pudding, 141
Almond and Cherries Pudding, 142
Cardamom Apples, 142
Bread and Berries Pudding, 149
Tapioca and Chia Pudding, 149
Dates and Rice Pudding, 149
Bread and Quinoa Pudding, 151

ALMONDS
Almond and Quinoa Bowls, 20
Cauliflower and Almonds Mix, 53
Saffron Risotto, 61
Almond Bowls, 74
Almond Spread, 75
Nuts Bowls, 75
Almond Shrimp and Cabbage, 133
Almond Rice Pudding, 138
Orange Bowls, 141
Quinoa Pudding, 141
Almond and Cherries Pudding, 142
Almonds, Walnuts and Mango Bowls, 149
Greek Cream Cheese Pudding, 150

APPLE JUICE
Ginger Pears Mix, 140

APPLES
Buttery Oatmeal, 14
Cabbage Mix, 58
Apple, Avocado and Mango Bowls, 148
Apple and Chia Mix, 15
Ginger Apple Bowls, 21
Apple Spread, 23
Apple and Carrot Dip, 79
Chicken and Apples Mix, 90
Cinnamon Apples, 137
Cinnamon Apples, 137
Apple Compote, 139
Cardamom Apples, 142
Pears and Apples Bowls, 150
Tomato Jam, 148

APRICOTS
Apricot and Peaches Cream, 143
Apricot Marmalade, 147

ARTICHOKES
Lemon Artichokes, 62
Asparagus Mix, 64
Chicken and Asparagus, 100
Asparagus Casserole, 28

AVOCADO
Squash Salsa, 70
Turkey and Avocado, 98
Shrimp and Avocado, 124
Avocado Cake, 137
Chia and Avocado Pudding, 141
Apple, Avocado and Mango Bowls, 148

AVOCADO OIL
Chocolate Breakfast Bread, 20
Chicken and Peach Mix, 41
Creamy Coconut Potatoes, 53
Baby Carrots and Parsnips Mix, 65
Macadamia Nuts Snack, 77
Cinnamon Pecans Snack, 80
Chicken and Broccoli, 91
Rosemary Chicken, 91
Balsamic Turkey, 91
Turkey and Scallions Mix, 92
Turkey Chili, 92
Chicken and Mango Mix, 98
Turkey and Carrots, 102
Turkey and Kidney Beans, 102
Garlic Turkey, 103
Honey Pork Chops, 107
Turmeric Lamb, 107
Chili Lamb, 107
Pork and Green Beans, 108

Beef and Artichokes, 109
Lamb and Potatoes, 109
Lamb and Fennel Mix, 111
Creamy Lamb, 111
Beef and Capers Sauce, 111
Lamb and Cabbage, 112
Balsamic Lamb Mix, 112
Beef and Endives, 113
Lamb and Lime Zucchinis, 113
Parsley and Chili Lamb, 114
Paprika Lamb, 114
Chili Salmon, 120
Rosemary Shrimp, 120
Coriander Salmon Mix, 121
Cod and Corn, 122
Creamy Shrimp, 123
Orange Cod, 123
Garlic Sea Bass, 124
Chives Mackerel, 125
Balsamic Tuna, 126
Shrimp and Pineapple Bowls, 127
Lime Crab, 127
Shrimp and Eggplant, 127
Coconut Mackerel, 128
Italian Shrimp, 129
Shrimp and Mushrooms, 129
Salmon and Berries, 130
Vanilla Pears, 137
Cinnamon Lamb, 116

BACON
Hash Brown and Bacon Casserole, 13
Corn Sauté, 51
Bacon Potatoes Mix, 59

BANANA
Maple Banana Oatmeal, 14

BEANS
Bbq Beans, 57
Beans Breakfast Bowls, 25

BEANS (BLACK)
Italian Black Beans Mix, 50
Black Beans Mix, 55

BEANS (GREEN)
Mixed Pork and Beans, 40
Butter Green Beans, 51
Creamy Beans, 57
Paprika Green Beans and Zucchinis, 67
Garlic Chicken and Green Beans, 85
Pork and Green Beans, 108
Beef with Green Beans and Cilantro, 118
Tuna and Green Beans, 122

Salmon, Tomatoes and Green Beans, 130

BEANS (LIMA)
Lime Beans Mix, 56

BEANS BLACK (CANNED)
Beans Salad, 24
Peppers Rice Mix, 24
Beans Breakfast Bowls, 25
Pork Soup, 38
Beans Chili, 38
Mixed Pork and Beans, 40
Beans Spread, 70
Beets Salad, 74
Chicken and Beans, 93
Pork and Beans Mix, 105

BEANS RED KIDNEY (CANNED)
Beans Salad, 24
Beans Breakfast Bowls, 25
Beans Chili, 38
Salsa Beans Dip, 72
Turkey and Kidney Beans, 102

BEANS WHITE (CANNED)
Beans Chili, 38
White Beans Mix, 57

BEEF
Beef and Artichokes Stew, 47
Beef Dip, 82
Beef Meatloaf, 22
Roasted Beef and Cauliflower, 33
Soy Pork Chops, 33
Beef Stew, 34
Beef and Celery Stew, 35
Tomato Pasta Mix, 35
Honey Lamb Roast, 35
Worcestershire Beef Mix, 35
Pork Soup, 38
Mustard Short Ribs, 39
Creamy Brisket, 39
Mixed Pork and Beans, 40
Pork Chops and Butter Sauce, 40
Mustard Pork Chops and Carrots, 41
Cinnamon Pork Ribs, 43
Pesto Pork Shanks, 44
Potato Stew, 44
Paprika Pork and Chickpeas, 45
Beef and Cabbage, 46
Balsamic Beef Stew, 46
Beef Curry, 46
Beef and Artichokes Stew, 47
Beef Soup, 48
Masala Beef Mix, 49

Dill Mushroom Sauté, 52
Beef Dip, 81
Pork Chops and Mango Mix, 104
Beef and Zucchinis Mix, 104
Pork and Soy Sauce Mix, 104
Beef and Sauce, 105
Beef with Spinach, 105
Mustard Ribs, 106
Beef and Corn Mix, 106
Cider Beef Mix, 106
Tarragon Pork Chops, 106
Honey Pork Chops, 107
Turmeric Lamb, 107
Beef and Red Onions Mix, 107
Pork and Okra, 108
Oregano Beef, 108
Pork and Green Beans, 108
Mint Lamb Chops, 109
Beef and Artichokes, 109
Lamb and Potatoes, 109
Lamb and Tomatoes Mix, 110
Pork and Eggplant Mix, 110
Rosemary Lamb with Olives, 110
Nutmeg Lamb and Squash, 111
Creamy Lamb, 111
Beef and Capers Sauce, 111
Masala Beef and Sauce, 112
Lamb and Cabbage, 112
Pork and Lentils, 112
Balsamic Lamb Mix, 112
Beef and Endives, 113
Beef and Endives, 113
Lamb and Lime Zucchinis, 113
Beef and Peas, 113
Maple Beef, 113
Rosemary Beef, 114
Cumin Pork Chops, 114
Paprika Lamb, 114
Beef with Peas and Corn, 115
Lime Pork Chops, 115
Lamb with Capers, 115
Lamb and Zucchini Mix, 115
Beef and Peppers, 116
Cinnamon Lamb, 116
Lamb and Kale, 116
Beef and Sprouts, 117
Green Curry Lamb, 117
Oregano Lamb, 117
Pesto Lamb Chops, 118
Beef with Green Beans and Cilantro, 118
Balsamic Lamb Chops, 118
Creamy Beef, 119
Walnut and Coconut Beef, 119
Walnut and Coconut Beef, 119

BEETS
Beets Salad, 74

BELL PEPPER (GREEN)
Sausage and Potato Mix, 12
Stuffed Peppers Platter, 72
Eggs and Sweet Potato Mix, 23
Peppers Rice Mix, 24
Beans Breakfast Bowls, 25
Peppers and Eggs Mix, 27
Creamy Cod Stew, 30
Salsa Chicken, 31
Shrimp Gumbo, 37
Squash and Chicken Soup, 37
Beans Chili, 38
Mushroom Soup, 39
Beans and Mushroom Stew, 42
Beef Soup, 48
Shrimp Salad, 78
Peppers Salsa, 84
Pork and Chilies Mix, 105
Beef and Peppers, 116
Shrimp and Rice Mix, 131

BELL PEPPER (ORANGE)
Peppers Rice Mix, 24
Peppers Salsa, 84
Beef and Peppers, 116

BELL PEPPER (RED)
Broccoli Casserole, 17
Hot Eggs Mix, 18
Eggs and Sweet Potato Mix, 23
Beans Salad, 24
Peppers Rice Mix, 24
Beans Breakfast Bowls, 25
Peppers and Eggs Mix, 27
Sweet Potato and Clam Chowder, 31
Salsa Chicken, 31
Squash and Chicken Soup, 37
Pork Soup, 38
Beans Chili, 38
Mushroom Soup, 39
Beans and Mushroom Stew, 42
Chicken and Eggplant Stew, 42
Pork Chili, 43
Potato Stew, 44
Italian Black Beans Mix, 50
Tomato and Corn Mix, 51
Veggie Mix, 60
Lemon Kale Mix, 65
Bulgur and Beans Salsa, 73
Eggplant Salad, 76
Shrimp Salad, 78
Peppers Salsa, 84

155

Chives Duck, 97
Pork and Beans Mix, 105
Pork and Chilies Mix, 105
Beef and Peppers, 116
Chicken and Peppers, 99
Eggs and Sweet Potato Mix, 23
Italian Black Beans Mix, 50
Lime Beans Mix, 56
Mustard Brussels Sprouts, 67
Shrimp Salad, 78
Spinach Frittata, 18

BELL PEPPER (YELLOW)
Peppers and Eggs Mix, 27
Pork Chili, 43
Lemon Kale Mix, 65

BLACKBERRIES
Cinnamon Berries Oatmeal, 12
Coconut Quinoa, 12
Pumpkin and Berries Bowls, 24
Salmon and Berries, 130
Creamy Berries Mix, 139
Strawberry and Blackberry Jam, 147
Bread and Berries Pudding, 149
Berries Salad, 150
Cocoa and Berries Quinoa, 15
Berry Cream, 138
Blueberries Jam, 141
Berries Salad, 150
Creamy Berries Mix, 139

BOK CHOY
Coconut Bok Choy, 62

BROCCOLI
Broccoli Casserole, 17
Basil Sausage and Broccoli Mix, 25
Curry Broccoli Mix, 63
Broccoli Dip, 81
Chicken and Broccoli, 91
Cod and Broccoli, 136

BRUSSELS SPROUTS
Chicken and Brussels Sprouts Mix, 46
Mustard Brussels Sprouts, 54
Brussels Sprouts and Cauliflower, 65
Mustard Brussels Sprouts, 67
Chicken with Brussels Sprouts, 98
Beef and Sprouts, 117
Tuna and Brussels Sprouts, 124

BUTTER
Cinnamon French Toast, 13
Chia Oatmeal, 14

Buttery Oatmeal, 14
Chocolate Breakfast Bread, 20
Almond and Quinoa Bowls, 20
Pork Chops and Butter Sauce, 40
Mustard Pork Chops and Carrots, 41
Cheddar Potatoes Mix, 50
Butter Green Beans, 51
Corn Sauté, 51
Mashed Potatoes, 56
Buttery Spinach, 59
Cauliflower Mash, 60
Cumin Quinoa Pilaf, 60
Nuts Bowls, 75
Strawberry Cake, 140
Almond and Cherries Pudding, 142
Cherry and Rhubarb Mix, 143
Buttery Pineapple, 144
Cantaloupe Cream, 145
Bread and Berries Pudding, 149

BUTTERNUT
Squash and Chicken Soup, 37
Butternut Squash and Eggplant Mix, 52

BUTTERNUT SQUASH
Garlic Squash Mix, 64
Squash Salsa, 70
Nutmeg Lamb and Squash, 111
Sea Bass and Squash, 128

CABBAGE (GREEN)
Beef and Cabbage, 46
Cabbage and Onion Mix, 63
Cabbage and Kale Mix, 66

CABBAGE (RED)
Beef and Cabbage, 46
Cabbage Mix, 58
Cabbage and Onion Mix, 63
Chicken and Cabbage Mix, 99
Lamb and Cabbage, 112
Almond Shrimp and Cabbage, 133

CABBAGE (SAVOY)
Savoy Cabbage Mix, 68

CALAMARI RINGS
Calamari Rings Bowls, 78
Spinach, Walnuts and Calamari Salad, 80
Calamari and Sauce, 132
Calamari Curry, 134

CANNED ARTICHOKE
Artichoke Soup, 42
Beef and Artichokes Stew, 47

Artichoke Dip, 69
Artichoke Dip, 84
Paprika Chicken and Artichokes, 86
Beef and Artichokes, 109
Cod and Artichokes, 130

CANNED CHICKPEAS
Chickpeas Stew, 36

CAPERS
Veggie Mix, 60
Eggplant Salsa, 75
Eggplant Salsa, 82
Beef and Capers Sauce, 111
Lamb with Capers, 115
Veggie Medley, 66
Parmesan Quinoa, 17
Creamy Shrimp Bowls, 17
Seafood Soup, 29
Creamy Cod Stew, 30
Sweet Potato and Clam Chowder, 31
Slow Cooked Thyme Chicken, 33
Roasted Beef and Cauliflower, 33
Beef Stew, 34
Lentils Soup, 36
Parsley Chicken Stew, 39
Mushroom Soup, 39
Artichoke Soup, 42
Turmeric Lentils Stew, 43
Pork Chili, 43
Potato Stew, 44
Salmon Stew, 45
Beef and Cabbage, 46
Balsamic Beef Stew, 46
Beef Soup, 48
Veggie Soup, 48
Oregano Turkey Stew, 48
Corn Sauté, 51
Dill Mushroom Sauté, 52
Marjoram Rice Mix, 56
Lime Beans Mix, 56
White Beans Mix, 57
Veggie Mix, 60
Savoy Cabbage Mix, 68
Beef Dip, 81
Lamb and Zucchini Mix, 115
Salmon Salad, 132
Carrots Oatmeal, 13
Carrots Casserole, 20
Scallions Quinoa and Carrots Bowls, 26
Lamb and Onion Stew, 34
Pork Roast and Olives, 34
Beef and Celery Stew, 35
Chickpeas Stew, 36
Mushroom Stew, 38

Mustard Pork Chops and Carrots, 41
Beef Curry, 46
Chickpeas Stew, 47
Hot Zucchini Mix, 52
Carrots and Spinach Mix, 53
Orange Carrots Mix, 55
Garlic Carrots Mix, 63
Baby Carrots and Parsnips Mix, 65
Beets Salad, 74
Lentils Dip, 76
Apple and Carrot Dip, 79
Carrots Spread, 83
Turkey and Carrots, 102
Hot Salmon and Carrots, 127
Shrimp and Rice Mix, 131

CASHEW BUTTER
Granola Bowls, 21
Maple Pudding, 138

CASHEWS
Cashew Butter, 24
Berry Cream, 138

CAULIFLOWER
Cauliflower Casserole, 22
Roasted Beef and Cauliflower, 33
Balsamic Cauliflower, 50
Cauliflower and Almonds Mix, 53
Sweet Potato and Cauliflower Mix, 58
Cauliflower Mash, 60
Cauliflower and Potatoes Mix, 64
Brussels Sprouts and Cauliflower, 65
Cauliflower Spread, 70
Cauliflower Bites, 81
Cauliflower Dip, 83
Shrimp and Cauliflower Bowls, 135

CELERY
Beef and Celery Stew, 35
Roasted Beef and Cauliflower, 33
Chicken Soup, 36
Chickpeas Stew, 47
Italian Black Beans Mix, 50
White Beans Mix, 57

CHEESE (CHEDDAR)
Sausage and Potato Mix, 12
Veggie Hash Brown Mix, 13
Cauliflower and Eggs Bowls, 16
Broccoli Casserole, 17
Creamy Shrimp Bowls, 17
Chili Eggs Mix, 19
Zucchini and Cauliflower Eggs Mix, 26
Mushroom Quiche, 26

Scallions Quinoa and Carrots Bowls, 26
Ham Omelet, 27
Peas and Rice Bowls, 28
Asparagus Casserole, 28
Cheddar Potatoes Mix, 50

CHEESE (FETA)
Cheesy Eggs, 19

CHEESE (GOAT)
Baby Spinach Rice Mix, 27
Spinach Rice, 61

CHEESE (MOZZARELLA)
Thyme Hash Browns, 14
Spinach Frittata, 18
Mushroom Casserole, 21
Leek Casserole, 22
Baby Spinach Rice Mix, 27
Herbed Egg Scramble, 28
Artichoke Dip, 69
Lemon Shrimp Dip, 69
Salsa Beans Dip, 72
Hash Brown and Bacon Casserole, 13

CHEESE (PARMESAN)
Quinoa and Veggies Casserole, 16

CHEESE (SWISS)
Spinach Spread, 69

CHERRIES
Cherries and Cocoa Oats, 23
Farro Mix, 60
Cherry Bowls, 138
Almond and Cherries Pudding, 142
Cherry and Rhubarb Mix, 143

CHERRY JUICE
Cherry Bowls, 138

CHIA SEEDS
Chia Oatmeal, 14
Apple and Chia Mix, 15
Quinoa and Chia Pudding, 25
Chia and Orange Pudding, 139
Orange Bowls, 141
Chia and Avocado Pudding, 141
Strawberry and Orange Mix, 145
Tapioca and Chia Pudding, 149

CHICKEN
Sausage and Potato Mix, 12
Creamy Shrimp Bowls, 17
Peppers Rice Mix, 24

Baby Spinach Rice Mix, 27
Seafood Soup, 29
Sesame Salmon Bowls, 29
Garlic Shrimp and Spinach, 30
Ginger Salmon, 30
Creamy Cod Stew, 30
Sweet Potato and Clam Chowder, 31
Maple Chicken Mix, 31
Maple Chicken Mix, 31
Salsa Chicken, 31
Turkey and Mushrooms, 32
Indian Chicken and Tomato Mix, 32
Slow Cooked Thyme Chicken, 33
Tomato Pasta Mix, 35
Chickpeas Stew, 36
Chicken Soup, 36
Lime and Thyme Chicken, 37
Shrimp Gumbo, 37
Squash and Chicken Soup, 37
Squash and Chicken Soup, 37
Parsley Chicken Stew, 39
Mushroom Soup, 39
Creamy Potato Soup, 40
Chicken with Corn and Wild Rice, 40
Chicken with Corn and Wild Rice, 40
Chicken and Peach Mix, 41
Chicken and Peach Mix, 41
Chicken Drumsticks and Buffalo Sauce, 41
Chicken Drumsticks and Buffalo Sauce, 41
Artichoke Soup, 42
Chicken and Eggplant Stew, 42
Chicken and Rice, 45
Salmon Stew, 45
Chicken and Brussels Sprouts Mix, 46
Chicken and Brussels Sprouts Mix, 46
Chickpeas Stew, 47
Oregano Turkey Stew, 48
Garlic Risotto, 54
Marjoram Rice Mix, 56
Cabbage Mix, 58
Kale Mix, 59
Farro Mix, 60
Cumin Quinoa Pilaf, 60
Mint Farro Pilaf, 61
Parmesan Rice, 61
Spinach Rice, 61
Mango Rice, 62
Coconut Bok Choy, 62
Calamari Rings Bowls, 78
Chicken Salad, 79
Chicken Meatballs, 80
Lentils Hummus, 83
Garlic Chicken and Green Beans, 85
Garlic Chicken and Green Beans, 85
Oregano Turkey and Tomatoes, 85

Mustard Chicken Mix, 85
Lemon Turkey and Spinach, 86
Paprika Chicken and Artichokes, 86
Paprika Chicken and Artichokes, 86
Chives Chicken Wings, 86
Lime Chicken Mix, 87
Chicken and Olives, 87
Turkey, Tomato and Fennel Mix, 87
Chicken with Tomatoes and Eggplant Mix, 88
Chicken and Onions Mix, 88
Pesto Chicken Mix, 88
Ginger Turkey Mix, 89
Turkey and Plums Mix, 89
Creamy Turkey Mix, 89
Chicken and Apples Mix, 90
Chicken and Endives, 90
Basil Chicken Wings, 90
Chicken and Broccoli, 91
Rosemary Chicken, 91
Chicken Curry, 91
Balsamic Turkey, 91
Turkey and Scallions Mix, 92
Parsley Chicken Mix, 92
Parsley Chicken Mix, 92
Turkey Chili, 92
Masala Turkey, 93
Chicken and Beans, 93
Turkey and Corn, 93
Coriander Turkey Mix, 94
Dill Turkey and Peas, 94
Turkey with Rice, 94
Italian Turkey, 95
Duck and Mushrooms, 95
Turkey and Tomato Sauce, 95
Tomato Chicken and Chickpeas, 95
Turkey with Leeks and Radishes, 96
Coconut Turkey, 96
Hot Chicken and Zucchinis, 96
Hot Chicken and Zucchinis, 96
Turkey with Radishes, 97
Chives Duck, 97
Cilantro Chicken and Eggplant Mix, 97
Chicken with Brussels Sprouts, 98
Chicken and Mango Mix, 98
Turkey and Avocado, 98
Chicken and Peppers, 99
Chicken and Cabbage Mix, 99
Lime Turkey and Chard, 99
BBQ Turkey mix, 100
Chicken and Asparagus, 100
Chicken and Asparagus, 100
Lemon Turkey and Potatoes, 100
Turkey and Okra, 101
Mustard Duck Mix, 101
Orange Chicken Mix, 101

Turkey and Carrots, 102
Rosemary Chicken Thighs, 102
Turkey and Kidney Beans, 102
Coriander and Turmeric Chicken, 103
Garlic Turkey, 103
Cumin Chicken Mix, 103
Cumin Chicken Mix, 103
Chili Salmon, 120
Rosemary Shrimp, 120
Paprika Cod, 120
Spicy Tuna, 121
Ginger Tuna, 121
Chives Shrimp, 121
Coriander Salmon Mix, 121
Tuna and Green Beans, 122
Cod and Corn, 122
Turmeric Salmon, 122
Sea Bass and Chickpeas, 122
Creamy Shrimp, 123
Garlic Sea Bass, 124
Tuna and Brussels Sprouts, 124
Shrimp with Spinach, 124
Shrimp and Avocado, 124
Chives Mackerel, 125
Shrimp and Mango Mix, 125
Balsamic Tuna, 126
Lime Trout Mix, 126
Creamy Tuna and Scallions, 126
Cod and Mustard Sauce, 126
Shrimp and Pineapple Bowls, 127
Hot Salmon and Carrots, 127
Shrimp and Eggplant, 127
Sea Bass and Squash, 128
Italian Shrimp, 129
Basil Cod and Olives, 129
Tuna and Fennel, 129
Shrimp and Mushrooms, 129
Cod and Artichokes, 130
Salmon, Tomatoes and Green Beans, 130
Shrimp and Rice Mix, 131
Chives Mussels, 131
Calamari and Sauce, 132
Salmon Salad, 132
Walnut Tuna Mix, 132
Indian Shrimp, 133
Shrimp, Tomatoes and Kale, 133
Calamari Curry, 134
Balsamic Trout, 134
Shrimp, Salmon and Tomatoes Mix, 135
Shrimp and Cauliflower Bowls, 135
Cinnamon Trout, 136
Lime Shrimp, 120

CHICKPEAS
Chickpeas Spread, 71

CHICKPEAS (CANNED)
Paprika Pork and Chickpeas, 45
Chickpeas Stew, 47
Chickpeas Salsa, 73
Tomato Chicken and Chickpeas, 95
Sea Bass and Chickpeas, 122

CHIVES
Thyme Hash Browns, 14
Quinoa and Veggies Casserole, 16
Parmesan Quinoa, 17
Creamy Shrimp Bowls, 17
Chili Eggs Mix, 19
Eggs and Sweet Potato Mix, 23
Zucchini and Cauliflower Eggs Mix, 26
Mushroom Quiche, 26
Ham Omelet, 27
Herbed Egg Scramble, 28
Asparagus Casserole, 28
Seafood Soup, 29
Creamy Cod Stew, 30
Maple Chicken Mix, 31
Indian Chicken and Tomato Mix, 32
Chicken Soup, 36
Mushroom Soup, 39
Creamy Potato Soup, 40
Chicken with Corn and Wild Rice, 40
Pork Chili, 43
Pork and Mushroom Stew, 44
Pork and Tomatoes Mix, 44
Potato Stew, 44
Beef and Cabbage, 46
Beef and Artichokes Stew, 47
Veggie Soup, 48
Butter Green Beans, 51
Corn Sauté, 51
Tomato and Corn Mix, 51
Cauliflower and Almonds Mix, 53
Potatoes and Leeks Mix, 55
Cabbage and Onion Mix, 63
Garlic Carrots Mix, 63
Cauliflower and Potatoes Mix, 64
Paprika Green Beans and Zucchinis, 67
Mustard Brussels Sprouts, 67
Minty Peas and Tomatoes, 68
Squash Salsa, 70
Rice Snack Bowls, 70
Chickpeas Spread, 71
Corn Dip, 72
Tomato and Mushroom Salsa, 72
Lentils Salsa, 74
Broccoli Dip, 81
Zucchini Spread, 82
Eggplant Salsa, 82
Garlic Chicken and Green Beans, 85

Mustard Chicken Mix, 85
Chives Chicken Wings, 86
Chicken and Olives, 87
Chicken and Onions Mix, 88
Creamy Turkey Mix, 89
Chicken and Apples Mix, 90
Rosemary Chicken, 91
Balsamic Turkey, 91
Turkey and Scallions Mix, 92
Duck and Mushrooms, 95
Tomato Chicken and Chickpeas, 95
Hot Chicken and Zucchinis, 96
Chives Duck, 97
Chicken and Mango Mix, 98
Turkey and Avocado, 98
Lemon Turkey and Potatoes, 100
Turkey and Carrots, 102
Coriander and Turmeric Chicken, 103
Cumin Chicken Mix, 103
Beef and Zucchinis Mix, 104
Pork and Olives Mix, 104
Beef and Sauce, 105
Mustard Ribs, 106
Turmeric Lamb, 107
Chives Lamb, 108
Pork and Green Beans, 108
Pork and Eggplant Mix, 110
Lemon Lamb, 110
Beef and Endives, 113
Cumin Pork Chops, 114
Beef with Peas and Corn, 115
Lamb and Zucchini Mix, 115
Beef and Peppers, 116
Cinnamon Lamb, 116
Lamb and Kale, 116
Beef and Sprouts, 117
Balsamic Lamb Chops, 118
Creamy Beef, 119
Lime Shrimp, 120
Spicy Tuna, 121
Ginger Tuna, 121
Chives Shrimp, 121
Tuna and Green Beans, 122
Cod and Corn, 122
Turmeric Salmon, 122
Pesto Cod and Tomatoes, 123
Shrimp with Spinach, 124
Shrimp and Avocado, 124
Chives Mackerel, 125
Shrimp and Mango Mix, 125
Creamy Tuna and Scallions, 126
Cod and Mustard Sauce, 126
Lime Crab, 127
Hot Salmon and Carrots, 127
Shrimp and Eggplant, 127

Salmon and Peas, 128
Chili Shrimp and Zucchinis, 128
Italian Shrimp, 129
Basil Cod and Olives, 129
Shrimp and Mushrooms, 129
Chives Mussels, 131
Calamari and Sauce, 132
Salmon Salad, 132
Salmon and Strawberries Mix, 135
Cod and Broccoli, 136
Cinnamon Trout, 136

CHOCOLATE (DARK)
Chocolate Breakfast Bread, 20
Chocolate Mango Mix, 146

CLAMS (CANNED)
Sweet Potato and Clam Chowder, 31

COCONUT
Coconut Jam, 148

COCONUT CREAM
Granola Bowls, 21
Squash Bowls, 21
Apple Spread, 23
Cashew Butter, 24
Pumpkin and Berries Bowls, 24
Quinoa and Chia Pudding, 25
Cinnamon Squash, 58
Nuts Bowls, 75
Apple and Carrot Dip, 79
Sweet Potato Dip, 79
Spinach Dip, 83
Masala Turkey, 93
Coconut Turkey, 96
Mint Lamb Chops, 109
Walnut and Coconut Beef, 119
Coconut Mackerel, 128
Coconut Cream, 137
Mandarin Cream, 144
Cranberries Cream, 144
Cantaloupe Cream, 145
Coconut Jam, 148
Pears and Apples Bowls, 150
Creamy Rhubarb and Plums Bowls, 150
Ginger Cream, 151
Cherry and Rhubarb Mix, 143

COCONUT MILK
Coconut Quinoa, 12
Buttery Oatmeal, 14
Seafood Soup, 29
Sweet Potato and Clam Chowder, 31
Beef Curry, 46

Eggplant Curry, 47
Creamy Coconut Potatoes, 53
Red Curry Veggie Mix, 54
Creamy Beans, 57
Sweet Potato and Cauliflower Mix, 58
Curry Pork Meatballs, 78
Carrots Spread, 83
Calamari Curry, 134
Coconut Cream, 137
Strawberry Cake, 140
Melon Pudding, 151

COCONUT OIL
Coconut Bok Choy, 62
Avocado Cake, 137
Berry Cream, 138
Maple Pudding, 138
Chia and Orange Pudding, 139
Raisin Cookies, 140
Chia and Avocado Pudding, 141
Yogurt Cheesecake, 145
Cinnamon and Chocolate Peaches, 148

COD
Pesto Cod and Tomatoes, 123
Creamy Cod Stew, 30
Paprika Cod Sticks, 77
Paprika Cod, 120
Cod and Corn, 122
Parsley Cod, 123
Orange Cod, 123
Dill Cod, 125
Cod and Mustard Sauce, 126
Basil Cod and Olives, 129
Cod and Artichokes, 130
Cod and Broccoli, 136

CORN
Beans Breakfast Bowls, 25
Beans Chili, 38
Chicken with Corn and Wild Rice, 40
Corn Sauté, 51
Tomato and Corn Mix, 51
Rice and Corn, 64
Thyme Mushrooms and Corn, 66
Stuffed Peppers Platter, 72
Corn Dip, 72
Turkey and Corn, 93
Turkey with Olives and Corn, 94
Beef and Corn Mix, 106
Beef with Peas and Corn, 115
Cod and Corn, 122

CORN (CANNED)
Italian Black Beans Mix, 50

CRAB
Crab Dip, 69
Lime Crab, 127

CRANBERRIES
Cranberry Maple Oatmeal, 20
Pork and Cranberries, 34
Cranberries Cream, 144
Berries Salad, 150

CREAM
Thyme Hash Browns, 14
Cocoa and Berries Quinoa, 15
Parmesan Quinoa, 17
Creamy Shrimp Bowls, 17
Potato and Ham Mix, 18
Chili Eggs Mix, 19
Ginger Apple Bowls, 21
Mushroom Quiche, 26
Scallions Quinoa and Carrots Bowls, 26
Peppers and Eggs Mix, 27
Herbed Egg Scramble, 28
Peas and Rice Bowls, 28
Asparagus Casserole, 28
Creamy Cod Stew, 30
Creamy Brisket, 39
Pork Chops and Butter Sauce, 40
Cheddar Potatoes Mix, 50
Creamy Beans, 57
Zucchini Mix, 59
Buttery Spinach, 59
Cauliflower Mash, 60
Italian Eggplant, 62
Parmesan Spinach Mix, 68
Spinach Spread, 69
Artichoke Dip, 69
Lemon Shrimp Dip, 69
Cauliflower Spread, 70
Mushroom Dip, 71
Spinach Dip, 71
Dill Potato Salad, 71
Dill Potato Salad, 71
Creamy Mushroom Spread, 73
Almond Spread, 75
Onion Dip, 75
Spinach and Walnuts Dip, 77
Broccoli Dip, 81
Beef Dip, 81
Zucchini Spread, 82
Carrots Spread, 83
Cauliflower Dip, 83
Lentils Hummus, 83
Artichoke Dip, 84
Creamy Turkey Mix, 89
Turkey and Corn, 93

Duck and Mushrooms, 95
Beef and Corn Mix, 106
Beef and Red Onions Mix, 107
Creamy Lamb, 111
Beef and Capers Sauce, 111
Creamy Beef, 119
Creamy Shrimp, 123
Creamy Tuna and Scallions, 126
Cod and Mustard Sauce, 126
Calamari and Sauce, 132
Berry Cream, 138
Cinnamon Peach Mix, 140
Orange Bowls, 141
Almond and Cherries Pudding, 142
Vanilla Peach Cream, 142
Apricot and Peaches Cream, 143
Pomegranate and Mango Bowls, 144
Buttery Pineapple, 144
Lemon Peach Mix, 146
Pear Cream, 147
Apple, Avocado and Mango Bowls, 148
Cinnamon and Chocolate Peaches, 148
Coconut Jam, 148
Bread and Berries Pudding, 149
Almonds, Walnuts and Mango Bowls, 149
Berries Salad, 150
Corn Dip, 72
Chives Duck, 97
Greek Cream, 151
Chocolate Mango Mix, 146

CREAM CHEESE
Cinnamon French Toast, 13
Creamy Shrimp Bowls, 17
Worcestershire Beef Mix, 35
Creamy Potato Soup, 40
Chicken with Corn and Wild Rice, 40
Crab Dip, 69
Lemon Shrimp Dip, 69
Corn Dip, 72
Tomato and Mushroom Salsa, 72
Broccoli Dip, 81
Beef and Sauce, 105
Yogurt Cheesecake, 145
Greek Cream Cheese Pudding, 150

CURRY PASTE (YELLOW)
Beef Curry, 46
Chicken Curry, 91
Calamari Curry, 134

DATES
Dates and Rice Pudding, 149

DUCK
Duck and Mushrooms, 95
Chives Duck, 97
Mustard Duck Mix, 101

EGGPLANT
Pork and Eggplant Casserole, 23
Turmeric Lentils Stew, 43
Eggplant Curry, 47
Veggie Soup, 48
Masala Beef Mix, 49
Butternut Squash and Eggplant Mix, 52
Red Curry Veggie Mix, 54
Veggie Mix, 60
Veggie Medley, 66
Mushroom Dip, 71
Eggplant Salsa, 75
Eggplant Salsa, 82
Pork and Eggplant Mix, 110
Shrimp and Eggplant, 127
Salmon Salad, 132
Chicken and Eggplant Stew, 42
Italian Eggplant, 62
Eggplant Salad, 76
Chicken with Tomatoes and Eggplant Mix, 88
Cilantro Chicken and Eggplant Mix, 97

EGGS
Turkey Meatballs, 76
Hash Brown and Bacon Casserole, 13
Cinnamon French Toast, 13
Thyme Hash Browns, 14
Quinoa and Veggies Casserole, 16
Cauliflower and Eggs Bowls, 16
Sausage and Eggs Mix, 16
Broccoli Casserole, 17
Hot Eggs Mix, 18
Potato and Ham Mix, 18
Spinach Frittata, 18
Chili Eggs Mix, 19
Cheesy Eggs, 19
Tomato and Zucchini Eggs Mix, 19
Chocolate Breakfast Bread, 20
Carrots Casserole, 20
Mushroom Casserole, 21
Lamb and Eggs Mix, 22
Cauliflower Casserole, 22
Beef Meatloaf, 22
Leek Casserole, 22
Eggs and Sweet Potato Mix, 23
Pork and Eggplant Casserole, 23
Basil Sausage and Broccoli Mix, 25
Zucchini and Cauliflower Eggs Mix, 26
Mushroom Quiche, 26
Scallions Quinoa and Carrots Bowls, 26

Ham Omelet, 27
Peppers and Eggs Mix, 27
Herbed Egg Scramble, 28
Asparagus Casserole, 28
Curry Pork Meatballs, 78
Chicken Meatballs, 80
Avocado Cake, 137
Raisin Cookies, 140
Chia and Avocado Pudding, 141
Almond and Cherries Pudding, 142
Yogurt Cheesecake, 145
Bread and Berries Pudding, 149
Tapioca and Chia Pudding, 149
Greek Cream Cheese Pudding, 150
Ginger Cream, 151
Paprika Cod Sticks, 77

ENDIVES
Chicken and Endives, 90
Beef and Endives, 113

FENNEL
Fennel Soup, 41
Turkey, Tomato and Fennel Mix, 87
Lamb and Fennel Mix, 111
Tuna and Fennel, 129

FIGS
Turkey and Figs, 32

GARAM MASALA
Pork and Eggplant Casserole, 23
Beans Salad, 24
Indian Chicken and Tomato Mix, 32
Chicken and Rice, 45
Chickpeas Stew, 47
Masala Beef Mix, 49
Spinach Mix, 57
Buttery Spinach, 59
Rice and Corn, 64
Artichoke Dip, 69
Chickpeas Salsa, 73
Sweet Potato Dip, 79
Spinach Dip, 83
Garlic Chicken and Green Beans, 85
Creamy Turkey Mix, 89
Masala Turkey, 93
Dill Turkey and Peas, 94
Chicken with Brussels Sprouts, 98
Chicken and Asparagus, 100
Cumin Chicken Mix, 103
Beef and Sauce, 105
Mint Lamb Chops, 109
Masala Beef and Sauce, 112
Tuna and Green Beans, 122

Creamy Shrimp, 123
Lime Trout Mix, 126
Coconut Mackerel, 128
Indian Shrimp, 133
Lemon Turkey and Spinach, 86
Rosemary Chicken Thighs, 102

GRANOLA
Granola Bowls, 21

GRAPES
Vanilla Grapes Mix, 143

HAM
Potato and Ham Mix, 18
Ham Omelet, 27

HAZELNUTS
Nuts Bowls, 75

HONEY
Cinnamon French Toast, 13
Ginger Raisins Oatmeal, 15
Pumpkin and Quinoa Mix, 15
Honey Lamb Roast, 35
Chicken Drumsticks and Buffalo Sauce, 41
Mustard Pork Chops and Carrots, 41
Basil Chicken Wings, 90
Pork and Soy Sauce Mix, 104
Honey Pork Chops, 107
Pear Cream, 147
Bread and Quinoa Pudding, 151
Melon Pudding, 151

KALE
Mushroom Casserole, 21
Kale Mix, 59
Lemon Kale Mix, 65
Cabbage and Kale Mix, 66
Veggie Medley, 66
Lamb and Kale, 116
Shrimp, Tomatoes and Kale, 133

LAMB
Lamb and Eggs Mix, 22
Lamb and Onion Stew, 34
Honey Lamb Roast, 35
Turmeric Lamb, 107
Chili Lamb, 107
Chives Lamb, 108
Mint Lamb Chops, 109
Lamb and Potatoes, 109
Lamb and Tomatoes Mix, 110
Lemon Lamb, 110
Rosemary Lamb with Olives, 110

Nutmeg Lamb and Squash, 111
Lamb and Fennel Mix, 111
Creamy Lamb, 111
Lamb and Cabbage, 112
Balsamic Lamb Mix, 112
Lamb and Lime Zucchinis, 113
Parsley and Chili Lamb, 114
Paprika Lamb, 114
Lamb with Capers, 115
Lamb and Zucchini Mix, 115
Beef and Peppers, 116
Cayenne Lamb Mix, 116
Cinnamon Lamb, 116
Lamb and Kale, 116
Green Curry Lamb, 117
Oregano Lamb, 117
Pesto Lamb Chops, 118
Balsamic Lamb Chops, 118

LEEKS
Leek Casserole, 22
Fennel Soup, 41
Turkey with Leeks and Radishes, 96
Rosemary Leeks, 54
Potatoes and Leeks Mix, 55

LEMON
Salmon and Strawberries Mix, 135
Lemon Jam, 146
Cashew Butter, 24
Masala Beef Mix, 49
Balsamic Cauliflower, 50
Lemon Artichokes, 62
Garlic Carrots Mix, 63
Lemon Kale Mix, 65
Squash Salsa, 70
Apple and Carrot Dip, 79
Walnuts Bowls, 81
Turkey and Scallions Mix, 92
Lemon Lamb, 110
Maple Pudding, 138
Strawberry Cake, 140
Peaches and Wine Sauce, 143
Cantaloupe Cream, 145
Lemon Peach Mix, 146
Rhubarb Stew, 146
Strawberry and Blackberry Jam, 147
Pear Cream, 147
Bread and Berries Pudding, 149
Tapioca and Chia Pudding, 149

LEMON JUICE
Apple Spread, 23
Sesame Salmon Bowls, 29
Turkey and Walnuts, 33

Chicken Soup, 36
Veggie Soup, 48
Masala Beef Mix, 49
Carrots and Spinach Mix, 53
Parmesan Rice, 61
Garlic Carrots Mix, 63
Asparagus Mix, 64
Lemon Kale Mix, 65
Lemon Shrimp Dip, 69
Squash Salsa, 70
Chickpeas Spread, 71
Lentils Dip, 76
Chicken Salad, 79
Eggplant Salsa, 82
Cauliflower Dip, 83
Turkey and Scallions Mix, 92
Lemon Turkey and Potatoes, 100
Mustard Duck Mix, 101
Oregano Beef, 108
Lemon Lamb, 110
Lamb and Fennel Mix, 111
Rosemary Beef, 114
Lime Trout Mix, 126
Salmon and Peas, 128
Calamari Curry, 134
Cinnamon Apples, 137
Maple Pudding, 138
Vanilla Grapes Mix, 143
Pomegranate and Mango Bowls, 144
Cantaloupe Cream, 145
Lemon Jam, 146
Lemon Peach Mix, 146
Rhubarb Stew, 146
Strawberry and Blackberry Jam, 147
Pear Cream, 147
Rhubarb Jam, 147
Apricot Marmalade, 147
Apple, Avocado and Mango Bowls, 148
Coconut Jam, 148
Creamy Rhubarb and Plums Bowls, 150
Ginger Cream, 151
Slow Cooked Thyme Chicken, 33
Chicken Drumsticks and Buffalo Sauce, 41
Chicken and Eggplant Stew, 42
Pesto Pork Shanks, 44
Lemon Artichokes, 62
Cauliflower Spread, 70
Chickpeas Salsa, 73
Eggplant Salad, 76
Apple and Carrot Dip, 79
Sweet Potato Dip, 79
Lentils Hummus, 83
Artichoke Dip, 84
Mustard Chicken Mix, 85
Lemon Turkey and Spinach, 86

Balsamic Turkey, 91
Parsley Chicken Mix, 92
Dill Cod, 125

LENTILS
Lentils Soup, 36

LENTILS (CANNED)
Hot Lentils, 55
Lentils Salsa, 74
Lentils Dip, 76
Lentils Hummus, 83
Pork and Lentils, 112
Turmeric Lentils Stew, 43

LIME
Lime Chicken Mix, 87
Blueberries Jam, 141
Peppers Rice Mix, 24
Lime and Thyme Chicken, 37
Mustard Pork Chops and Carrots, 41
Eggplant Curry, 47
Crab Dip, 69
Chicken and Olives, 87
Lime Turkey and Chard, 99
Turkey and Okra, 101
Coriander and Turmeric Chicken, 103
Cider Beef Mix, 106
Masala Beef and Sauce, 112
Lime Pork Chops, 115
Lime Trout Mix, 126
Chives Mussels, 131
Indian Shrimp, 133
Berries Salad, 150
Melon Pudding, 151

LIME JUICE
Lentils Soup, 36
Squash and Chicken Soup, 37
Mustard Pork Chops and Carrots, 41
Black Beans Mix, 55
Lime Chicken Mix, 87
Chicken Curry, 91
Masala Turkey, 93
Lime Turkey and Chard, 99
Turkey and Okra, 101
Coriander and Turmeric Chicken, 103
Honey Pork Chops, 107
Pork and Green Beans, 108
Masala Beef and Sauce, 112
Lamb and Lime Zucchinis, 113
Beef and Peas, 113
Parsley and Chili Lamb, 114
Beef with Peas and Corn, 115
Lime Pork Chops, 115

Lime Shrimp, 120
Ginger Tuna, 121
Coriander Salmon Mix, 121
Shrimp and Mango Mix, 125
Lime Crab, 127
Shrimp and Eggplant, 127
Italian Shrimp, 129
Basil Cod and Olives, 129
Shrimp and Mushrooms, 129
Salmon and Berries, 130
Cod and Artichokes, 130
Shrimp and Red Chard, 131
Chives Mussels, 131
Calamari and Sauce, 132
Indian Shrimp, 133
Shrimp, Tomatoes and Kale, 133
Trout Bowls, 134
Oregano Shrimp Bowls, 134
Vanilla Pears, 137
Chia and Avocado Pudding, 141
Berries Salad, 150
Lime and Thyme Chicken, 37
Crab Dip, 69
Chicken and Olives, 87
Pork and Olives Mix, 104
Cod and Corn, 122
Parsley Cod, 123
Shrimp and Avocado, 124
Chives Mackerel, 125

MACADAMIA NUTS
Macadamia Nuts Snack, 77

MACKEREL
Chives Mackerel, 125
Coconut Mackerel, 128

MANDARINS
Mandarin Cream, 144

MANGO
Mango Rice, 62
Chicken and Mango Mix, 98
Pork Chops and Mango Mix, 104
Shrimp and Mango Mix, 125
Pomegranate and Mango Bowls, 144
Maple Plums and Mango, 145
Chocolate Mango Mix, 146
Apple, Avocado and Mango Bowls, 148
Almonds, Walnuts and Mango Bowls, 149

MAPLE SYRUP
Coconut Quinoa, 12
Maple Banana Oatmeal, 14
Apple and Chia Mix, 15

Chocolate Breakfast Bread, 20
Cranberry Maple Oatmeal, 20
Pumpkin and Berries Bowls, 24
Maple Chicken Mix, 31
Pork and Cranberries, 34
Mustard Brussels Sprouts, 54
Maple Beef, 113
Almond Rice Pudding, 138
Cherry Bowls, 138
Berry Cream, 138
Maple Pudding, 138
Vanilla Peach Cream, 142
Maple Plums and Mango, 145

MELON
Melon Pudding, 151

MILK
Cheesy Eggs, 19
Chocolate Breakfast Bread, 20
Mashed Potatoes, 56

MUSHROOMS
Turkey and Mushrooms, 32
Beef and Celery Stew, 35
Mushroom Soup, 39
Pork and Mushroom Stew, 44
Balsamic Beef Stew, 46
Tomato and Mushroom Salsa, 72
Creamy Mushroom Spread, 73
Chicken Salad, 79

MUSHROOMS (BELLA)
Mushroom Quiche, 26

MUSHROOMS (BROWN)
Parsley Mushroom Mix, 58

MUSHROOMS (BUTTON)
Red Curry Veggie Mix, 54

MUSHROOMS (PORTOBELLO)
Stuffed Mushrooms, 76

MUSHROOMS (WHITE)
Thyme Mushrooms and Corn, 66
Veggie Hash Brown Mix, 13
Mushroom Casserole, 21
Mushroom Stew, 38
Beans and Mushroom Stew, 42
Dill Mushroom Sauté, 52
Sweet Potato and Cauliflower Mix, 58
Mushroom Dip, 71
Beef Dip, 82
Cauliflower Dip, 83

Mushroom Salsa, 84
Duck and Mushrooms, 95
Shrimp and Mushrooms, 129

NUTMEG
Almond and Quinoa Bowls, 20
Granola Bowls, 21
Pumpkin and Berries Bowls, 24
Ginger Salmon, 30
Pork and Mushroom Stew, 44
Beets Salad, 74
Apple and Carrot Dip, 79
Nutmeg Lamb and Squash, 111
Cinnamon Apples, 137
Creamy Berries Mix, 139
Plums Stew, 139
Chia and Avocado Pudding, 141
Bread and Quinoa Pudding, 151

OATS
Cinnamon Berries Oatmeal, 12
Carrots Oatmeal, 13
Maple Banana Oatmeal, 14
Chia Oatmeal, 14
Buttery Oatmeal, 14
Ginger Raisins Oatmeal, 15
Peach, Vanilla and Oats Mix, 18
Cranberry Maple Oatmeal, 20
Cherries and Cocoa Oats, 23

OKRA
Balsamic Okra Mix, 63
Minty Peas and Tomatoes, 68
Turkey and Okra, 101
Pork and Okra, 108

ONION
Veggie Soup, 48
Lentils Salsa, 74

ONION (PEARL)
Italian Turkey, 95

ONION (RED)
Sausage and Eggs Mix, 16
Broccoli Casserole, 17
Carrots Casserole, 20
Mushroom Casserole, 21
Lamb and Eggs Mix, 22
Cauliflower Casserole, 22
Beef Meatloaf, 22
Eggs and Sweet Potato Mix, 23
Pork and Eggplant Casserole, 23
Asparagus Casserole, 28
Shrimp Stew, 29

Turkey and Mushrooms, 32
Indian Chicken and Tomato Mix, 32
Turkey and Figs, 32
Lamb and Onion Stew, 34
Beef Stew, 34
Beef and Celery Stew, 35
Tomato Pasta Mix, 35
Chickpeas Stew, 36
Lentils Soup, 36
Chicken Soup, 36
Shrimp Gumbo, 37
Mushroom Stew, 38
Fennel Soup, 41
Beans and Mushroom Stew, 42
Chicken and Eggplant Stew, 42
Turmeric Lentils Stew, 43
Pork Chili, 43
Pork and Mushroom Stew, 44
Pesto Pork Shanks, 44
Potato Stew, 44
Chicken and Rice, 45
Salmon Stew, 45
Paprika Pork and Chickpeas, 45
Balsamic Beef Stew, 46
Beef Curry, 46
Chicken and Brussels Sprouts Mix, 46
Chickpeas Stew, 47
Beef and Artichokes Stew, 47
Beef Soup, 48
Oregano Turkey Stew, 48
Masala Beef Mix, 49
Italian Black Beans Mix, 50
Sage Peas, 51
Tomato and Corn Mix, 51
Dill Mushroom Sauté, 52
Butternut Squash and Eggplant Mix, 52
Barley Mix, 56
Parmesan Rice, 61
Cabbage and Onion Mix, 63
Garlic Carrots Mix, 63
Curry Broccoli Mix, 63
Asparagus Mix, 64
Lemon Kale Mix, 65
Cabbage and Kale Mix, 66
Savoy Cabbage Mix, 68
Rice Snack Bowls, 70
Dill Potato Salad, 71
Stuffed Peppers Platter, 72
Stuffed Mushrooms, 76
Curry Pork Meatballs, 78
Chicken Salad, 79
Garlic Chicken and Green Beans, 85
Turkey, Tomato and Fennel Mix, 87
Chicken with Tomatoes and Eggplant Mix, 88
Creamy Turkey Mix, 89

Chicken and Apples Mix, 90
Turkey Chili, 92
Chicken and Beans, 93
Turkey and Corn, 93
Turkey with Olives and Corn, 94
Tomato Chicken and Chickpeas, 95
Turkey with Leeks and Radishes, 96
Hot Chicken and Zucchinis, 96
Chicken with Brussels Sprouts, 98
Lemon Turkey and Potatoes, 100
Mustard Duck Mix, 101
Pork and Olives Mix, 104
Beef with Spinach, 105
Pork and Chilies Mix, 105
Turmeric Lamb, 107
Pork and Okra, 108
Oregano Beef, 108
Mint Lamb Chops, 109
Lemon Lamb, 110
Creamy Lamb, 111
Lamb and Lime Zucchinis, 113
Cayenne Lamb Mix, 116
Cinnamon Lamb, 116
Beef and Sprouts, 117
Beef with Green Beans and Cilantro, 118
Creamy Beef, 119
Ginger Tuna, 121
Turmeric Salmon, 122
Tuna and Brussels Sprouts, 124
Basil Cod and Olives, 129
Tuna and Fennel, 129
Shrimp and Rice Mix, 131
Shrimp and Red Chard, 131
Salmon Salad, 132
Walnut Tuna Mix, 132
Cod and Broccoli, 136
Chicken and Onions Mix, 88
Beef and Red Onions Mix, 107

ONION (YELLOW)
Veggie Hash Brown Mix, 13
Cauliflower and Eggs Bowls, 16
Hot Eggs Mix, 18
Beans Breakfast Bowls, 25
Basil Sausage and Broccoli Mix, 25
Ham Omelet, 27
Seafood Soup, 29
Sweet Potato and Clam Chowder, 31
Salsa Chicken, 31
Indian Chicken and Tomato Mix, 32
Slow Cooked Thyme Chicken, 33
Pork Roast and Olives, 34
Squash and Chicken Soup, 37
Pork Soup, 38
Beans Chili, 38

Mushroom Soup, 39
Creamy Potato Soup, 40
Chicken with Corn and Wild Rice, 40
Mixed Pork and Beans, 40
Artichoke Soup, 42
Carrots and Spinach Mix, 53
Cauliflower and Almonds Mix, 53
Spinach Mix, 57
Kale Mix, 59
Tomato and Mushroom Salsa, 72
Chickpeas Salsa, 73
Bulgur and Beans Salsa, 73
Turkey Meatballs, 76
Peppers Salsa, 84
Chicken and Broccoli, 91
Chicken Curry, 91
Coconut Turkey, 96
Chives Duck, 97
Cumin Chicken Mix, 103
Pork and Beans Mix, 105
Cider Beef Mix, 106
Pork and Lentils, 112
Lamb and Kale, 116
Onion Dip, 75
Sausage and Potato Mix, 12

ONIONS (GREEN)
Mustard Short Ribs, 39
Corn Sauté, 51
Dill Mushroom Sauté, 52
Marjoram Rice Mix, 56
Mint Farro Pilaf, 61
Minty Peas and Tomatoes, 68
Artichoke Dip, 69
Crab Dip, 69
Salsa Beans Dip, 72
Turkey with Rice, 94

ORANGE JUICE
Ginger Raisins Oatmeal, 15
Sage Sweet Potatoes, 53
Orange Carrots Mix, 55
Orange Chicken Mix, 101
Orange Cod, 123
Salmon and Strawberries Mix, 135
Strawberry and Orange Mix, 145
Maple Plums and Mango, 145
Cinnamon Plums, 142

ORANGES
Lemon Jam, 146
Ginger Raisins Oatmeal, 15
Orange Carrots Mix, 55
Strawberry and Orange Mix, 145
Maple Plums and Mango, 145

Orange Chicken Mix, 101
Chia and Orange Pudding, 139
Orange Bowls, 141
Vanilla Grapes Mix, 143

PARMESAN
Parmesan Quinoa, 17
Tomato and Zucchini Eggs Mix, 19
Parmesan Rice, 61
Parmesan Spinach Mix, 68

PASTE (TAHINI)
Chickpeas Spread, 71
Beans Spread, 70
Mushroom Dip, 71
Lentils Dip, 76
Zucchini Spread, 82
Cauliflower Dip, 83
Lentils Hummus, 83

PASTE CURRY (GREEN)
Curry Pork Meatballs, 78
Green Curry Lamb, 117

PASTE CURRY (RED)
Eggplant Curry, 47
Red Curry Veggie Mix, 54
Sweet Potato and Cauliflower Mix, 58
Curry Broccoli Mix, 63

PEACHES
Peach, Vanilla and Oats Mix, 18
Chicken and Peach Mix, 41
Cinnamon Peach Mix, 140
Vanilla Peach Cream, 142
Peaches and Wine Sauce, 143
Apricot and Peaches Cream, 143
Lemon Peach Mix, 146
Cinnamon and Chocolate Peaches, 148

PEANUTS (GREEN)
Seasoned Peanuts, 80

PEARS
Buttery Oatmeal, 14
Vanilla Pears, 137
Ginger Pears Mix, 140
Pear Cream, 147
Pears and Apples Bowls, 150

PEAS
Peas and Rice Bowls, 28
Sage Peas, 51
Beef and Peas, 113
Beef with Peas and Corn, 115

PEAS (GREEN)
Dill Turkey and Peas, 94

PEAS (SNAP)
Salmon and Peas, 128

PECANS
Nuts Bowls, 75
Cinnamon Pecans Snack, 80
Chia and Orange Pudding, 139

PEPPER (CAYENNE)
Chicken Soup, 36
Pork Chili, 43
Nuts Bowls, 75
Lentils Dip, 76
Chicken and Peppers, 99
Cayenne Lamb Mix, 116
Spicy Tuna, 121
Cinnamon Trout, 136
Indian Chicken and Tomato Mix, 32

PEPPER (CHILI)
Beef Soup, 48
Chicken Salad, 79
Shrimp and Avocado, 124
Cinnamon Trout, 136

PEPPER (JALAPENO)
Beef Soup, 48
Garlic Shrimp and Spinach, 30
Cabbage and Onion Mix, 63

PEPPER CHILI
Turkey Chili, 92
Hot Chicken and Zucchinis, 96
Chickpeas Stew, 36
Shrimp Gumbo, 37
Chili Salmon, 120
Parsley and Chili Lamb, 114

PEPPER CHILI (GREEN)
Chili Eggs Mix, 19
Broccoli Dip, 81
Chili Lamb, 107
Garlic Sea Bass, 124
Chili Shrimp and Zucchinis, 128

PEPPER CHILI GREEN (CANNED)
Peppers Rice Mix, 24
Squash and Chicken Soup, 37
Pork and Chilies Mix, 105
Beans and Mushroom Stew, 42
Bulgur and Beans Salsa, 73
Chicken and Beans, 93

PEPPER FLAKES (HOT)
Italian Eggplant, 62

PEPPER FLAKES (RED)
Shrimp Stew, 29
Turkey and Mushrooms, 32
Chickpeas Stew, 36
Artichoke Soup, 42
Pork Chili, 43
Veggie Mix, 60
Garlic Squash Mix, 64
Lentils Salsa, 74
Chicken Meatballs, 80
Chicken with Tomatoes and Eggplant Mix, 88
BBQ Turkey mix, 100
Spicy Tuna, 121

PINE NUTS
Black Beans Mix, 55
Rice Snack Bowls, 70
Beef Dip, 82
Parsley Chicken Mix, 92

PINEAPPLE
Pineapple and Tofu Salsa, 73
Shrimp and Pineapple Bowls, 127
Buttery Pineapple, 144

PINEAPPLE JUICE
Pineapple and Tofu Salsa, 73

PISTACHIOS
Carrots and Spinach Mix, 53

PLUMS
Turkey and Plums Mix, 89
Plums Stew, 139
Cinnamon Plums, 142
Maple Plums and Mango, 145
Creamy Rhubarb and Plums Bowls, 150

POMEGRANATE
Pomegranate and Mango Bowls, 144

PORK
Pork and Eggplant Casserole, 23
Soy Pork Chops, 33
Pork and Cranberries, 34
Pork Roast and Olives, 34
Pork Soup, 38
Mixed Pork and Beans, 40
Pork Chops and Butter Sauce, 40
Mustard Pork Chops and Carrots, 41
Pork Chili, 43
Cinnamon Pork Ribs, 43

Pork and Mushroom Stew, 44
Pork and Tomatoes Mix, 44
Pesto Pork Shanks, 44
Paprika Pork and Chickpeas, 45
Curry Pork Meatballs, 78
Pork Chops and Mango Mix, 104
Pork and Olives Mix, 104
Pork and Soy Sauce Mix, 104
Pork and Beans Mix, 105
Pork and Chilies Mix, 105
Tarragon Pork Chops, 106
Honey Pork Chops, 107
Pork and Okra, 108
Pork and Green Beans, 108
Pork and Eggplant Mix, 110
Pork and Lentils, 112
Cumin Pork Chops, 114
Lime Pork Chops, 115

POTATO
Seafood Soup, 29
Sweet Potato and Clam Chowder, 31
Salmon Stew, 45
Red Curry Veggie Mix, 54
Sausage and Potato Mix, 12
Eggs and Sweet Potato Mix, 23
Potato Stew, 44
Veggie Soup, 48
Cheddar Potatoes Mix, 50
Creamy Coconut Potatoes, 53
Sage Sweet Potatoes, 53
Potatoes and Leeks Mix, 55
Mashed Potatoes, 56
Sweet Potato and Cauliflower Mix, 58
Bacon Potatoes Mix, 59
Cauliflower and Potatoes Mix, 64
Tarragon Sweet Potatoes, 67
Dill Potato Salad, 71
Sweet Potato Dip, 79
Lemon Turkey and Potatoes, 100
Lamb and Potatoes, 109
Veggie Mix, 60

POTATOES (RED)
Potato and Ham Mix, 18
Creamy Potato Soup, 40
Chicken with Corn and Wild Rice, 40

PUMPKIN
Pumpkin and Berries Bowls, 24
Pumpkin and Quinoa Mix, 15
Potatoes and Leeks Mix, 55

QUINOA
Coconut Quinoa, 12

Pumpkin and Quinoa Mix, 15
Cocoa and Berries Quinoa, 15
Quinoa and Veggies Casserole, 16
Parmesan Quinoa, 17
Almond and Quinoa Bowls, 20
Quinoa and Chia Pudding, 25
Scallions Quinoa and Carrots Bowls, 26
Cumin Quinoa Pilaf, 60
Quinoa Pudding, 141
Bread and Quinoa Pudding, 151

RADISHES
Turkey with Leeks and Radishes, 96
Turkey with Radishes, 97

RAISINS
Coconut Quinoa, 12
Ginger Raisins Oatmeal, 15
Rice Snack Bowls, 70
Raisin Cookies, 140

RHUBARB
Cherry and Rhubarb Mix, 143
Rhubarb Stew, 146
Rhubarb Jam, 147
Creamy Rhubarb and Plums Bowls, 150

RICE
Peppers Rice Mix, 24
Parmesan Rice, 61
Mango Rice, 62

RICE (ARBORIO)
Saffron Risotto, 61
Spinach Rice, 61

RICE (BROWN)
Rice Snack Bowls, 70

RICE (WHITE)
Stuffed Peppers Platter, 72
Almond Rice Pudding, 138
Maple Pudding, 138
Dates and Rice Pudding, 149
Melon Pudding, 151

RICE (WILD)
Peas and Rice Bowls, 28
Chicken with Corn and Wild Rice, 40
Chicken and Rice, 45
Garlic Risotto, 54
Marjoram Rice Mix, 56
Rice and Corn, 64
Rice Snack Bowls, 70
Turkey with Rice, 94

Shrimp and Rice Mix, 131

SALMON
Seafood Soup, 29
Sesame Salmon Bowls, 29
Ginger Salmon, 30
Salmon Stew, 45
Salmon Bites, 77
Chili Salmon, 120
Coriander Salmon Mix, 121
Turmeric Salmon, 122
Hot Salmon and Carrots, 127
Salmon and Peas, 128
Salmon and Berries, 130
Salmon, Tomatoes and Green Beans, 130
Salmon Salad, 132
Salmon and Strawberries Mix, 135
Shrimp, Salmon and Tomatoes Mix, 135

SALSA
Beans Salad, 24
Peppers Rice Mix, 24
Salsa Chicken, 31
Salmon Stew, 45
Salsa Beans Dip, 72
Bulgur and Beans Salsa, 73
Lentils Salsa, 74
Eggplant Salsa, 75
Eggplant Salad, 76
Shrimp Salad, 78
Chicken Salad, 79
Spinach, Walnuts and Calamari Salad, 80
Beef Dip, 82
Eggplant Salsa, 82
Peppers Salsa, 84
Mushroom Salsa, 84
Chicken Meatballs, 80

SAUCE (BBQ)
Mustard Short Ribs, 39
Bbq Beans, 57
BBQ Turkey mix, 100

SAUCE (CHILI)
Tacos, 74
Salmon Bites, 77

SAUCE (HOT)
Beans Breakfast Bowls, 25
Creamy Beans, 57
Beef Dip, 81

SAUCE (SRIRACHA)
Sweet Potato and Cauliflower Mix, 58
Beef Dip, 81

SAUCE (TOMATO)
Maple Chicken Mix, 31
Turkey and Figs, 32
Roasted Beef and Cauliflower, 33
Lamb and Onion Stew, 34
Pork Roast and Olives, 34
Beef Stew, 34
Beef and Celery Stew, 35
Lime and Thyme Chicken, 37
Shrimp Gumbo, 37
Mushroom Stew, 38
Parsley Chicken Stew, 39
Chickpeas Stew, 47
Beef and Artichokes Stew, 47
Sage Peas, 51
Tomato and Corn Mix, 51
Dill Mushroom Sauté, 52
Rosemary Leeks, 54
Veggie Mix, 60
Garlic Carrots Mix, 63
Cauliflower and Potatoes Mix, 64
Veggie Medley, 66
Paprika Green Beans and Zucchinis, 67
Stuffed Peppers Platter, 72
Tomato and Mushroom Salsa, 72
Stuffed Mushrooms, 76
Cauliflower Bites, 81
Oregano Turkey and Tomatoes, 85
Lime Chicken Mix, 87
Chicken and Olives, 87
Turkey, Tomato and Fennel Mix, 87
Chicken and Broccoli, 91
Turkey and Scallions Mix, 92
Chicken and Beans, 93
Dill Turkey and Peas, 94
Turkey and Tomato Sauce, 95
Tomato Chicken and Chickpeas, 95
Cilantro Chicken and Eggplant Mix, 97
Chicken and Peppers, 99
Coriander and Turmeric Chicken, 103
Cumin Chicken Mix, 103
Pork and Beans Mix, 105
Oregano Beef, 108
Lamb and Potatoes, 109
Pork and Eggplant Mix, 110
Lemon Lamb, 110
Pork and Lentils, 112
Beef and Peas, 113
Rosemary Beef, 114
Parsley and Chili Lamb, 114
Cayenne Lamb Mix, 116
Shrimp and Red Chard, 131
Shrimp, Salmon and Tomatoes Mix, 135

SAUCE (WING)
Chicken Drumsticks and Buffalo Sauce, 41

SAUCE (WORCESTERSHIRE)
Sweet Potato and Clam Chowder, 31
Worcestershire Beef Mix, 35

SAUSAGE (BEEF)
Leek Casserole, 22

SAUSAGE (PORK)
Sausage and Eggs Mix, 16
Basil Sausage and Broccoli Mix, 25
Shrimp Gumbo, 37

SAUSAGES
Cauliflower and Eggs Bowls, 16

SCALLIONS
Scallions Quinoa and Carrots Bowls, 26
Baby Spinach Rice Mix, 27
Turkey and Walnuts, 33
Pork Chops and Butter Sauce, 40
Creamy Coconut Potatoes, 53
Lime Beans Mix, 56
Farro Mix, 60
Spinach Rice, 61
Eggplant Salad, 76
Oregano Turkey and Tomatoes, 85
Paprika Chicken and Artichokes, 86
Pesto Chicken Mix, 88
Chicken and Endives, 90
Balsamic Turkey, 91
Turkey and Scallions Mix, 92
Masala Turkey, 93
Coriander Turkey Mix, 94
Dill Turkey and Peas, 94
Turkey with Radishes, 97
Cilantro Chicken and Eggplant Mix, 97
Chicken and Mango Mix, 98
Chicken and Asparagus, 100
Orange Chicken Mix, 101
Turkey and Carrots, 102
Coriander and Turmeric Chicken, 103
Beef and Corn Mix, 106
Chili Lamb, 107
Chives Lamb, 108
Beef and Artichokes, 109
Pork and Eggplant Mix, 110
Rosemary Lamb with Olives, 110
Beef and Capers Sauce, 111
Paprika Lamb, 114
Beef with Peas and Corn, 115
Lamb with Capers, 115
Oregano Lamb, 117

Creamy Beef, 119
Walnut and Coconut Beef, 119
Lime Shrimp, 120
Chili Salmon, 120
Paprika Cod, 120
Coriander Salmon Mix, 121
Tuna and Green Beans, 122
Sea Bass and Chickpeas, 122
Creamy Shrimp, 123
Parsley Cod, 123
Orange Cod, 123
Shrimp with Spinach, 124
Creamy Tuna and Scallions, 126
Shrimp and Pineapple Bowls, 127
Hot Salmon and Carrots, 127
Coconut Mackerel, 128
Chili Shrimp and Zucchinis, 128
Shrimp and Mushrooms, 129
Salmon and Berries, 130
Cod and Artichokes, 130
Calamari and Sauce, 132
Indian Shrimp, 133
Salmon and Strawberries Mix, 135

SEA BASS
Sea Bass and Squash, 128
Sea Bass and Chickpeas, 122
Garlic Sea Bass, 124

SHALLOT
Creamy Brisket, 39
Garlic Risotto, 54
Shrimp and Mango Mix, 125
Lime Crab, 127

SHORT PASTA
Tomato Pasta Mix, 35

SHRIMP
Creamy Shrimp Bowls, 17
Seafood Soup, 29
Shrimp Stew, 29
Garlic Shrimp and Spinach, 30
Shrimp Gumbo, 37
Lemon Shrimp Dip, 69
Shrimp Salad, 78
Lime Shrimp, 120
Rosemary Shrimp, 120
Chives Shrimp, 121
Creamy Shrimp, 123
Shrimp with Spinach, 124
Shrimp and Avocado, 124
Shrimp and Mango Mix, 125
Shrimp and Pineapple Bowls, 127
Shrimp and Eggplant, 127

Chili Shrimp and Zucchinis, 128
Italian Shrimp, 129
Shrimp and Mushrooms, 129
Shrimp and Rice Mix, 131
Shrimp and Red Chard, 131
Almond Shrimp and Cabbage, 133
Indian Shrimp, 133
Shrimp, Tomatoes and Kale, 133
Oregano Shrimp Bowls, 134
Shrimp, Salmon and Tomatoes Mix, 135
Shrimp and Cauliflower Bowls, 135

SOUR CREAM
Veggie Hash Brown Mix, 13
Hash Brown and Bacon Casserole, 13
Hot Eggs Mix, 18
Ham Omelet, 27
Beef and Sauce, 105

SPINACH
Quinoa and Veggies Casserole, 16
Spinach Frittata, 18
Baby Spinach Rice Mix, 27
Garlic Shrimp and Spinach, 30
Carrots and Spinach Mix, 53
Spinach Mix, 57
Buttery Spinach, 59
Spinach Rice, 61
Parmesan Spinach Mix, 68
Spinach Spread, 69
Spinach Dip, 71
Chicken Salad, 79
Spinach, Walnuts and Calamari Salad, 80
Spinach Dip, 83
Artichoke Dip, 84
Lemon Turkey and Spinach, 86
Shrimp with Spinach, 124
Oregano Shrimp Bowls, 134
Creamy Shrimp Bowls, 17
Beans Salad, 24
Rice Snack Bowls, 70
Spinach and Walnuts Dip, 77
Beef with Spinach, 105
Trout Bowls, 134
Sesame Salmon Bowls, 29

SPRING ONIONS
Spinach Frittata, 18
Chili Eggs Mix, 19
Cheesy Eggs, 19
Tomato and Zucchini Eggs Mix, 19
Beans Salad, 24
Peppers Rice Mix, 24
Beans Breakfast Bowls, 25
Basil Sausage and Broccoli Mix, 25

173

Zucchini and Cauliflower Eggs Mix, 26
Ham Omelet, 27
Peppers and Eggs Mix, 27
Peas and Rice Bowls, 28
Sesame Salmon Bowls, 29
Creamy Cod Stew, 30
Maple Chicken Mix, 31
Lamb and Onion Stew, 34
Parsley Chicken Stew, 39
Chicken and Rice, 45
Balsamic Cauliflower, 50
Tomato and Corn Mix, 51
Hot Zucchini Mix, 52
Cabbage and Onion Mix, 63
Rice and Corn, 64
Garlic Squash Mix, 64
Shrimp Salad, 78
Beef Dip, 81
Beef Dip, 82
Spinach Dip, 83
Peppers Salsa, 84
Artichoke Dip, 84
Mushroom Salsa, 84
Lemon Turkey and Spinach, 86
Lime Chicken Mix, 87
Chicken and Olives, 87

SQUASH
Cinnamon Squash, 58
Veggie Medley, 66

STRAWBERRIES
Salmon and Strawberries Mix, 135
Strawberry Cake, 140
Strawberry and Orange Mix, 145
Strawberry and Blackberry Jam, 147
Berries Salad, 150

TACO
Tacos, 74

TAPIOCA PEARLS
Tapioca and Chia Pudding, 149

TARRAGON
Tarragon Sweet Potatoes, 67
Turkey and Kidney Beans, 102
Tarragon Pork Chops, 106

TEMPEH
Beets Salad, 74

TOFU
Pineapple and Tofu Salsa, 73

TOMATO PASSATA
Chicken and Onions Mix, 88
Ginger Turkey Mix, 89
Turkey Chili, 92
Turkey with Olives and Corn, 94
Turkey with Radishes, 97
Turkey and Kidney Beans, 102
Pork and Olives Mix, 104
Beef with Spinach, 105
Pork and Chilies Mix, 105
Pork and Okra, 108
Chives Lamb, 108
Beef and Artichokes, 109
Lamb and Fennel Mix, 111
Beef and Endives, 113
Lamb with Capers, 115
Beef and Sprouts, 117
Shrimp with Spinach, 124
Dill Cod, 125
Salmon and Peas, 128
Chili Shrimp and Zucchinis, 128
Salmon, Tomatoes and Green Beans, 130
Chives Mussels, 131
Almond Shrimp and Cabbage, 133
Shrimp and Cauliflower Bowls, 135
Chicken with Corn and Wild Rice, 40
Artichoke Soup, 42
Chicken and Eggplant Stew, 42
Turmeric Lentils Stew, 43
Pork Chili, 43
Cinnamon Pork Ribs, 43
Pork and Mushroom Stew, 44
Pork and Tomatoes Mix, 44
Pesto Pork Shanks, 44
Potato Stew, 44
Salmon Stew, 45
Paprika Pork and Chickpeas, 45
Beef and Cabbage, 46
Chicken and Brussels Sprouts Mix, 46
Beef Soup, 48
Veggie Soup, 48
Oregano Turkey Stew, 48
Italian Black Beans Mix, 50
Butternut Squash and Eggplant Mix, 52
Cauliflower and Almonds Mix, 53
Hot Lentils, 55
Lime Beans Mix, 56
Kale Mix, 59
Cabbage and Onion Mix, 63
Curry Broccoli Mix, 63
Baby Carrots and Parsnips Mix, 65
Brussels Sprouts and Cauliflower, 65
Lentils Salsa, 74
Lime Turkey and Chard, 99
Garlic Turkey, 103

Lamb and Cabbage, 112
Beef with Peas and Corn, 115
Lamb and Zucchini Mix, 115
Sea Bass and Chickpeas, 122
Basil Cod and Olives, 129
Shrimp and Mushrooms, 129
Cod and Broccoli, 136

TOMATOES
Creamy Cod Stew, 30
Chili Eggs Mix, 19
Tomato and Zucchini Eggs Mix, 19
Beans Chili, 38
Fennel Soup, 41
Beans and Mushroom Stew, 42
Turmeric Lentils Stew, 43
Balsamic Beef Stew, 46
Beef Soup, 48
Veggie Soup, 48
Oregano Turkey Stew, 48
Tomato and Corn Mix, 51
Cabbage and Onion Mix, 63
Minty Peas and Tomatoes, 68
Savoy Cabbage Mix, 68
Spinach, Walnuts and Calamari Salad, 80
Chicken and Endives, 90
Turkey and Avocado, 98
Chicken and Asparagus, 100
Shrimp and Eggplant, 127
Tomato Jam, 148

TOMATOES (CANNED)
Turkey Meatballs, 76
Shrimp Stew, 29
Turkey and Mushrooms, 32
Beef Stew, 34
Tomato Pasta Mix, 35
Chickpeas Stew, 36
Pork Soup, 38
White Beans Mix, 57
Balsamic Okra Mix, 63
Cabbage and Kale Mix, 66
Thyme Mushrooms and Corn, 66
Chicken with Tomatoes and Eggplant Mix, 88

TOMATOES (CHERRY)
Quinoa and Veggies Casserole, 16
Hot Eggs Mix, 18
Spinach Frittata, 18
Sesame Salmon Bowls, 29
Indian Chicken and Tomato Mix, 32
Chicken and Peach Mix, 41
Pork and Tomatoes Mix, 44
Spinach Mix, 57
Veggie Mix, 60

Balsamic Okra Mix, 63
Veggie Medley, 66
Squash Salsa, 70
Rice Snack Bowls, 70
Tomato and Mushroom Salsa, 72
Pineapple and Tofu Salsa, 73
Beets Salad, 74
Chicken Salad, 79
Eggplant Salsa, 82
Peppers Salsa, 84
Oregano Turkey and Tomatoes, 85
Turkey, Tomato and Fennel Mix, 87
Tomato Chicken and Chickpeas, 95
Lamb and Tomatoes Mix, 110
Pesto Cod and Tomatoes, 123
Shrimp and Mango Mix, 125
Salmon, Tomatoes and Green Beans, 130
Salmon Salad, 132
Almond Shrimp and Cabbage, 133
Shrimp, Tomatoes and Kale, 133
Oregano Shrimp Bowls, 134
Shrimp, Salmon and Tomatoes Mix, 135
Mushroom Salsa, 84

TROUT
Lime Trout Mix, 126
Trout Bowls, 134
Balsamic Trout, 134
Cinnamon Trout, 136

TUNA
Spicy Tuna, 121
Ginger Tuna, 121
Tuna and Green Beans, 122
Tuna and Brussels Sprouts, 124
Balsamic Tuna, 126
Creamy Tuna and Scallions, 126
Tuna and Fennel, 129
Walnut Tuna Mix, 132

TURKEY
Turkey and Mushrooms, 32
Turkey and Figs, 32
Turkey and Walnuts, 33
Oregano Turkey Stew, 48
Turkey Meatballs, 76
Oregano Turkey and Tomatoes, 85
Lemon Turkey and Spinach, 86
Turkey, Tomato and Fennel Mix, 87
Ginger Turkey Mix, 89
Turkey and Plums Mix, 89
Creamy Turkey Mix, 89
Balsamic Turkey, 91
Turkey and Scallions Mix, 92
Turkey Chili, 92

Masala Turkey, 93
Turkey and Corn, 93
Coriander Turkey Mix, 94
Turkey with Olives and Corn, 94
Dill Turkey and Peas, 94
Turkey with Rice, 94
Italian Turkey, 95
Turkey and Tomato Sauce, 95
Turkey with Leeks and Radishes, 96
Coconut Turkey, 96
Turkey with Radishes, 97
Turkey and Avocado, 98
Lime Turkey and Chard, 99
BBQ Turkey mix, 100
Lemon Turkey and Potatoes, 100
Turkey and Okra, 101
Turkey and Carrots, 102
Turkey and Kidney Beans, 102
Garlic Turkey, 103

WALNUTS
Carrots Oatmeal, 13
Chocolate Breakfast Bread, 20
Squash Bowls, 21
Turkey and Walnuts, 33
Spinach and Walnuts Dip, 77
Spinach, Walnuts and Calamari Salad, 80
Walnuts Bowls, 81
Zucchini Spread, 82
Walnut and Coconut Beef, 119
Walnut Tuna Mix, 132
Cinnamon Apples, 137
Creamy Berries Mix, 139
Quinoa Pudding, 141
Almonds, Walnuts and Mango Bowls, 149
Pears and Apples Bowls, 150

WHIPPING CREAM
Zucchini and Cauliflower Eggs Mix, 26
Creamy Potato Soup, 40

Chicken with Corn and Wild Rice, 40
Corn Sauté, 51
Creamy Berries Mix, 139

WINE (RED)
Pork and Cranberries, 34
Beef and Celery Stew, 35
Peaches and Wine Sauce, 143

WINE (WHITE)
Turkey and Figs, 32
Paprika Cod, 120

YOGURT (GREEK)
Cinnamon Berries Oatmeal, 12
Sausage and Potato Mix, 12
Spinach Dip, 71
Yogurt Cheesecake, 145
Greek Cream Cheese Pudding, 150
Greek Cream, 151
Ginger Cream, 151

ZUCCHINIS
Tomato and Zucchini Eggs Mix, 19
Zucchini and Cauliflower Eggs Mix, 26
Creamy Cod Stew, 30
Veggie Soup, 48
Veggie Mix, 60
Veggie Medley, 66
Hot Chicken and Zucchinis, 96
Chili Shrimp and Zucchinis, 128
Salmon Salad, 132
Hot Zucchini Mix, 52
Red Curry Veggie Mix, 54
Zucchini Mix, 59
Paprika Green Beans and Zucchinis, 67
Zucchini Spread, 82
Beef and Zucchinis Mix, 104
Lamb and Lime Zucchinis, 113
Lamb and Zucchini Mix, 115

Copyright 2019 by Nicole Coleman All rights reserved.

All rights Reserved. No part of this publication or the information in it may be quoted from or reproduced in any form by means such as printing, scanning, photocopying or otherwise without prior written permission of the copyright holder.

Disclaimer and Terms of Use: Effort has been made to ensure that the information in this book is accurate and complete, however, the author and the publisher do not warrant the accuracy of the information, text and graphics contained within the book due to the rapidly changing nature of science, research, known and unknown facts and internet. The Author and the publisher do not hold any responsibility for errors, omissions or contrary interpretation of the subject matter herein. This book is presented solely for motivational and informational purposes only.

Made in the USA
Monee, IL
02 January 2020